make it with
paper

make it with
paper

Oceana

AN OCEANA BOOK

This book is produced by
Quantum Publishing Ltd
6 Blundell Street
London N7 9BH

ISBN 0-681-28897-3

QUMMIWP

Manufactured in Singapore by
Pica Digital Pte. Ltd

Printed in Singapore by
Star Standard Industries Pte. Ltd

CONTENTS

GENERAL INTRODUCTION

Each project in this book begins with a list of materials and a picture of the finished item. For your first attempts, the papers provided are marked with folding lines and the templates at the back of the book can be traced to make an endless supply of patterns.

To get the best possible results, the three most important things to keep in mind are:

• Cut slowly and carefully
• Fold precisely
• Get to know the keys which explain the fold lines and arrows

Begin each exercise by cutting out all paper elements for the desired project from the supply sheets provided and use sharp, conformable scissors. Protect your work surface by placing a piece of cardboard under your work if you are cutting with a blade and take great care to use it in small sections. You should use a ruler or something straight-edged for most projects, along with a tool such as a letter opener to score fold lines on the back of the elements. Carefully study the step-by-step photos to visually check your work. It is often helpful to look ahead to the next diagram or picture to see the results of a fold in advance. Take time to make neat, accurate folds. If you follow all these tips, and remember not to get frustrated if things do not go to plan on your first few attempts, you will find that you are able to make beautiful paper objects without any problem at all.

Though adhesives are not always necessary, you may wish to make your creations last longer by adding a little white glue or paste at key contact points. Apply adhesive sparingly and neatly and have a damp cloth handy to wipe away spills. Tracing templates are provided for each project, so that you can make additional examples from whatever material you choose.

7

PAPER FLOWERS

INTRODUCTION

Flowers are splendid subjects to render in paper and their forms are open to wide interpretation. When working on the projects in this chapter, it is a good idea to have different types of paper to hand. This will allow you to achieve different effects and will also give you an idea of what type of paper you feel most comfortable working with. It is also a good idea to practice the project on cheap scrap paper before you make the final piece, allowing you to perfect the techniques involved before you use more expensive paper.

Many methods of paper flower-making require special materials such as crepe paper, wire, florist's tape, and dowels. Not so with these patterns. The simple techniques will produce stunning results with even the most ordinary papers. Experiment with differnt types of paper, then use the templates in the back of the book to make flowers from any material you choose. Alternatively adapt these flower designs to create dozens of other plants of your own. The projects in this chapter are perfect for adding color and visual interest to your home, from adorning a dinner table to livening up a windowsill.

Enjoy

GLOSSARY AND KEY

Because the illustrations can show only a segment of a project's folding procedure, it is helpful to know whether the paper is being folded in front or from behind. The origami system of valley-folds and mountain-folds uses two kinds of broken lines (see key diagram) to show when to fold toward the project's surface (valley-fold) and when to fold behind the surface (mountain-fold).

Valley-fold—Relative to the display view of the paper being folded, a valley-fold is always folded in front of the project's surface. If you were to unfold a valley-fold you would see a valley-crease, which dents into the paper's surface forming a valley.

Mountain-fold—Relative to the displayed view of the paper being folded, a mountain-fold is always folded behind the project's surface. If you were to unfold a mountain-fold you would see a mountain-crease, which rises up from the paper's surface forming a mountain ridge.

Various types of arrows help make the folding instructions even clearer. These arrows are easy to understand with a quick study of the illustrated key. Whenever you see the repeat arrow in a diagram, you must apply the demonstrated folding procedure to all indicated parts of the project. If, when embarking on a project, you are unsure what a diagram is instructing you to do, simply refer back to these pages before continuing. Once you have completed a couple of projects, you will find that you will be able to interpret the diagrams easily.

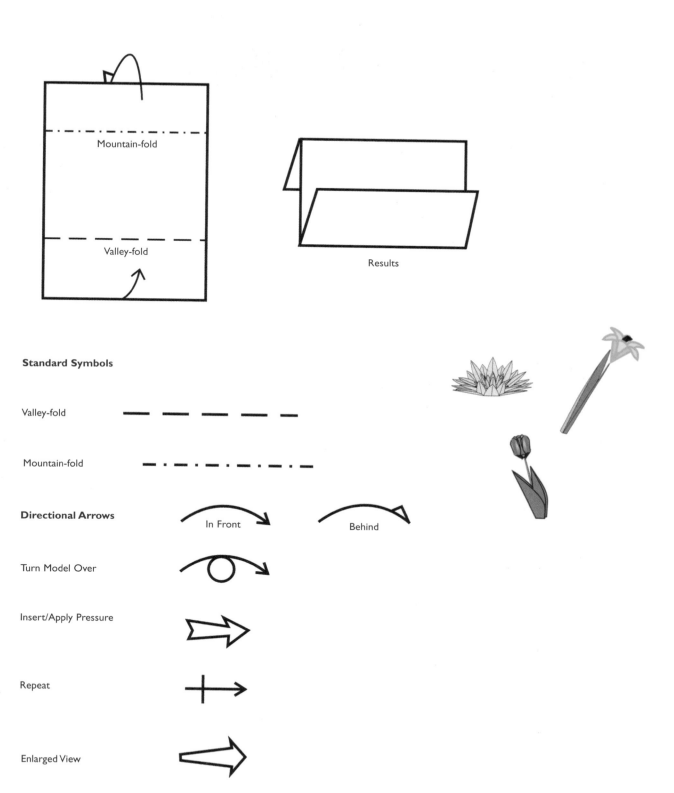

Mountain-fold

Valley-fold

Results

Standard Symbols

Valley-fold

Mountain-fold

Directional Arrows

In Front

Behind

Turn Model Over

Insert/Apply Pressure

Repeat

Enlarged View

PAPER ROSE

Although they are not as fragrant, paper roses last much longer than the real ones do. Since real roses come in all shapes and sizes, there is a lot of room for creative license when making a paper rose. When we think of roses we usually think of the classic shades of pink and red, but these diverse flowers come in a wide variety of colors. Yellow, white, peach, and even near-black garnet, are all shades that can be found in real roses and that can be adopted for a banquet of the paper variety.

If you like long-stemmed roses, such as tea roses, remember that they can look spindly on their own, so it is important that they are displayed alongside other plants. Fill in your arrangement with shorter-stemmed primroses or luxuriously petaled cabbage roses. Since roses have layers of beautifully unfurling petals, you will get the best results if you study a few real roses before attempting this project.

YOU WILL NEED

- **Rose template**
- **Scissors**
- **White glue**
- **Ruler or other straightedge**
- **Scoring tool (such as a letter opener)**
- **Pencil or toothpick (to open a hole in base of blossom)**

HOW TO BUILD A ROSE

The blossom shown here requires only four pieces to complete. You may scale the pattern down to create charming miniature roses or, if you are after a design with a much bigger impact, make the scale larger for a really dramatic display. Adding paper stems and leaves will make your flowers even more beautiful and realistic, and these are relatively easy to achieve. The rose pattern can be used as it appears or adapted to create carnations by using pinking shears to cut the pattern from tissue paper. Double or triple the tissue for each layer of the blossom pattern, to provide extra petals and more support for the flower, then fluff open the layers after assembly. The effect is very lifelike.

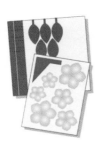 

And although this is a book about papercraft, you needn't limit yourself to this medium alone. Projects like this lend themselves to other materials as well. For instance, colorful fabrics make wonderful roses: if you lightly coat the back of the selected fabric with spray adhesive and apply a thin backing, the rose pattern will look like fabric and fold like paper. Use these fabric roses as coordinated interior accents.

Once you have mastered the folded rose by using the special pattern at the end of the book, try experimenting with other paper textures, colors, and patterns. This simple method produces stunning results from even the most ordinary paper. Try newspapers, magazine pages, or book covers; or use coupons, concert tickets, or seed packets—the list is endless. After a time, you may find yourself going beyond the scope of this book and applying the rose technique to create dozens of other plant and butterfly designs.

Design Tips

- Once all of the elements are cut out, clean the work area of any scraps of paper or debris that could later be confused with the actual flower cutouts.
- For maximum "grab", make only a small hold in the bottom of each part of the blossom, then let the paper stem enlarge the hole by itself.
- The leaves may be arranged any way that you feel. Try making additional pockets and leaves, or skip the pockets altogether and glue the leaves to the outside of the stem.
- You may choose to glue the stem closed once the blossom is inserted. Blossoms and leaves can also be used alone, without a stem.

1 Following the fold-lines, score the backs of petals using a letter opener and straightedge. Turn the paper over.

2 Make pleats, starting on the left side of the petal and working left to right. The score lines will guide you. Fold loosely at first, then tighten the entire piece to finish.

3 Fold each petal down, to make the shape pictured here. This fold extends only halfway across each petal. You may curl the petals, for a softer effect.

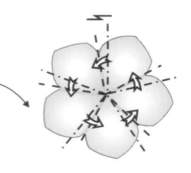

4 Pierce a small hole in the center of each unit (a sharp pencil works well for this); keep the hole as small as possible.

5 *Make the center spike by repeatedly folding triangle in half (a-c). Be sure that your folds are tight and sharp. Curl the flag tightly around the top of spike and make a cone shape (d & e). You may loosen this curled paper after the blossom has been assembled.*

6 *Assemble blossom. You may apply a small amount of glue where the petals meet the spike (optional, but recommended for permanent displays). White glue works best.*

Optional glue points

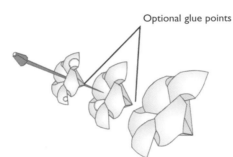

7 *Fold each leaf in half, lengthwise. Make an angled crease as a guide. The angled crease sets the direction and spread for veins in the leaves. Make all crease sharp.*

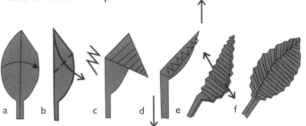

8 *Next, tightly fan-fold the leaves. You may vary the width of each pleat, narrower toward the tip and wide at the center. Open out each leaf completely and shape it with your fingers. If you want to add a stem, follow the folding method as shown in the line drawings below.*

Fan fold

Fold and unfold

Fold edges to center

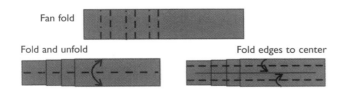

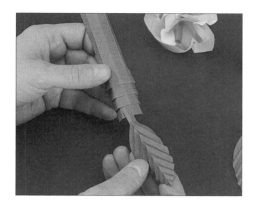

9 *Insert leaves into stem. Be sure that you insert the leaves on the smooth, outside of the stem (side with no raw edges showing). Pay close attention to which side of each leaf is uppermost. Glue is not necessary here.*

10 *Fold the stem in half (lengthwise) once again, on the existing centerfold line. Hide the raw edges inside and narrow the stem.*

12 *Perfect roses— ready for display.*

11 *Finally, insert the blossom into the top end of the finished stem. Choose a secure group of layers to do this. You may apply a small amount of white glue for performance.*

ROSE GALLERY

Heart-shaped boxes can be decorated with simplified versions of the complete rose. Each rose blossom has only two petal segments and no center spike. If you are using heavy, cover-weight paper, dampening it with water first will make it easy to form the petal shapes.

Richly colored and velvety, handmade oriental papers make these roses look real. Oriental papers are strong but soft in texture. Make them easier to work with by pasting two sheets together, as suggested for newspapers.

Decorate a cake. Plastic-coated decorative foils come in many colors and are excellent for making flowers and leaves. Prevent grease stains by placing small pieces of wax paper between the flowers and frosting. Use only food-grade materials on edible cakes.

Rose brooch with green and gold foil leaves. Brooch pins may be purchased as blanks (check local craft stores). Assemble the floral decoration, then attach it to the pin with hot-melt glue.

Newspapers, or printed pages from any source, are great for making flowers. Prepare magazines or newsprint papers by pasting together two layers for a thicker, more durable sheet. Very effective in advertising and for point-of-sale displays.

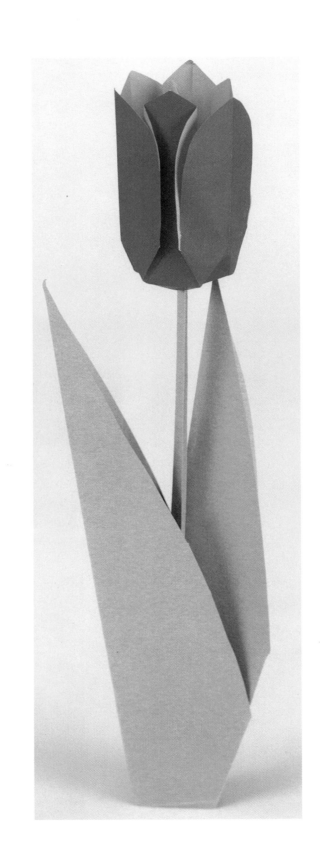

PAPER TULIP

There are more than a thousand—and counting—variations of tulip. This helps to make life easy for the would-be paper tulip maker. Choosing paper colors for these flowers is simple: almost anything goes. The stems, however, are a different story, since tulips bloom early in the spring their paper counterparts should have pale-green paper stems. If you want to achieve realistic, lifelike results, it is important that the colors you use match the real thing as much as possible.

A newly popular tulip variety, the Parrot tulip, has bright, striped and fringed petals that are worth trying to recreate in paper. The trick for making any variety of tulip is paper is keeping the shapes of the flowers from being too uniform. Copy real tulips and make each paper bloom with a slight imperfection, a few odd-size petals, petals that are tightly shut or slightly shallow and open petals. Varying the size and form of paper tulips takes away the stiffness their cupped shape is prone to, and makes them seem airy and light. Paper tulips give you the feeling of spring all year round.

YOU WILL NEED

- **Tulip template**
- **Scissors**
- **White glue**
- **Ruler or other straightedge**
- **Scoring tool (such as a letter opener)**
- **Pencil or toothpick (to open a hole in base of blossom)**

HOW TO BUILD A TULIP

Fields of colorful tulips are easy to make with method described here. Use any type of brightly colored paper. Once mastered, this paper tulip will surely become a firm favorite. You will be surprised at how easily they can be made, and at how lifelike they look. They look wonderful in a variety of colors.

These tulips are especially good for table-top and window displays, since they stand up very well on their own. Like the paper rose, tulips can easily be scaled up or down—to create miniature or life-size collections.

Feel free to experiment with the final shapes of the petals and leaves; adding a curl here and there or possibly changing the outlines as you cut out the paper patterns; as long as the final result looks good, it doesn't really mattter what you try. Photographs of real tulips in garden catalogs and books are great for inspiration: so are visits to gardens and nursery centers, where you can gather ideas about color combinations and display.

Design Tips

- When using the $1/2$ leaf pattern, first fold the paper in half and align the short edge of the pattern shape to the folded edge of the paper. Cut out the shape and you will have the first fold of the leaf set already done.
- Make longer stems from heavy paper for arrangements with cut flowers in containers. Glue the blossoms in place for permanence.
- For a more interesting and dramatic tulip, use spray cement to glue contrasting colors of thin papers back-to-back. Cut and fold the blossom from this paper as usual. The center of the finished tulip will be a different color than the petals.
- Bright, solid colors work best for most tulips, but include some variegated colors in large displays. Vary the hue of the green stems and leaves in large displays, to add depth. In any arrangement, make some blossoms more open than others. This adds a natural touch.

1   *Following the lines, score the inside (light-colored side) of the petal using a letter opener and straightedge. Do not press so hard that you tear the paper.*

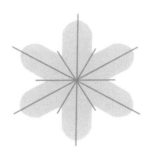

2   *Select any petal and fold it upward to its opposite partner, matching the V-notches (on either side of the petal) to the horizontal center line.*

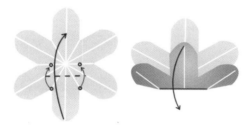

3   *Open up the folded paper. The blue line in the illustration for Step Two indicates the crease you have just made. Repeat steps two and three for the remaining five petals. For more control, rotate the paper as you work, folding each petal away from you—from the bottom to the top. Open the paper flat. There will be a six-pointed, star-shaped crease pattern in the center of the flower. Make a small hole in the center of the flower, using a sharp pencil or other such tool. Turn the paper over.*

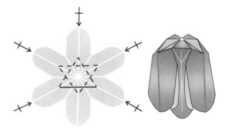

Study the folding pattern. You will be mountain-folding the outline of the hexagon in the center of the paper, you will also be mountain-folding the short lines from the corners of the hexagon to the V-notches. The valley-fold lines are creased by folding the outside edges of every other petal to the center of the line of that petal.

4 *Observe the diamond-shaped creases on the bottom outside of the blossom (there are six). With a little pressure from your finger, dent in the three outside petals. This will give the bottom of the blossom a pleasing, rounded shape.*

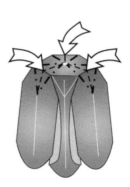

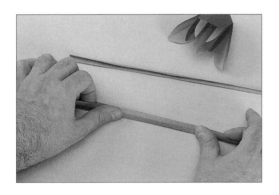

5 *Fold the stem as follows: Crease in a center line, then fold the outside edges to this center line. Finally, fold in half again, lengthwise.*

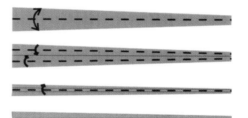

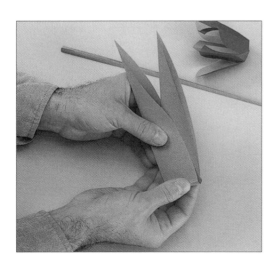

6 *Prepare a leaf base by folding the leaf paper in half, tip to tip (a). Fold in half the long way, curved edges together (b). Grasp the inner point and swivel it out, allowing the base line to change position (c). Fold the bottom corners of the leaf section inside. This secures the shape and adds a more dynamic stance (d). The leaf set should stand on its own (e).*

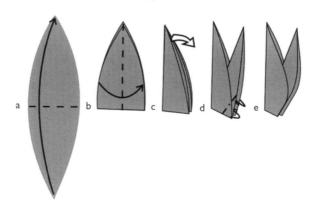

7 Fit the wide end of the stem into the base (glue is optional) and insert the narrow end of the stem into the hole in the bottom of the tulip. Slide the tulip blossom down the stem until it is well seated. Cut off any excess stem.

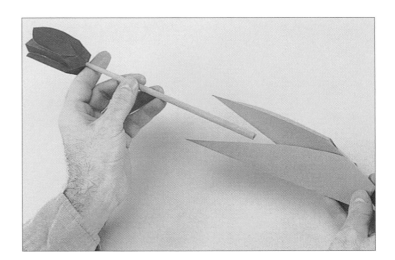

8 The completed tulip—ready for display.

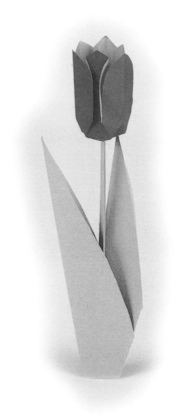

Tulip Shortcuts

Once you are comfortable with the full folding and shaping method of the tulip blossom, you may wish to try a more direct method and save some time. Omit the creasing of the six-pointed star. Go directly to the procedure pictured in the third photo and fold the petal edges parallel to and against the center line of the petals between them. Remember to form a flat base at the bottom center of the blossom.

TULIP GALLERY

Only three-inches tall, these tiny tulip plantsbecome charming ornaments with the addition of a loop of thread attached to the top of the stem inside the blossom.

Long-stem arrangements of tulips and roses. The tulips provide bright colors while the roses fill in the composition. Slender iris leaves add touches of green.

Use a small cluster of tulip blooms as ornaments on a gift package. To add a dramatic contrast of color, insert yellow paper posies in the base of each tulip. For small flowers, reduce and simplify the shapes of the leaves.

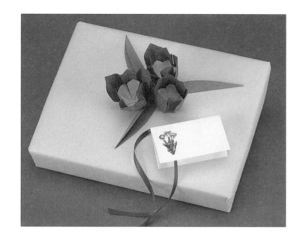

Miniature tulips can also be worn as a smart lapel pin. Glue the tulip to a small clasp pin or attach them directly with a straight pin.

A free-standing table-top display of paper tulips. The green plant parts of these life-size tulips were created with a heavy, cover-stock paper. Very sturdy and stable, these flowers require no additional support.

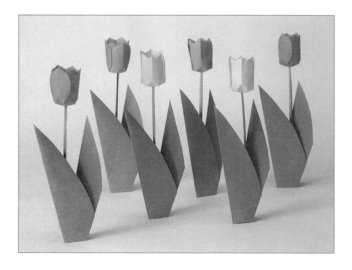

PAPER DAISY

Whether you think of them as weeds or wildflowers, daisies have been crowding lawns and filling out bouquets for as long as either was invented. You may not wish to pick wild daisies, so these plants are the perfect subject to make out of paper. There are daisies to fit every personality; they can be small, dainty white flowers, or brash, saucer-size Shasta daisies in neon pink, yellow, and lavender. The variety is such that you'll never get bored of creating these wonderful little flowers. If you pull apart a blossom of a real daisy, you'll find the center is made up of many little "flowers" that give it a fuzzy look. Daisies belong to the same group of flowers as asters, marigolds, goldenrods, and sunflowers—so you can take color cues from any of these for making paper daisies; or, if you like, experiment and let your imagination run wild. Snip paper petals into a tight fringe to mimic English daisies, or make them smooth and generously overlapping for Shasta and Michaelmas daisies.

YOU WILL NEED

- **Tulip template**
- **Scissors**
- **White glue**
- **Ruler or other straightedge**
- **Scoring tool (such as a letter opener)**
- **Pencil or toothpick (to open a hole in base of blossom)**
- **Toothpick (to wind paper strip for the center)**

HOW TO BUILD A DAISY

Daisies come in all colors and sizes, which allows you great freedom when making them out of paper. The contrasting color of the center "button" gives these flowers a perky, wide-awake effect. It is no wonder that we equate daisies with a cheerful outlook and use them for creating "get well" and "congratulations" bouquets for friends and loved ones. As well as being great fun to look at, they are also highly enjoyable to make.

This daisy form is especially suited for arrangements that are wide and shallow, which is the ideal shape for a dining table centerpiece. Coordinate daisy centerpieces to the occasion or season by choosing appropriately colored papers: pastels for a spring bouquet or golds and russets for an autumn arrangement. You can also coordinate the color of the flowers with the colors of your table setting or room interior.

Daisies are the perfect filler item in floral arrangements, they make a good background for long-stemmed flowers. Short-stemmed daisies are ideal as boutonnieres or package ornaments: if you add longer stems, they work well with slim flowers such as irises and lilies. For a bright accent or pretty garland, string single blossoms together in a classic daisy chain.

Design Tips

- When selecting papers to make daisies, choose colors that match the season or theme. Dark green paper leaves and stems will emphasize the perky effect of the blossoms.
- Make longer stems and extra leaves for arrangements of flowers in tall containers, or for mixing with the other paper flowers in this book.
- For a faster finish, glue leaves directly to the flower stems. You can also glue the blossoms in place to make the daisy more durable.
- If you cut out small blossoms with an X-acto knife the results will be neater and the work will go faster.

1   *Following the fold lines, score the back (light-colored side) of the paper between the petals with a scoring tool and straightedge. Turn the paper over. Score the front (dark-colored side) from tip to tip, across the center line of the petals. Repeat scoring steps on another paper cutout; you will need two for each daisy.*

2   *Using a pencil or toothpick, piece a hole in the center of the daisy. Be careful not to make the hole too large—since the paper must be snug enough for the stem to get a good hold.*

3   *Make stems by folding the paper strip in half twice, lengthwise, to get a thin, four-layered paper spear.*

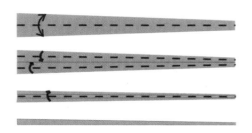

4 *Glue two yellow strips end-to-end for each daisy center. Wind this strip tightly around a toothpick and glue the outside end to the body of the coil. Carefully remove the toothpick when the glue has dried, this leaving a hole in the center of the coil button.*

5 *Fold the leaves in half lengthwise (a). Make an angled crease as a guide (b). Fan-fold the leaf parallel to the angle guide (c). Open the leaf completely and shape (d-f).*

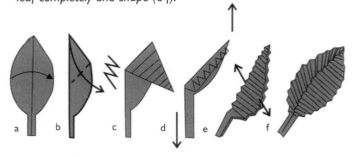

6 *To assemble, place one daisy cutout over the other. Take care to stagger the petals so that all sixteen petals are visible. Spear the set of petals and the button-center with the paper stem.*

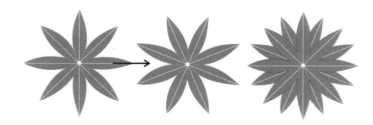

7 Make sure that the stem is snugly in place, then trim any excess paper from the center. You may use glue to make the flower more durable.

8 The finished daisy—ready for display.

DAISY GALLERY

Informal arrangements of daisies bring a touch of summer to any room.

Make a centerpiece of large daisy forms and leaves. Use heavy "artist" papers to make your designs even more graceful.

A classic daisy chain worn as a crown. Glue paper daisies to ribbon, or string them together to create a decorative border, garland or wreath.

In place of a box, paper daisies are a cheerful surprise as a package ornament. Perfect for decorating a summertime birthday, or shower gift.

PAPER IRIS

Irises are related to lilies, and come in nearly as many shapes, sizes, and colors as do roses. Bearded iris, dwarf iris, Dutch, French and Japanese irises, each has its own distinct appearance. To recreate lifelike irises in paper, use a paper with high rag content for bearded varieties, and a stiff, slightly shiny paper for making the crisp, dwarf varieties of iris. A quick glance at a garden catalog will supply enough color inspiration for a whole field of flowers: bright violet *Ruffled*; *Breathless*, with flamingo-pink blossoms; *China Maid*, petals in a blend of pink, buff and lilac; *Crystal*, in bright, frosty blue; or *Frost and Flame*, pure white flowers with tangerine-colored beards.

Of the irises listed, dwarf irises are the easiest to mimic in paper, bearded irises are more difficult and the Japanese variety is trickiest of all. Japanese irises are wide and flat, but soft in appearance. It takes careful planning to find (or adapt) paper that can be cut to so large a shape without excessive stiffness or without drooping under its own weight.

YOU WILL NEED

- **Iris paper template**
- **Scissors or X-acto knife**
- **White glue**
- **Ruler or other straightedge**
- **Scoring tool**

HOW TO BUILD A PAPER IRIS

Named after Iris, the Greek goddess of the rainbow, this flower was the source of inspiration for the highly stylized fleur-de-lis design. Large, bold, and showy, the iris is an outstanding addition to any garden or flower arrangement and a must on the list of paper flowers gathered for this collection.

The slim, graceful profile of the iris shows best when displayed as a single stem or in a small grouping of three. If you want to make a larger spray of flowers you will need extra leaves or some more open paper flower-shapes, to fill out the bouquet.

The iris shown is a simplified rendition, requiring only a single piece of paper for the blossom. Although any color is suitable, remember that the iris is a spring and early summer plant. Paper in hues of pale pink and mauve, deep purple and lavender, or rich tints of yellow will offer the most natural-looking results.

Once attached to its stem and leaf, the simple lines of this flower form become quite striking. Just a few of these blooms will add drama to any arrangement.

Design Tips

- For best effect, choose two-tone paper with contrasting hues on either side. Use bright or dusty greens for the stems and leaves.
- A round pencil will curl flower petals better than a six-sided one; the facets leave unsightly horizontal rib marks.
- As noted before, the blossom is more durable fit is glued to the stem. Try to leave as little stem as possible showing inside the flower.
- When using the iris as the only flower in an arrangement, cut stems to varying lengths. Use iris leaves separately and insert into mixed arrangements of paper flowers.

1 *On the outside (light hue side) of the paper, mountain-fold and unfold across gap notches between petals. Repeat with the other two sets of opposing gap notches, folding the shape in half three times in this manner.*

2 *Pierce the center to make s small hole for the stem.*

3 *The blossom papers provided for this project have a line dividing three petals in half. I will refer to this as a centerline. Notice also that these three lines are arranged in a symmetrical triangle. Fold each mountain-crease against and aligned to its corresponding centerline, Repeat with the other two sets of centerlines and mountain-folds. You will end up with three petals on the outside and three petals on the inside.*

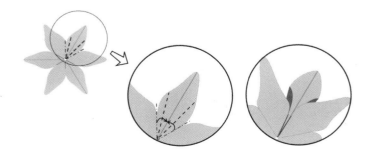

4   *Fold down the three outside petals as far as they can go. Make a sharp, horizontal crease at the point where each petal attaches to the flower. Make sure all of the creases made thus far are crisp.*

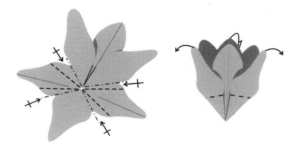

5   *If your folding is neat and sharp, you will not need glue to keep the blossom in a good form. Give the three outer petals a slight downward curl. Curl the three inner petals toward the center of the flower.*

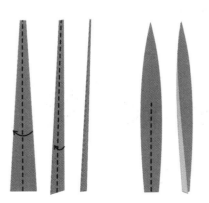

6   *Make stems by folding the stem paper in half twice, lengthwise, to get a thin, four-layered paper spear. Two-thirds from the bottom of the leaf, fold the leaf in half lengthwise. You may then leave the leaf straight, or gently curl it downward.*

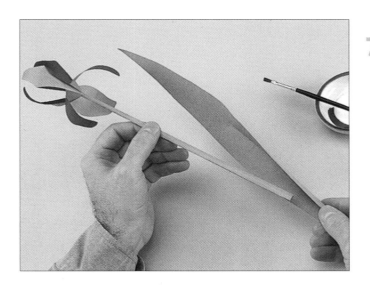

7 Insert the stem through the center hole from the bottom. Glue the leaf to the base of the stem. More than one leaf per stem and flower is a nice touch. You may also use iris leaves by themselves, to add green to other arrangements. Make extra leaves so that you can adjust the final composition of your flowers.

8 The finished iris—ready for display.

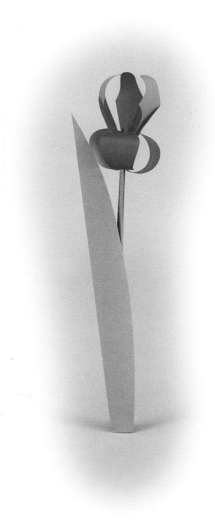

Iris Shortcuts

To cut folding time in half, fold two petal sets at once by stacking two cutouts together. Make sure all the petals are lined up and hold the layers firmly together as you cut. Make all the creases sharp and clean. Pull the two papers apart just before curling and shaping the petals.

IRIS GALLERY

Irises and leaves in a basket. The iris is a plant that carries itself well in a simple, uncluttered arrangement. A good balance of leaves supports the composition. If you stand the flowers up in aquarium gravel, the arrangement is easier to modify.

Long-stem vase arrangements can support more numerous blooms and a mix of colors. Long stems are best made from sturdier papers—or by folding more layers with lightweight papers.

Framed arrangements of irises and a paper butterfly make an elegant wall decoration. Choose a deep frame to emphasize the 3-D effect of the flowers.

Give gift packages oriental grace by wrapping them in handmade Japanese paper with iris ornaments.

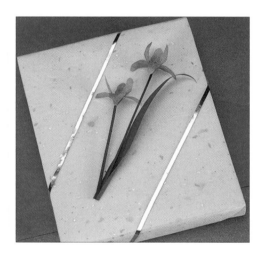

To make your compositions dynamic, always use an odd number of blooms and keep them few in number.

PAPER DAYLILY

Daylily trumpets look like graceful butterflies that have landed on green stems. Although their blooms last only a day in the garden, the paper variety keep well indoors. Thanks to hybrid flower breeders, there are many variations on the trumpet shape of the daylily: some have wide overlapping petals, some frilled, crinkled and ruffled petals, some are shaped like cups, others like small bells. In nature, daylily colors range from pale lemon through soft tones of ivory to deep burgundy, maroon, and even purple. With so much variety in both color and form, the daylily is the perfect flower to create in paper.

Real daylilies are edible, paper daylilies are naturals as pretty garnishes for desserts, formal place settings, or summer luncheon tables. They are elegant flowers that look great in a wide variety of colors.

YOU WILL NEED

- **Daylily paper template**
- **Scissors and/or X-acto knife**
- **White glue**
- **Ruler or other straightedge**
- **Scoring tool**
- **Toothpick**

HOW TO BUILD A PAPER DAYLILY

Daylilies often grow wild along the edges of fields and roadways. Their short-lived blossoms are daily replaced by the successive bloom of abundant buds, which provides a long lasting summer display. The main difference between daylilies and cultivated lilies is the appearance of their leaves; daylilies have long, grass-like leaves extending from the base of the plant. Easter and other cultivated lilies have short leaves that collar the stem. If you wish to create the cultivated variety, you can modify the design described here.

The paper daylily method shown here is a simple way to get these showy blooms without having to water. Use them to quickly fill out a large flower arrangement. Life-size versions are also excellent for stage or window dressing. The simple leaf shape is easy to make in quantity by stacking together several layers of green paper and cutting freehand. Use the leaves by themselves to fill in and support arrangements of other long-stemmed flowers.

The daylily pattern is an especially good one to use on paper-backed fabrics. To create your own paper-backed fabric, choose a lightweight, small print gingham or calico fabric and apply a light coating of spray adhesive to the back. Next, press a sheet of colored tissue or other lightweight paper against the adhesive side of the fabric. Cut out the flower patterns from this material and create floral displays coordinated with the room interiors of your home. The daylily will give you a feeling of summer all year round.

Design Tips
- For best efect, use two-tone paper with a light and dark hue of the same color. Use bright or dusty greens for the stems and leaves.
- Make long stems from heavyweight papers or extra folded-layers to keep them sturdy. Florist's wire is also useful.
- When using the lily as the only flower in an arrangement, cut stems to vary the length. Use lily leaves by themselves, as a graceful green accent in mixed paper flower arrangements.

1   *Score the center of three petals, along the three printed lines. These are the centerlines.*

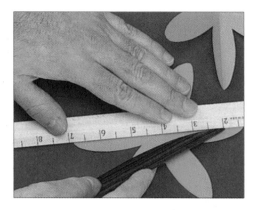

2   *On the outside (light hue side) of the paper, mountain-fold and unfold across gap notches (between petals). Repeat with the other two sets of opposing gap notches. Fold the shape in half three times, then pierce the center to make a small hole for the stem.*

3   *On either side of the three centerlines is a mountain-crease. Fold each mountain-crease against and aligned to its corresponding centerline. Repeat with the other two sets of centerlines and mountain-folds. You will end up with three petals on the outside and three petals on the inside.*

4   *Glue together the overlapping paper of the outside petals, to keep the lily's trumpet shape tight. Let dry. Curl down the outside petals. Make some lilies more open than others. You may also have a few with the petals curled.*

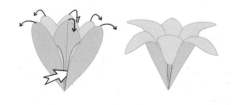

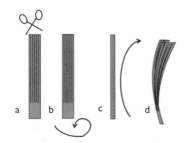

5 To make the filaments for the center, cut the provided paper into thin strips that remain connected at the bottom (a). Curl this paper into a tight cylinder by wrapping it around a toothpick (b&c). Fan out for filaments and give each a slight curl (d).

6 Make stems by folding stem paper in half twice, lengthwise, to make a thin, four-layered paper spear. Two-thirds from the bottom of the leaf, fold the leaf in half lengthwise. You may then leave the leaf straight or gently curl in downward.

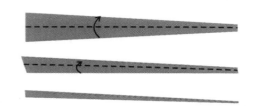

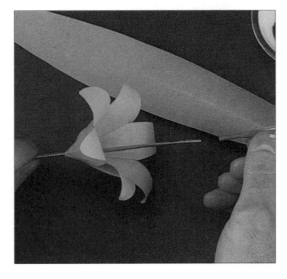

7 Insert the stem through the center hole from the bottom. Spear the cylinder end of the filament bundle with the protruding point of the stem, inside the trumpet of the flower. Use glue to keep the assembly secure.

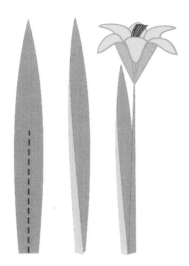

8 *Glue the leaf to the base of the stem. More than one leaf per stem and flower is a nice touch.*

9 *The finished daylily—ready for display.*

Daylily Shortcuts

You can make long stems quickly by folding paper in half lengthwise, then cutting the folded edge of the paper away as a long and tapered stem shape. This stem paper will already be folded in half the long way. Also, try folding several layers of lightweight paper together and cutting out several stems at once.

DAYLILY GALLERY

A paper butterfly lights on an arrangement of daylilies. The butterfly may be attached to a thin wire or glued directly to one of the blooms.

Daylily made of paper-backed fabric. Choose a light weight fabric and attach a thin but strong backing paper with spray adhesive or glue. You can coordinate arrangements and colors with any room or occasion.

Miniature lilies make elegant gift ties. Gifts may be simply enclosed in a cloth or paper sack and decorated with a gift tie attached with ribbon.

Miniature daylilies make an attractive lapel pin. Glue the lily to a small clasp pin or attach it directly to your lapel with a straight pin.

Daylilies made of handmade Japanese papers. A long-stem arrangement in a tall vase is a quick and simple way to make a large accent piece. Notice that paper leaves are used as the support media and show through the glass vase in an attractive way.

PAPER POSIES

Posies are small wildflowers, such as buttercups, that bloom in the late spring and summer. Lady-smock and cuckoo-flower are traditional names for posies. Fields of posies growing wild are a sign of high summer in many parts of the world, but with the designs suggested here they are accessible to everyone. Common to grassy slopes, and growing in hues of silver-white, delicate pink and rich yellow, posies—whether paper or perennial—look best arranged together in small vases, or in a small nosegay, tied-up with a ribbon. Without scent, but sweet in their appearance, posies suggest innocence and informality; they may not be as grand as some flowers, but they have a charm that is all their own. Paper with a subtle sheen is best to reflect the silky, slightly waxy quality of posy flower petals.

HOW TO BUILD A POSY

Posies can be a single, small, fragrant flower or a bunch of them. Posy is the informal name for wildflowers, gathered during a pleasant stroll and assembled into a spontaneous bouquet. The appeal of posies is their informality and innocent charm. And, because they come in such variety, they present us with a wide selection of design options.

The posy selection here contains two types of small flowers: daisies and buttercups. Each is quick and easy to make—you can fill a May basket in no time at all. Do not hesitate to add these little paper flowers to any dried flower arrangement; they will fit in quite nicely and will help give it a natural look.

Some paper butterflies are also included, to add to the effect of a bright, summer afternoon. You may wish to create your own butterflies by painting butterfly wing patterns on watercolor paper and using the cut-and-fold method as indicated on the pattern sheet.

YOU WILL NEED

- **Posy paper elements**
- **Scissors**
- **White glue**
- **Ruler or other straightedge**
- **Scoring tool**
- **Pencil—to open a hole in the base of the blossom**
- **Toothpick**

Design Tips

- Choose colors typical of wildflowers, especially violet, yellow and white. Use drab or deep greens for the stems, to reflect that these are summer plants.
- The two-tone paper supplied for this project has a different color on each side. You can fold the project with either side outward.
- Add leaves from the other flower patterns in this book. Glue the leaves and blossoms in place for permanence.
- Tie together a bouquet of posies with ribbon and lace for a formal occasion or string them together to make garlands and leis.
- Cut butterfly shapes out of any brightly colored or patterned papers. Butterflies make great accents to any arrangement. Use them to decorate packages or as a brooch.

I Following the lines indicated, score one side of the paper buttercup pattern. This will be the "show side". You may lightly pencil these lines in first if you are not sure you are clear on their arrangement. Turn paper over.

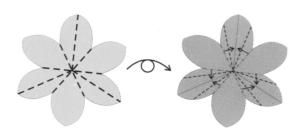

2 Fold the short creases (located between each petal) to touch and align with the long creases (running through the center of three of the petals). Notice that there are only three long creases and each long crease has a short crease on either side. If you fold correctly, the finished piece will look like an upside-down, conical paper cup. Turn the form over.

3 From this view you can see inside the buttercup - the three narrow petals will be very distinct. Using a pencil or toothpick, pierce a hole in the center. Do not make this hole too large— leave the paper snug enough for the stem to get a good hold.

4 *Make stems by folding stem paper in half lengthwise, twice, to get a thin, four-layered paper spear.*

5 *Insert the paper stem into the hole.*

6 To Make a Daisy
Score or valley-fold creases up the center of each petal. Make sure that these folds are neat and crisp. Turn paper over. Score or valley-crease folds running straight between each petal. Using a pencil or toothpick, pierce a hole in the center. Do not make this hole too large—leave the paper snug enough for the stem to get a good hold. Put the stem paper through the center hole from the underside, working until the fit is very snug. Either side of the paper will work for the outside of the flower. You may also add the button center described in the Daisy project. Trim any excess stem paper from the flowerleaf center.

7 To Make a Butterfly
Mountain- and valley-fold, as indicated and bring the forewings to the hindwings (a). The forewings should overlap the hindwings slightly. Mountain-fold the center of the butterfly's body. Valley-fold along the body and wing attachment lines to bring the wings into a natural position (b).

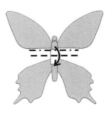

8   *The finished butterfly. Add a butterfly or two to any summer bouquet of flowers.*

9   *Cut out the paper vase elements and valley-fold on the dashed lines. Paste tab (a) to the inner edge (b) and tab (c) to the inner edge (d). Place the completed vase over a small can or plastic drinking cup and fill with paper flowers.*

10   *The completed project: paper vase, posies and butterfly.*

Posy Shortcuts

Save time cutting out flowerleaf elements by stacking up four sheets of colored paper and cutting them all at once. Trace the outline of the template onto the top layer of the paper stack, then cut. Be sure to keen all of the paper layers tightly together as you cut.

POSY GALLERY

Coffee cake garnish with daisy and buttercup blossoms. Use paper posies to garnish all types of salads and desserts.

A May basket filled with posies is a delightful project for young and old. The basket is a simple, construction paper cylinder wrapped around a paper cup. The edges of the basket were made fancy with scissor-cut fringe. A long strip of construction paper makes a good handle.

Posies arranged in a simple pitcher. A cheerful accent piece or gift. Make longer stems and create colorful arrangements in any container.

String together buttercup blossoms to make a lei or garland to grace an item or a setting. A needle and thread make quick work of this lovely floral accent piece.

A gathering of paper posies makes a fine nosegay. A ten-inch piece of green paper cut and folded in a buttercup pattern serves as collar and background to this handheld arrangement.

PAPER LOTUS

Exotic and mysterious are the words traditionally used to describe the lotus or water lily. Lotus blossoms set against the dark and quiet water of a secluded pond are one of natures most evocative and enchanting sights. This design will create a really atmospheric display.

Design Tips

- Any color is suitable for the blossom, in nature lotus colors range from deep crimson to stark white.

- To float paper lotus blossoms, make thin wax floats by dripping melted wax onto a cold water surface. Place the floats on the surface of a punch bowl or beverage and rest the lotus blossoms on top.

- Use only food-grade waxed papers for lotuses to garnish food. Glue the other elements together with drops of melted candle wax instead of paste or glue.

- Always use caution when working with melted wax and flame. Keep any candle flame away from paper ornaments.

YOU WILL NEED

- **Lotus paper elements**
- **Scissors**
- **White glue**
- **Ruler or other straightedge**
- **Scoring tool**
- **Pencil**

HOW TO BUILD A LOTUS

Although it appears complex, the lotus that follows is one of the easiest constructions in this section of the book. It is also the most beautiful. You will be surprised at how effectively a single lotus blossom and lily pad can cast splendid spell. Arrangements of water lilies are perfect for dinner table centerpieces, the coffee table or a display shelf in the book case. You can use your most elegant papers on this model. However, with the distinctive shape of this plant, even plain white shelf paper will be transformed when you fold it into a lotus. Scale the pattern as large or as small as needed for your arrangements—or make the flowers more lush by adding extra layers of paper.

1 Score or valley-fold the center petal. Do this to all three pink sets of petals and both yellow sets. It does not matter which side of the paper you choose, so long as all the creases are valley-folds. The valley-fold side will be the inner side of the finished flower.

2 Valley-fold along the base of each petal. Do this to all three pink sets of petals and both yellow sets.

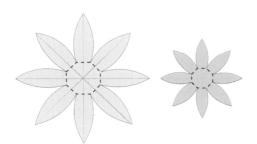

3 *Apply a little glue or paste to the center of the underside (mountain-fold side) of each element and stack them one on top of the other as shown. Be sure to rotate each petal set so that the petals from one layer show between the petals above it. Press together firmly and let dry. The petals in the center should be more tightly closed than the outer petals.*

4 *Put a valley-crease through the middle of the lily pad. This will be the outer side of the leaf.*

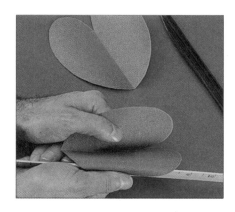

6 *The completed lotus—ready for display.*

5 *You may curl the outer edges of the leaves up or down for a more natural effect.*

LOTUS GALLERY

A lotus and paper frog in a display setting (the frog is displayed in a different chapter).

Make a decorative indoor wreath of lotus and rose elements. Alternate color layers of lotus elements to support and frame each rose blossom. Secure each piece to a cardboard ring and loop of cord attached to the back for hanging. A hot-melt glue gun makes quick work of the final assembly.

To beautify a formal dinner setting, use a paper lotus to fill each guest's empty plate. Each guest can then keep their lotus as a memento.

Float a lotus bloom in a punch bowl for an exotic touch. Make the blossom out of waxed paper or foil and set it on top of a wax float that is at least the diameter of the base of the bloom. Remove from bowl at serving time.

The lotus makes a wonderful table centerpiece because of its elegant and low height. You can also make blossoms to match your dinner napkins. Back fabric pieces with paper to make them suitably foldable. Practise on scrap material first.

PAPER CACTUS

The flowering cactus is romantic: one is reminded of painted deserts, western sunsets and the lone cry of the coyote. The beautiful blossoming of an otherwise drab and humble plant is a Cinderella story, illustrative of hope and self-confidence. The cactus is all this and more, and its interesting shape makes for an unusual yet eye-catching display.

Design Tips

- Choose rich green colors in glossy or semi-glossy materials. The cactus plant is succulent; the material should look appetising. Any color paper is suitable for the bloom.
- Make small cactus shapes and attach to large cacti as buds. Blossom and bud elements should be glued in place for permanence.
- Display finished cacti with sand or terra-cotta colors. Natural materials are especially effective. Fill a tray or planter with aquarium gravel or sand for an easy "anchor" medium.
- Vary the number and proportions of the radial arms of the cactus plant patterns to create cacti of all shapes and sizes.

YOU WILL NEED

- **Cactus paper elements**
- **Scissors**
- **White glue**
- **Ruler or other straightedge**
- **Scoring tool**
- **Pencil**
- **Flower pot, tray or planter**
- **Aquarium gravel or sand**

HOW TO BUILD A CACTUS

Our cactus is a simple construction; easily modified and quick to assemble, you can arrange a table-top desert in no time. Create cacti to accent a summer dinner party or to adorn gifts. Or present one to friends who have trouble keeping potted plants alive. They are not an obvious plant to make as part of a display, but that is part of their charm. Although these paper models look realistic, they are best kept from water completely.

Finally, be creative with the choice of materials and dimensions of the cacti you make on your own. Use paper-backed fabrics or vinyl wallpapers for their durability and texture. And the size of these materials will allow you to construct some very large specimens indeed, as you will see in the cactus gallery (pages 72-3).

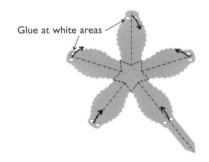

1 *Score or valley-fold the center of each petal and the area between each petal. Turn the paper over.*

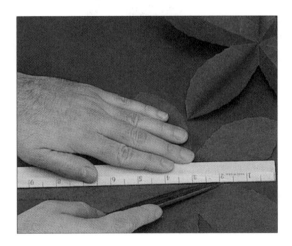

2 *Score a five pointed star (dotted lines provided) on the inside surface of the model paper. Use a pencil for this step, since the pencil marks will not be visible once the model is folded.*

Glue at white areas

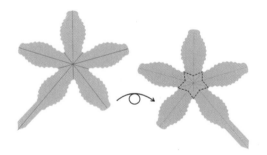

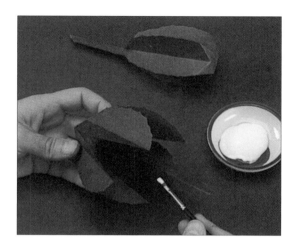

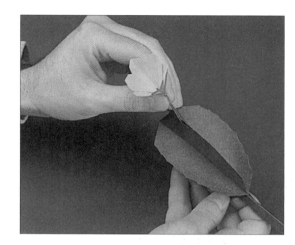

3 Apply glue or paste to the end of the inside paper surfaces (side of paper with the star). Mountain- and valley-fold on the crease lines to close and shape the cactus plant. Hold the crease lines to close and shape the cactus plant. Hold surfaces together until the glue sets.

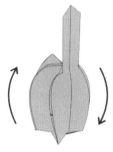

4 Rotate the model so that the anchoring spike points down. Create a cactus blossom from the provided material, following the folding and construction method of the buttercup in the posy instruction set. Insert the stem of the completed blossom between paper layers of cactus plant so that the blossom is seated firmly and attractively.

6 The finished cactus plant—ready for display.

5 Plant the paper spike into the selected medium. It is not necessary to have a blossom on each cactus if more than one plant is displayed in the same arrangement.

CACTUS GALLERY

The cactus makes an unusual yet eye-catching package ornament. Wrap the package first, then make a small slit through the wrapping paper whenever you want to place a cactus. Flatten the pointed planting tab and slip it into the slot in the wrap. Crease the base of the tab firmly, so the cactus will stand upright.

You can modify the basic cactus pattern proportions to create cacti of all sizes and dimensions. Make small cacti and attach as budding nodules, with or without blossoms.

A festive buffet setting. The cactus pictured is made of paper-backed fabric and the tortilla chips are handmade paper. The cactus coordinates with the cloth dinner napkins. Choose a lightweight fabric and apply a thin but strong backing paper with a spray adhesive or paste.

Arrange cacti on fabric, paper or sand for a background or display. Add some natural materials for texture and effect—scale from miniature to life-size.

Arrangements of cacti in terra-cotta pots looks very realistic. Mix and match blossom colors, you can even use different textures and shades of green among the cacti plants themselves. Fill pots with sand or gravel for easy "planting".

PAPER ANIMALS

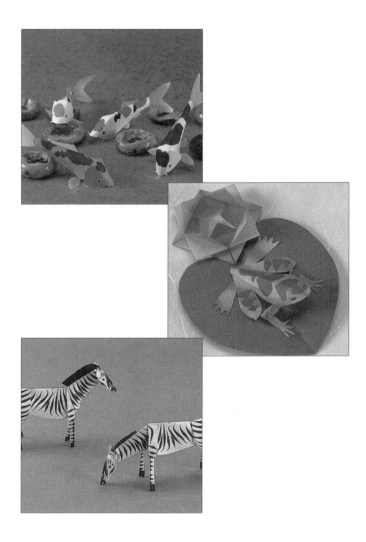

INTRODUCTION

The paper animals presented in this section were chosen carefully, with an eye toward offering projects with a range of construction techniques. Each animal is built with a unique folding method, and each method has its own particular strengths. Design tips and a gallery section round out the projects and demonstrate the many possibilities of the papers and templates provided. Printed templates are provided for all the projects in this book and can be found at the back. Trace the templates to create animals from any material you choose. Or adapt these animal shapes to design creatures of your own.

Enjoy

GLOSSARY AND KEY

If you have skipped the chapter on making paper flowers, you may not be aware of the different types of folds you will need to use in order to complete the projects; and if you have already worked your way through the paper flower projects, there is certainly no harm in recapping the techniques required before progressing to the paper animal projects.

Because the illustrations can show only a segment of a project's folding procedure, it is helpful to know whether the paper is being folded in front or from behind. The origami system of valley-folds and mountain-folds uses two kinds of broken lines (see key diagram) to show when to fold toward the project's surface (valley-fold) and when to fold behind the surface (mountain-fold).

Valley-fold—Relative to the display view of the paper being folded, a valley-fold is always folded in front of the project's surface. If you were to unfold a valley-fold you would see a valley-crease, which dents into the paper's surface forming a valley.

Mountain-fold—Relative to the displayed view of the paper being folded, a mountain-fold is always folded behind the project's surface. If you were to unfold a mountain-fold you would see a mountain-crease, which rises up from the paper's surface forming a mountain ridge.

Various types of arrows help make the folding instructions even clearer. These arrows are easy to understand with a quick study of the illustrated key. Whenever you see the repeat arrow in a diagram, you must apply the demonstrated folding procedure to all indicated parts of the project. If, when embarking on a project, you are unsure what a diagram is instructing you to do, simply refer back to these pages before continuing. Once you have completed a couple of projects, you will find that you will be able to interpret the diagrams easily.

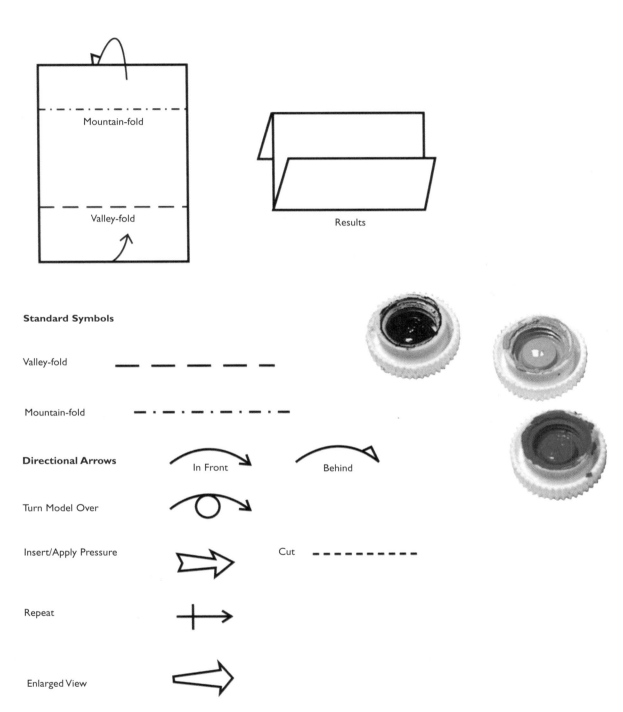

Mountain-fold

Valley-fold

Results

Standard Symbols

Valley-fold

Mountain-fold

Directional Arrows

In Front

Behind

Turn Model Over

Insert/Apply Pressure

Cut

Repeat

Enlarged View

PAINTING & DECORATING

Whether you choose plain or patterned paper, the animal shapes in these projects are distinct enough to stand on their own. If you would like to decorate the animals to make them more realistic or more fanciful, you can use acrylic paint, inks, markers, crayons, stencils, appliqués, and even monoprinting. When painting and decorating the projects, you don't have to limit yourself to realism—feel free to experiment with all kinds of colors and patterns.

Add Shine

Apply a rainbow of shimmering luster with iridescent acrylic paint. These paints come in many colors and are permanent and fade-resistant. For best results, paint a dark base-coat first. Paint on a smooth, seamless field of iridescence or try using brushes, rollers, sponges or rags to make textured and mottled effects. This paint works especially well to decorate the frog and the lizard projects.

Sponge Paint

Daubing on paint makes it easy to produce textures and multicolored effects. Use a sponge or wadded rag to dab or streak broken areas of color over the paper. Use a separate sponge or rag each color and apply dark colors first. Experiment with smudging or scraping the applied paints while they are wet. Acrylic tube colors are the best choice for this technique, since they are flexible and water resistant when dry. Use only non-toxic colors around children. This technique is also great for decorating paper turtles and fish.

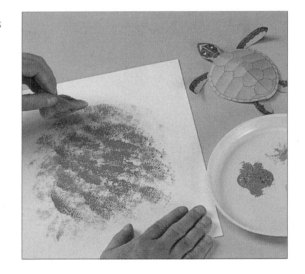

Add Texture

You can copy the texture of many different surfaces with the crayon rubbing technique. Place paper over the chosen texture and rub with a crayon. Oil pastels, colored pencils, and varying the amount of pressure and shape of stroke will produce different effects. A plastic mesh bag, such as a grocery fruit bag, is wonderful for making "reptile skin" textures.

Japanese Style

What better way to ornament koi than with a Japanese painting style, brush (fude) and ink (sumi). To get this effect, paint on heavyweight, bright white, absorbent paper. Black, crimson and vermilion inks are best for koi. Prepare a liquid painting solution, load the brush with ink or paint, and touch the tip to the surface of the paper. Allow the ink or paint to bleed into the paper as you go: aim for rounded shapes wth slightly soft edges. You may want to practise on ordinary newsprint first.

Appliqués

Appliqués decorate paper with very precise, rich patterns. Here, colored shapes for a parrot are cut out, then pasted in place. This can be done before or after cutting out the final paper form. Draw a light pencil line to indicate the proper placement of the various elements.

Monoprints

1 Monoprinting can generate a wide variety of effects on paper. The basic materials needed substrate, paint, paper and a burnishing tool. Many types of surfaces and paints will work to create monoprints: here, we used a stiff plastic board and acrylic tube paints. To get this effect, apply a color in parallel rows directly from the tube and smear with a piece of cardboard.

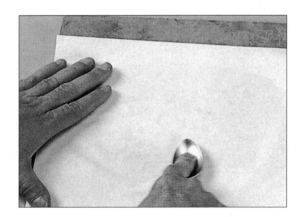

2 Place substrate-coated paper face-down on the cardboard and run with the back of a spoon to impress the paint on the surface of the paper.

3 Peel the paper up and let dry. It is possible to obtain several prints from one prepared surface.

Stencils

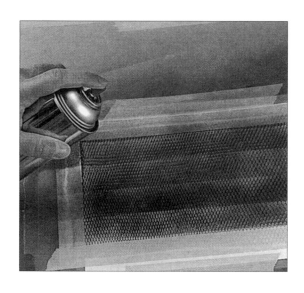

1 Stencils will also produce rich patterns and textures on paper. You can color or paint stencils by hand, or use spray paint for a fast finish. To stencil with spray paint, sandwich the chosen paper between the stencil and an "over-spray" sheet. The over-spray sheet will protect your work. Make sure that the stencil lies completely flat against the surface of the paper to be decorated. Spray paint in an even, controlled manner—or experiment by spraying short bursts, long and narrow bands, circular patterns, etc.

2 Each method will yield different results from the same stencil. Carefully remove the stencil and paper from the over-spray sheet and allow to dry. Always work in well-ventilated areas and use a respirator if suggested by the manufacturer.

PAPER FROG

Frogs and toads figure in many traditional tales and legends all over the world. Their amusing, odd shapes make them charming and sometimes irresistible, and make excellent subjects for artists and craftspeople alike. Over the years, frogs have been fashioned from every kind of material available: gold, silver, semiprecious stones, wood, porcelain, and, of course, paper. Some people like to collect frogs and toads, others may keep at least one for good luck.

The Japanese word for frog is *kaeru*, which sounds just like the Japanese word for "return home" and can be taken to mean: "hopefully you will return" (the likely explanation for this is that frogs usually return to the same ponds every year). A gift of the likeness of a frog means the same thing: give these paper frogs to friends as keepsakes that invite a return visit; or as mementos to wish travelers safe return home.

HOW TO BUILD A PAPER FROG

The frog project described here is easy to make and fun to decorate. Although we often associate frogs with the color green, real frogs come in every color of the rainbow, so anything goes for paper frogs. Bright or drab, speckled or striped, these frogs will liven up a table, bookcase, house plant, or windowsill.

Printed paper, to make both pond frogs and tree frogs, is provided in this book. Try your hand at decorating paper frogs and you'll see that they have a real charm all of their own.

YOU WILL NEED

- **Frog paper elements**
- **Scissors and/or X-acto knife**
- **Paste or glue stick**
- **Brush for applying paste**

Design Tips

- Use sharp scissors or an X-acto knife with a fresh blade to cut out the paper pattern. This will give you cleaner edges and a better looking model.
- When removing paper pieces, cut from the back side of the paper provided. Cut just inside the outlines and fold exactly on the indicated crease lines.
- Use very dark paper decorated with acrylic-based, iridescent paint to make frogs that look wet and slick.
- Create unusual jewelry by making frogs from foil or heavy aluminium embossing-sheets and then backing with a brooch pin.

1 *Score or valley-crease along the dashed lines on the underside of the frog pattern. This will give the frog's back a rounded shape. You can vary the degree of roundness by changing the angle of the folds.*

2 *Cut along the dotted lines to release the hind legs.*

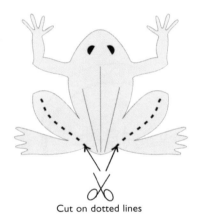

Cut on dotted lines

3 *Valley-fold the front legs inward, horizontally across the underside of the pattern.*

4 *Valley-fold the front legs at a downward angle away from the shoulder area.*

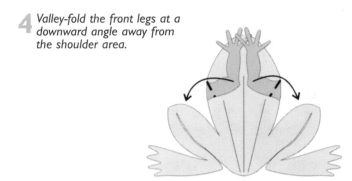

5 *Form "elbows" in the front legs by mountain-and valley-folding a V-shaped set of pleats. The completed folds will allow you to position the frog's legs in a variety of ways for a natural pose.*

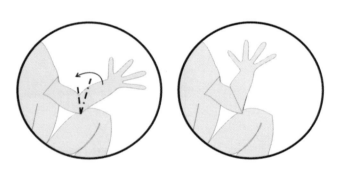

6 *Using an X-acto knife, cut a semi-circular line around the eyes of the frog. Turn the model over.*

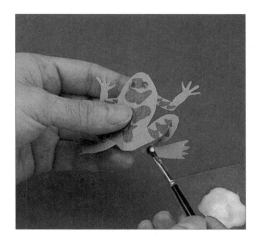

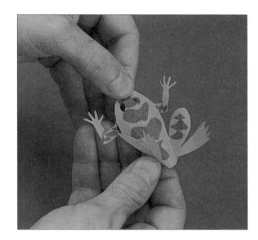

7 *Fold the eyelids up, away from this side of the paper. You can shape the paper lids with a slight curve or roundness. Apply a small dot of glue to the heel of each of the frog's back feet.*

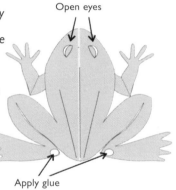

Open eyes

Apply glue

8 *Glue the heels under the rump of the frog to make the hind legs rounded and 3-dimensional. Valley-fold the hind legs at the waistline and adjust the all-over shape of the frog.*

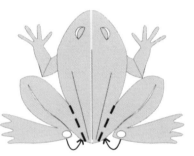

Glue heels under rump

9 *The finished frog.*

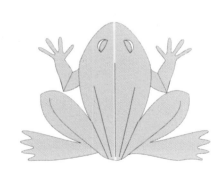

PAPER SEA TURTLE

There are more than two hundred species of turtles in the world. They live on land, in freshwater ponds, and in the sea. Since turtles are reputed to live a great many years, they are often used as symbols of longevity and security. Giving a gift with the figure of a turtle on it is a nice way to mark a christening, a wedding, or the opening of a new business. Turtles have a friendly charm, and people have reported feeling soothed simply by watching turtles. Who could possibly feel agitated when the pace of life is set by the turtle? Would that every day could be so calm.

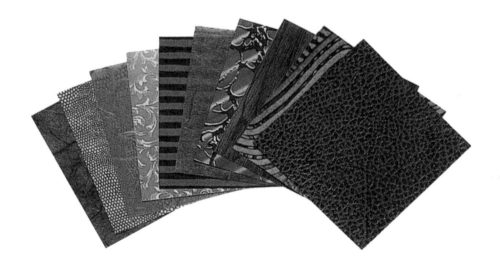

HOW TO BUILD A PAPER SEA TURTLE

As well as being an interesting project to make, the completed design also has a number of different uses. In addition to its decorative value, this turtle is also an unusual box that is handy for keeping small items on a desk or dresser top. You may choose to build just the top half of the sea turtle box—to make a wonderful gift package ornament or to string on a mobile.

Use the blue template to make sea turtles that coordinate with gift wrap, wallpaper, or any kind of paper you choose. The turtle is a symbol of wisdom, and the paper turtle box is a wise addition to any repertoire of gift creations.

YOU WILL NEED

- **Sea turtle box elements**
- **Scissors and/or X-acto knife**
- **Paste or glue stick**
- **Brush for applying paste**

Design Tips

- Use paste or a glue stick instead of liquid glue: paste will not warp paper as easily as liquid glue, and its slow drying time allows more time to posi tion elements.
- Work on only one tab at a time when making the base of the box. You will have better control if you proceed in order, one tab after the other, around the box perimeter.
- Center the box under the turtle-shell lid, so that the shell rim extends evenly beyond the edges of the box. Pre-flex the hinge before attaching the lid.
- Heavyweight paper with a surface texture works best for making the turtle box. Lightweight paper is fine for mobiles and package ornaments.

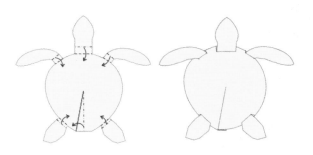

1 *Mountain and valley-fold the head and limbs of the sea turtle under the edge of the shell, as shown; you can swivel these parts to effect various swimming postures and to give each turtle more personality.*

2 *Round the shell of the turtle by mountain-folding a small ridge of paper at the back end. Make sure that no white paper remains visible on the other side of the shell. Secure folds with a little paste.*

3 *Pre-crease all the indicated fold lines on the paper for the box base. All but the tabs on the T-shaped extensions are valley folds.*

4 Valley-fold the T-shaped tab extensions inward. The top edge of each extension should touch the octagonal outline of the floor of the box.

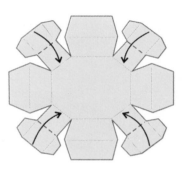

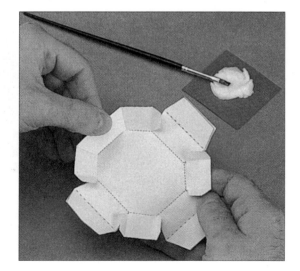

5 Apply paste to the outside of each of the eight tabs. The tabs to be pasted can be recognized by their slanted edges. There are two tabs on each of the T-shaped extensions.

Apply paste

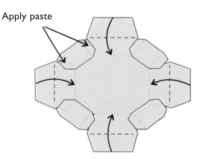

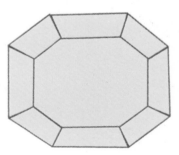

6 Press each pasted tab against its adjacent wall edge and fold the remaining extended edges of paper over all to cover. Press firmly to seal. The finished box bottom will have sloping sides and be somewhat dish-shaped.

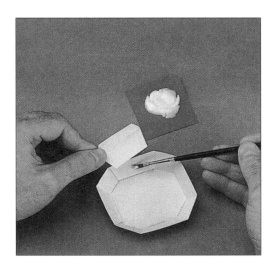

7 *Fold the paper hinge and paste one half to the inside of one the long walls of the box bottom.*

8 *Paste the other half of the paper hinge to the inside of the sea turtle shell. Align the box bottom with the center of the shell, so that the turtle's shell is centered over the box when the lid is closed.*

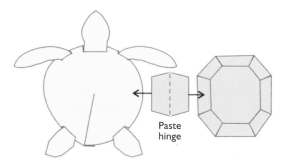

Paste
hinge

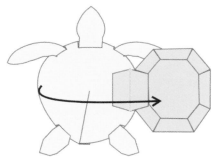

9 *The finished sea turtle box.*

PAPER LIZARD

Lizards and snakes are reptiles, cold-blooded animals that require warmth from the sun to get their day started. You may see these animals sunning themselves on rocks or stumps as if posing for a picture to be taken. Once startled, however, the show is quickly over and they flee for cover in the blink of an eye. Although they may not be the most popular animals with some people, lizards are a very interesting subject to make with paper. And, just like frogs, they come in all kinds of colors, not just green.

Salamanders, which resemble lizards in some ways, are amphibians and are more closely related to frogs and toads. They prefer watery or damp environments, and have no scales or claws. Because salamanders and lizards are shaped so similarly, you can adapt the same paper pattern to make either animal.

HOW TO BUILD A PAPER LIZARD

This lizard is modeled after a popular toy: you can assemble it without legs to make a snake. Use this pattern to make paper plastic lizards, salamanders, and snakes of every description. Use faux leather or crocodile and bright fabrics to make wonderful, durable versions of these toys, too. You don't have to stick with the standard green color that everyone associates with lizards—decorate with paint, sequins, glitter, and beads for fanciful and elaborate effects.

All of the projects in this chapter on paper animals are great inclusions in a mobile, and this lizard design is no exception: it will wiggle and sway in gentle air currents.

You can also make marionette lizards by attaching support threads to the feet.

YOU WILL NEED

- **Lizard paper elements**
- **Scissors and/or X-acto knife**
- **Paste or glue stick**
- **Brush for applying paste**

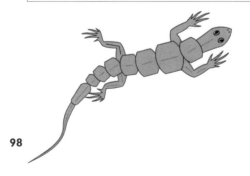

Design Tips

- Feel free to trim any paper that does not fit during assembly. The pattern is flexible and allows for variation.
- You can paste the leg elements on the top or bottom of any body segment, instead of assembling by the illustrated method. This simplifies construction and yields a different finished effect.
- As a shortcut, try simply cutting out the shape of the head at the eye area—instead of folding over the extra paper. You can then glue the simple paper head to the inside upper surface of the first body segment.
- Spread the body segments further apart for a more wiggly lizard.

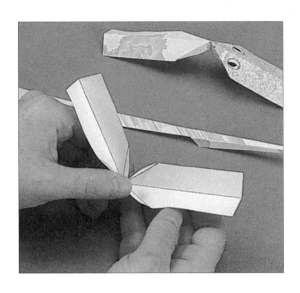

1 Work so that the lizard's face remains on the outside of the paper. Pre-crease all the lines on the lizard head paper and fold it in half, short edge to short edge. All but one of the pre-creases will be valley-folds. The short distance across the paper between the notches is a mountain-fold—it will be pushed into the larger fold to form a pointed nose.

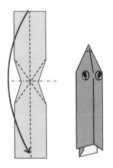

2 Before you attach the lizard's head to the tail, be sure that the edge of the tail with the raised "keel" is uppermost. Fold the paper over to form a neat edge: this is the top of the lizard's backbone. Apply paste to the wide end of the tail and slide it into the back of the lizard's head. Press the pasted papers together and flatten from side to side with your thumb.

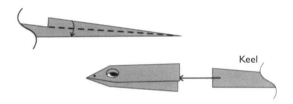

Keel

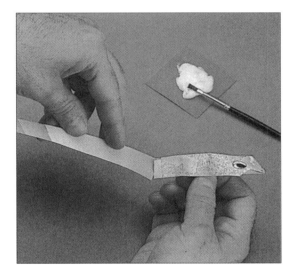

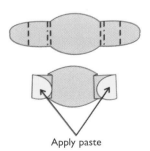

3 Mountain- and valley-fold each of the eight body segments, which are numbered on the underside. The number sequence begins at the head and ends with segment eight at the tail. Apply paste to each rounded tab just before you attach it to the tail strip.

Apply paste

4 *Pay careful attention to the proper attachment of the body segments. First, press a pasted tab on one side of the tail strip and secure. Bring the remaining tab around to the other side of the strip and attach it. Body segment number one should cover the joint between the head and the tail strip.*

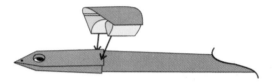

5 *Shape the front limbs of the lizard by mountain folding, then paste the limbs to the tail strip behind and slightly underneath the first body segment. Push the limbs under the body segment as far as possible without dislodging the segments.*

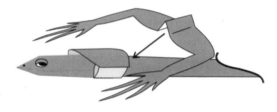

6 *Add body segments 2 through 4 in the same manner. Be sure that body segment number 2 covers the front limb attachment area. Add the hind limbs after segment 4, nesting them in the same manner as the front limbs. Attach the remaining body segment pieces.*

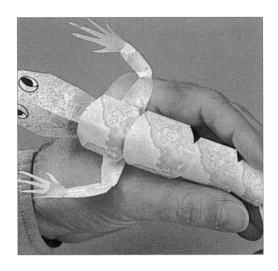

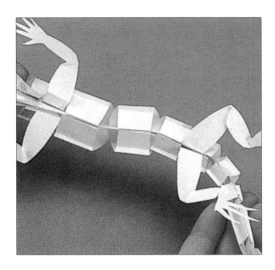

7 Once the hind limbs and the remaining body segments are in place, you can add detail by shaping each of the limbs: Make a few simple creases down the middle line of each limb, and accent "shoulder" and "elbow" joints with creases, too.

8 This flexible model can be posed in many ways.

9 The Finished lizard.

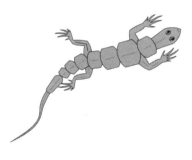

PAPER KOI

In Japan, the carp symbolizes strength. Colorful kites resembling carp are hoisted each year in celebration of Boy's Day, a national Japanese holiday. The Japanese treasure the beauty of carp, and have traditionally bred many beautiful ornamental varieties, called koi. Today, people of the world are discovering the beauty of koi—raising them in aquariums, garden pools, and simple backyard ponds. But you don't need to have a pond or aquarium to appreciate the beauty of these animals—you can stock an indoor garden with these charming paper substitutes. The standard white and orange-red patterns can be exchanged for all manner of colorful alternatives.

HOW TO BUILD A PAPER KOI

Koi are considered very intelligent and friendly fish, and koi fanciers have bred some exceptionally beautiful varieties. Since they are popular features of many public gardens, it is likely you will be able to find live koi for inspiration, but if not, images can be found in books and on the internet.

With a few sheets of paper and some paint you can create your very own paper koi pond at home. Decorating paper koi with signature patterns of crimson, black, and gold is nearly as much fun as building them. You can paint the paper before you cut out the pattern, or you may prefer to compose the design on a finished, blank paper model. Either way you will want variety in the collection, so try both.

YOU WILL NEED

- **Koi paper elements**
- **Scissors and/or X-acto knife**
- **Paste or glue stick**
- **Brush for applying paste**

Design Tips

- When pasting the rear ventral fins to each side of the keel in step 4, keep the sides of the body, near the tail, rounded as you paste. The body will remain nicely rounded once secured in this way.
- When bending the head down on step 6, remember to just hide the paper tabs with the gill covers—no further.
- When arranging groups of paper fish, curl the fins in a variety of ways, especially the tail fin.
- If you want to paint your koi, construct them from very white, slightly absorbent paper, such as watercolor paper. Apply paint with a light touch.

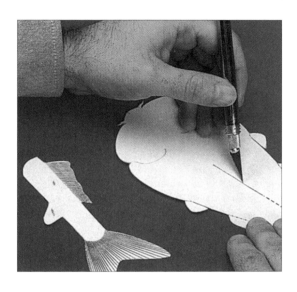

1 *Use an X-acto knife to cut carefully on the dotted lines for the gills and center slot of the koi. DO NOT cut on the dashed lines.*

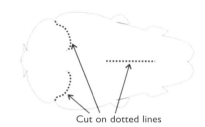

Cut on dotted lines

2 *Mountain-fold the fins flanking the paper shape, as shown and valley-fold the middle from the back end to the center slot.*

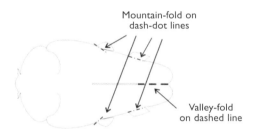

Mountain-fold on dash-dot lines

Valley-fold on dashed line

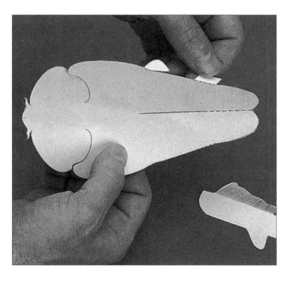

3 *Apply paste to both sides of the indicated keel of the fin. Keeping the body paper flat, slip top (dorsal) fin through the center slot that you cut in step 1.*

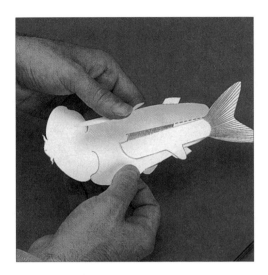

4 Fold the koi body paper in half and over the fin assembly. Keep the sides of the paper somewhat rounded as you attached the small, rectangular set of fins to the pasted keel. Carefully check the appearance of the koi at this point. The body should be conical and trim.

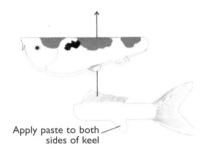

Apply paste to both
sides of keel

5 Trim any excess keel paper protruding from the pasted fin area. Fold back the rounded tabs near the gill covers.

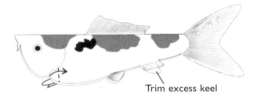

Trim excess keel

6 Apply paste to the outside of the folded tabs and bend the head just enough to attach the gill covers to the folded tabs.

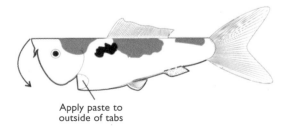

Apply paste to
outside of tabs

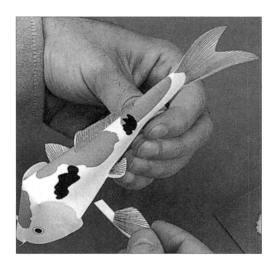

7 *The effect is a graceful, rounded fold for the slope of the koi's head. The gills should stand slightly open.*

8 *Apply paste to the tabs of the pectoral fins (they are labeled) and attach them to the inside walls of the open front, below and just behind the head. You can adjust these fins to any position that suits you.*

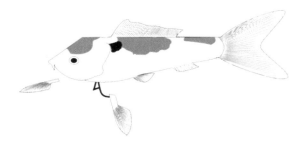

9 *The finished koi.*

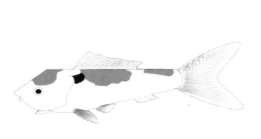

PAPER ZEBRA

Describe a zebra in three words, and you will probably come up with: wild, African horse. Contemplate each of these words and you will begin to understand the zebra. Wild: there is something inherently primitive and untamed about zebras. African: zebras live in the wild only in Africa, that huge and most exotic of continents. Horse: we connect with the zebra because we are so familiar with its cousin, the domestic horse. While this gives us some insight into zebras, their mystical quality remains. Even as still paper forms, they look exotic. Unlike many of the other projects in this chapter, there isn't a lot of scope for changing the colors and patterns here; however, the template can be easily modified to make horses and many other four-legged animals.

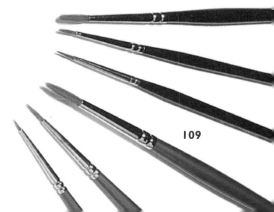

HOW TO BUILD A PAPER ZEBRA

The construction method demonstrated for the zebra adapts for creating most other four-legged animals: dogs, giraffes, elephants, cats, etc. If you choose to make a zebra and not a horse, don't be put off by trying to match up the stripes. The pattern is so busy that it hides slight imperfections in construction.

You can scale the pattern up or down on a copy machine, to make very large or miniature animals. Paper is provided for making one zebra and one horse. You can create ponies by shrinking the horse pattern slightly. The zebra is suited to constructing in herds—especially if you include a few small zebra colts.

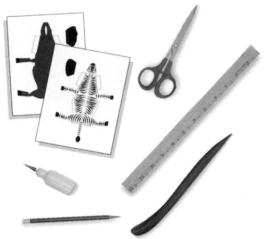

YOU WILL NEED

- **Zebra paper elements**
- **Scissors and/or X-acto knife**
- **Paste or glue stick**
- **Brush for applying paste**
- **Straightedge**
- **Letter opener**

Design Tips

- For practice, make multiple photocopies of the cutout and read through the steps before you begin.
- Experiment with poses for the head and legs. Consult photographs of horses and zebras for ideas.
- After final assembly, trim the bottoms of the hooves so that they are all even and neat. This is the best way to adjust the stance.
- Use glue or paste to keep the body closed and the legs close together.

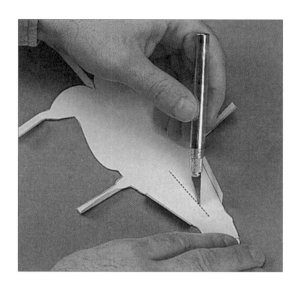

1 With an X-acto knife, cut open the slot for the mane. Valley-fold the leg and neck tabs in. Trim the bottom of the hooves if necessary. Turn the model over.

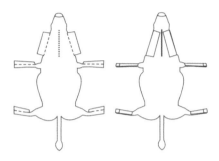

2 Using the X-acto knife, cut around the outer edges of the ears to partially separate them from the head.

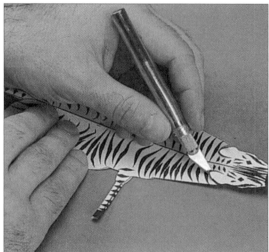

3 To form the rump, mountain- and valley-fold the hindquarters on the lines indicated.

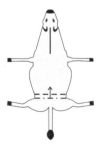

4   *Mountain- and valley-fold the forequarters, to form the shoulders.*

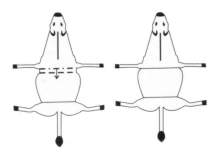

5   *Fold the neck back against the body. The fold line should run straight across the front line of the forelegs.*

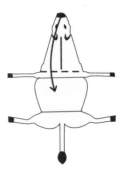

6   *Look carefully at the dashed lines on the underside of the neck in the illustration. Using a straightedge and letter opener, pre-crease lines like those on the model. The angle of these folds is adjustable, so there is no precise placement. After pre-creasing the paper, fold the neck forward while folding the zebra in half lengthwise.*

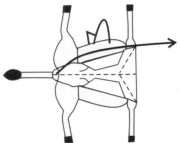

7 *Bend the head downward while allowing the ears to rotate upward. Once you are happy with the angle, gently press in the sides of the head to crease it in place. Here, too, you can make adjustments.*

8 *Insert the mane through the slot in the back of the neck. Secure it in place with a little glue. For added effect, you can snip the mane with scissors. Bend the tail down.*

9 *The finished zebra. The neck can be adjusted in different postures.*

PAPER GLIDING BIRD

Paper gliders become even more fun when you can take pride in the fact that you have built them yourself. Kites and toy gliders come in all shapes and colors, but none are more inspiring than those that resemble some wonderful bird, plying the winds and seeming to come to life in the breeze of a sunny day.

When building a new glider, always take care to fold very neatly. The number one axiom for best performance is balance! Once you understand the basics of good flight performance, you will want to make flocks of new flying creatures. Experience is the best teacher and don't waste any more time—test your wings!

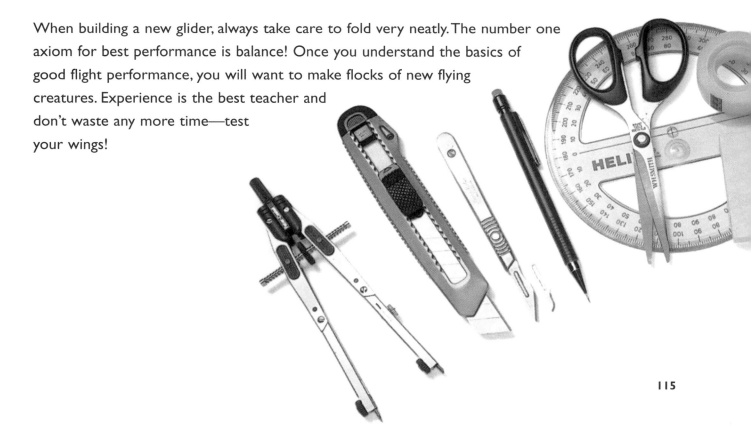

HOW TO BUILD A PAPER GLIDING BIRD

This graceful glider is fun to make and even more fun to fly. Use the gliding bird as a party favorite, or build a mobile and display a whole flock. If you are making a gliding bird purely for decorative purposes, you can use any kind of paper, but if you want to fly your bird, then lightweight paper makes the best gliders.

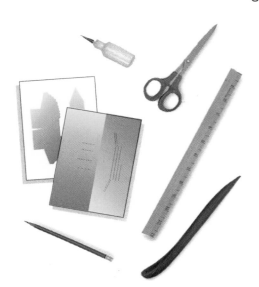

Once you master the simple method of construction, you can adapt this pattern to make gliders of your own devising. The front edges of the wings are thick, folded layers of paper for stiffness. The body of the bird also has layered folds, to weight the front and to provide stable seating for the wings. Paste and glue is not needed for assembly but we recommend it for performance.

YOU WILL NEED

- **Glider bird paper elements**
- **Scissors and/or X-acto knife**
- **Paste, glue stick or tape**
- **Brush for applying paste**

Design Tips
- Be sure to cut neatly to preserve the symmetry of the wings. The wings control the bird's balance during flight.
- For faster flights, weight the front of the bird by adding a few pieces of tape.
- Before launching, check that the wings and tail are evenly set and without any twists or dents.
- Small birds, made out of reasonably stiff paper, fly the best. Experiment with different launching techniques. Basically, any way that you are able to get this bird into the air should produce a gliding flight.

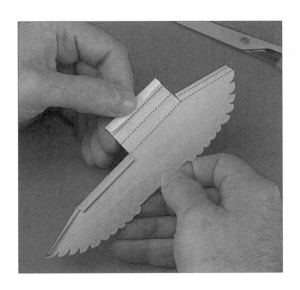

1. Begin by valley-folding the leading edges of the wing paper to make them dense and rigid. You should fold the narrow, flanking edges first, then the two large center areas. The larger edges will overlap the smaller edges and hold them in place. You can use the glue or tape to keep the folded, leading edges in place.

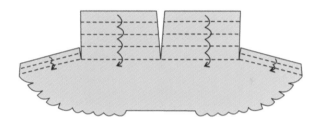

2. Valley-fold the outer wing areas. Mountain-fold the center of the wing. The resulting M-shape of the final wing will provide additional stability in flight.

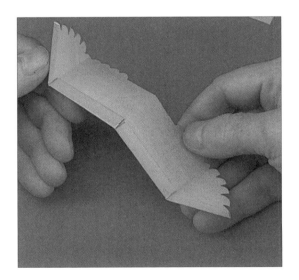

3. Begin to shape the body by mountain- and valley-folding the part of the body strip closest to the tail. Light-colored dashed lines are printed on the paper as a guide. The result of the first two folds will look like the figure in step 4.

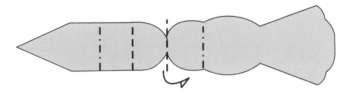

4 *Valley- and mountain-fold the remaining portion of the strip. The folds of paper at the front of the body provide the extra weight that will pull the model forward, through the air.*

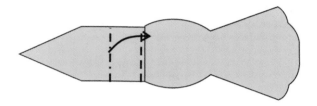

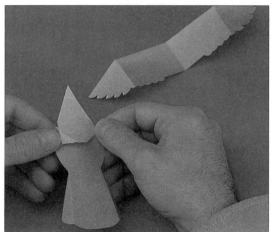

5 *Mountain-fold the two indicated corners of the layered paper as shown, so that they disappear under the square edge. This helps to lock these layers in place. Mountain-fold the tail edges to form the tail stabilizers.*

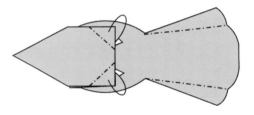

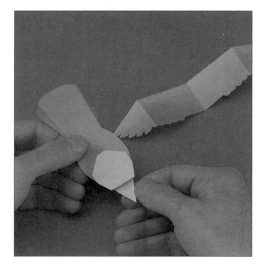

6 *Form the bird head and beak area by mountain- and valley-folding the pointed end of the body strip. There is no ideal placement for these particular folds, so just use your judgment. Mountain-fold the smaller side corners.*

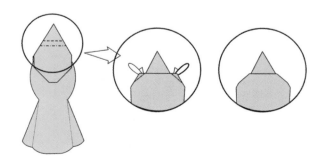

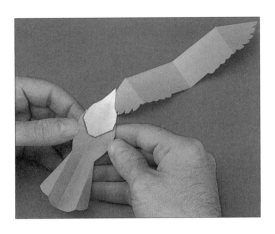

7 *Valley-fold the body in half, lengthwise, to make a V-shape channel. This channel forms a stabilizing keel and a center valley to cradle the wings of the bird.*

8 *Insert the paper wings under the heavy folded paper edge of the head. You can use a bit of glue or tape to secure the assembly, but it is often not necessary if you have folded the paper crisply and neatly.*

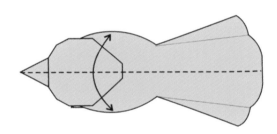

9 *The finished gliding bird. To launch, hold on to the front center edge of the wing assembly and toss the glider bird straight up, over your head in a backhand manner. The idea is to get the paper bird high in the air, where it will recover from a graceful loop and glide slowly to the ground.*

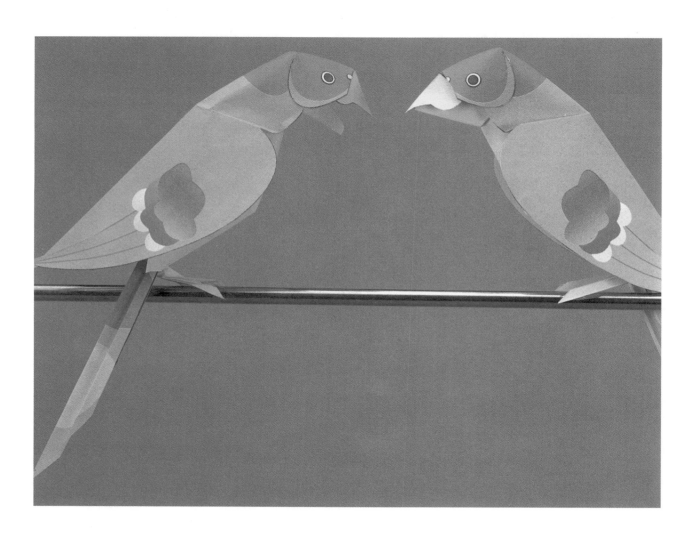

PAPER PARROT

Parakeets, macaws, cockatoos, and lorikeets are all members of the parrot family. They have hooked beaks and are among the most agile of birds. Often referred to as the clowns of the bird world, parrots are very entertaining and have long been favored as pets.

If you have ever had a parrot, you know that they can be very particular birds. When you try your hand at making parrots, keep in mind that paper sometimes behaves like a parrot and will try to have its own way. Your results may display some of your intentions and some of the paper's! Which is all for the best, since each paper parrot is bound to be unique.
One of the great things about making paper parrots is the variety of colors; in the wild, parrots come in all colors of the rainbow, so there is no limit to what you can use.

HOW TO BUILD A PAPER PARROT

The unusual construction of this bird allows you to pose the model with a sunflower seed in its beak. You can modify the beak and tail design to make other members of the parrot family, such as macaws and parakeets; or add a crest to make a cockatiel or a cockatoo. Parrots are among the most colorful of all birds—sporting plumage in vivid hues of emerald, azure, ruby, gold and amethyst—so you can select a wide variety of colored paper. You can find images of real parrots to base your designs on, or simply come up with color combinations of your own. Substitute paper-stiffened fabric for plain paper or decorate your creations with appliqués instead of paint. Make miniature parrots to use as a brooch or earrings.

YOU WILL NEED

- **Parrot bird paper elements**
- **Scissors and/or X-acto knife**
- **Paste, glue stick or tape**
- **Brush for applying paste**

Design Tips

- Use an adhesive, such as paste, that allows a little extra time for adjustments. This will give you flexibility in creating the best balance and expression.
- When cutting out the pattern, be sure to cut all the way to the end of the line on each side of the neck area. This is important for shaping the head.
- For more colorful birds, decorate paper with appliqués.
- You can modify the tail and beak shape or even add a crest to create different types of tropical birds.

1 *Begin on the underside of the paper. Pre-crease the indicated mountain- and valley-folds in the shoulder and beak areas. You can make these folds directly or score them first with a straight edge and letter opener.*

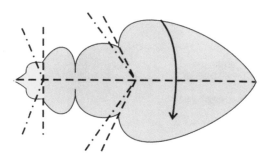

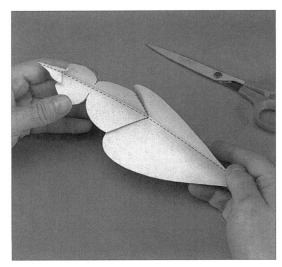

2 *When the shoulder and beak areas begin to bend inward, valley-fold along the center line and fold the model in half. Turn the model over.*

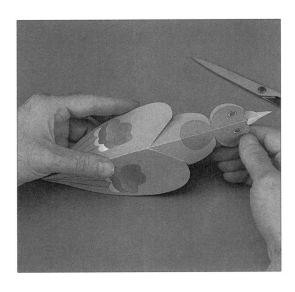

3 *This view of the back shows the outside shape of the shoulders. Notice that the model is left somewhat open.*

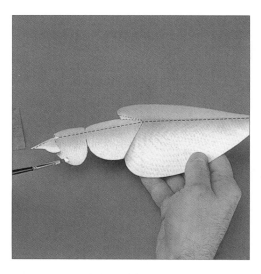

4 Apply a little paste to the inside of each "cheek" area, in preparation for securing the head. The cheeks will attach to the outside of the neck paper once the head is in position.

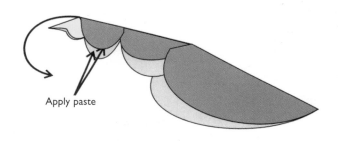

Apply paste

5 Bend the head downward and secure it in the desired position by pressing the pasted paper to the outside of the neck. You can alter the expression of the bird by changing the angle of the head.

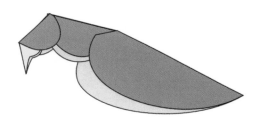

6 The solid yellow paper forms the belly, breast and lower bill of the parrot. Begin by pre-creasing the indicated mountain- and valley-folds at the narrow end of the paper, as shown. If you carefully crease only on the dashed lines provided and are sure to distinguish between valley- and mountain-folds, you will have no trouble folding the lower part of the bill.

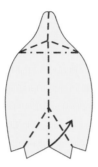

7 *Now work the paper at the other end by mountain- and valley-folding between the V-notched areas. The parrot's legs will protrude from each of these V-notches.*

8 *Fold the belly/breast area in half, allowing the beak paper to be at an angle on the outside and the leg area to fold inside.*

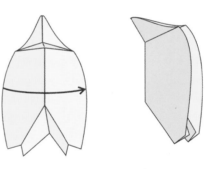

9 *Preparing the tail/leg paper is as easy as folding a paper fan. Maintain- and valley-fold it on the indicated dashed lines and compress it to make a narrow shape. Turn the paper over to display the brighter side.*

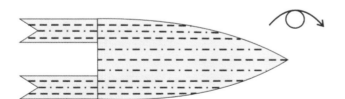

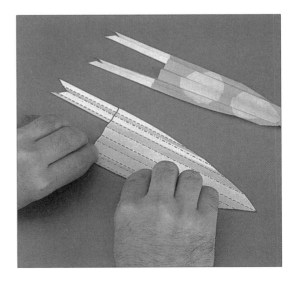

10 Fold the two yellow leg forms down on each side of the green paper where they join the top of the tail.

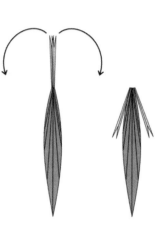

11 Apply paste on each side of the V-notched section on the lower inside of the yellow body form. Attach the top of the pale green (underside) surface of the tail form to the pasted edges of the V-notched paper. The two pasted edges will fit easily into the center valley-fold on the underside of the tail. Adjust the angle of the tail to your liking, but be sure to place each leg in its corresponding smaller V-notch opening, located to the right and left sides of the tail seating. Fold the body closed.

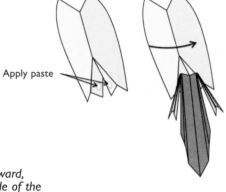

Apply paste

12 Fold each leg forward, around the outside of the lower body. The angle of the legs can be adjusted.

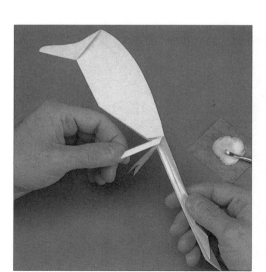

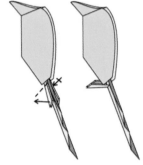

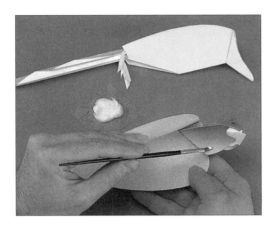

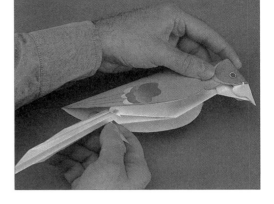

13 *Fit body and tail/beak sections together before applying paste, to determine whether any adjustments are needed. Apply paste to the inside of the neck paper and fit the body and tail/beak sections together. Press all layers together to secure. The body can be rounded after the paste has set.*

Apply paste

14 *Round out the body and adjust the leg positions for final placement.*

15 *The finished parrot can be perched on the edge of a table or bookcase. Use wire or tape to make a more permanent display.*

PAPER BAT

Bats are certainly one of the most amazing and misunderstood of mammals on the planet. Perhaps it is their secretive, nocturnal habits that cause concern, or maybe it is their odd form. Or, more likely, it could be their association with vampires in books and movies that has given them their undeserved reputation. But one need only take a look at these wonderful animals to begin to like them.

Fortunately for bats and people alike, society is realizing the important role bats play in nature: Insect-eating bats help keep bug populations down; and pollen-eating and fruit-eating bats are vital to many plants.

Many people have even built bat-houses to offer roosting sites for mosquito-eating bats. Paper bats are less intimidating than the real things, though not as effective against insects.

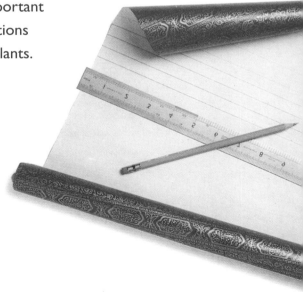

HOW TO BUILD A PAPER BAT

In China, the bat has long been a symbol of good luck. The image of the bat is a popular motif in oriental pottery, fabric, and building decoration. A dwelling with bats is considered fortunate. The origami bat is one of the most challenging of the projects in this chapter, but it is worth the effort. And when you successfully complete it, your confidence in this art form will be greatly enhanced. This sought-after design is very popular: Even people who don't find the image of a bat endearing warm up to these charming fellows. It is also, of course, the perfect Halloween decoration or package ornament.

Design Tips

- Always use paper that is the same color on both sides. If you have square origami paper that is colored on one side and white on the other, simply fold it in half, corner to corner, with the color on the outside; you will now have a triangle of the proper dimensions and color on both sides.
- If you are using heavyweight paper, dampen it first with a sponge and then fold; when the paper dries, the folds will remain. Wet-folding is also a good way to add expressive touches to your work.
- Make a small hole in the center of the top of the head and add a loop of thread to make bat ornaments.
- Experiment by modifying the wings, ears and faces of these bats, to make models that are large and scary, or small and delightful.

YOU WILL NEED

- **Bat paper elements**
- **Scissors and/or X-acto knife**
- **Paste or glue stick**

1   *Cut a square of paper diagonally in half, to make a triangle of the proper proportions to begin this project. This correct type of triangle has one square corner and two 45° angle corners. Any size will do. Valley-fold the triangle in half by bring the two 45° angles together as shown. Unfold. This creates a center line. Valley-fold all three corners to meet at the end of this center line where it touches the center of one of the triangles sides. Unfold. You will now have a set of valley-creases, as pictured.*

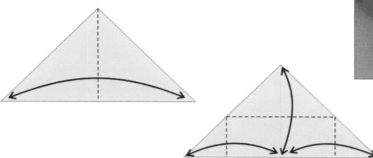

2   *Valley-fold the two, 45° angle corners to the square corner. Turn the paper over. Notice how this square has two open edges and two folded edges. Focus on the two folded edges of the square for the next step: Fold each of these edges to the center line and allow the triangular points from the underside to rotate around to the front of the paper. The model should now resemble the photo. Pay particular attention to the mountain-creases, which bisect each of the triangle shapes in front.*

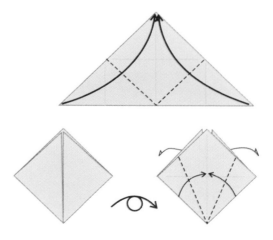

3   *Grasp one of the mountain-creases, align it with the center of the model and valley-fold the paper between the mountain-crease and the center line of the model. Do the same with the resulting paper triangle. Again, the model should resemble the photo. Turn the model over.*

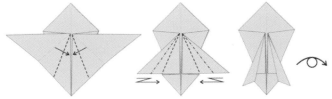

4   *Check to be sure that you have the correct side of the paper by looking at the center line: it should be a valley-fold. Open up the model, then valley-fold the top corner to the center of the bottom edge of the model. Valley-fold this square corner piece way back, toward the top of the model. Notice the black dots at the end of the two crease lines in the diagram. Align the end of each of the two crease lines with the folded edge of the paper on their way up (dot-to-dot in the diagram). This will show you how far to fold the corner back up.*

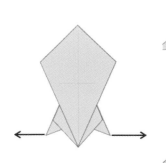

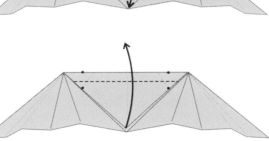

5 *Create a scalloped edge along the bottom of the wings by setting in the indicated mountain- and valley-folds (optional). Maintain-fold the left and right arm-edges (see the circle diagram for detail) under and out of sight.*

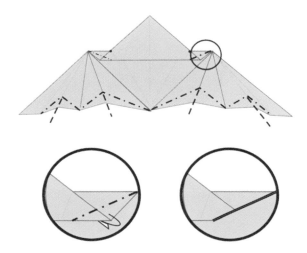

6 *Mountain- and valley-fold the top corner to make the nose and head. Fold the nose first and then valley-fold the whole shape down. Fold the wings closed over body. Use the diagram in step 7 as a guide.*

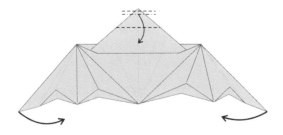

7 *Mountain-fold the arms in half, lengthwise, beginning from the corner point and working inward until you hit a mountain-crease in the area of the body. Swing this mountain-crease up to touch the nearest ear corner and valley-fold the paper between them.*

8 *The folding of the previous step defines the head area and supplies material for shaping the features.*

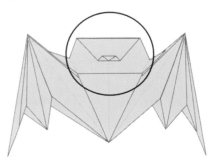

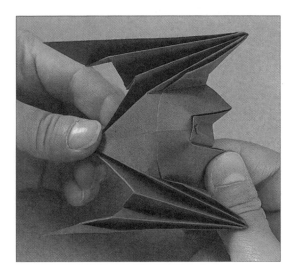

9 *Mountain-fold along the paper edge that runs from ear point to ear point. Valley-fold the two ear points across the top of the head and make them stand straight up.*

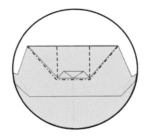

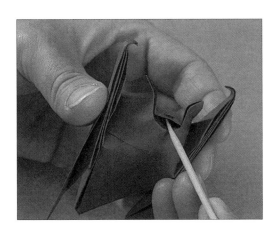

10   *Twist the ear points so that the flat sides face foward (optional). Open the mouth using a toothpick or similar tool (also optional).*

11   *Open the wings out and tightly curl the end of each wing around a toothpick to shape. You may wish to make a few roosting bats by folding the wings closed.*

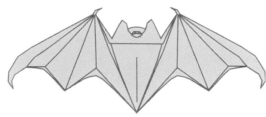

PAPER ANIMALS GALLERY

A paper frog brooch makes a simple accessory that is suitable for all ages.

Use the Sea Turtles Box as a party favorite and a friendly surprise filled with treats.

Make an authentic bat mobile! These excellent models are cheerful and friendly, hardly the types to cause alarm.

Try using a paper frog on a lily pad as a package ornament. Adding a paper frog is a quick and easy way to make any gift more fun.

An elegant arrangement of good-luck bats in a framed wall hanging. Bats and the color red are both highly regarded by the Chinese as symbols of good luck.

Arrange fancy ornamental koi on a table-top or create a beautiful mobile of colorful, swimming koi. The river stones pictured are actually examples of raku, a Japanese ceramic glaze technique. Stones created by Paul Rossi, Essex, New York.

The segmented bodies of toy paper lizards wiggle when handled. They make great accent pieces for a southwestern- or tropical-theme parties and are lots of fun at children's birthday parties, too.

Adorn the lid of a simple jewelry box with a zebra and her colt; or substitute horses or ponies for equestrian-minded friends.

3

PAPER BOXES

INTRODUCTION

The projects here were designed to be fun and simple to make. Easy to construct from almost any type of paper, these eight projects provide a versatile platform for creative invention. Triangle, square, rectangle, pentagon, hexagon, heart: all of these basic box shapes have been addressed in this section. The box designs and presentation ideas range from the classic to the unusual and offer something to suit every occasion.

Our method will allow you to produce winning results from even the most ordinary papers. Experiment with the paper provided, then use the templates in the back of the book to create boxes from a wide variety of paper and other materials. The folded-wall construction provides added support to the box walls, as well as a neat, finished rim. Each of the box lid patterns has a reinforced rim and our unique appliqué slot system, which allows for the insertion of an infinite variety of decorative paper elements to customize your own creations. An added bonus is that these boxes are super simple to make and a lot of fun, too! You will enjoy experimenting with the possibilities provided by different paper, and after a time you may go beyond the scope of this section and apply these techniques to create dozens of other boxes and containers of your own, whether as gifts or for use around the home or office.

Enjoy

GLOSSARY AND KEY

If you have skipped the chapters on making paper flowers and paper animals and come straight to this chapter on paper boxes, you may not be aware of the different types of folds you will need to use in order to complete the projects; and even if you have already worked your way through the paper flower and paper animal projects, there is certainly no harm in recapping the techniques required before progressing to the paper box designs.

Because the illustrations can show only a segment of a project's folding procedure, it is helpful to know whether the paper is being folded in front or from behind. The origami system of valley-folds and mountain-folds uses two kinds of broken lines (see key diagram) to show when to fold toward the project's surface (valley-fold) and when to fold behind the surface (mountain-fold).

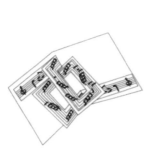

Valley-fold—Relative to the display view of the paper being folded, a valley-fold is always folded in front of the project's surface. If you were to unfold a valley-fold you would see a valley-crease, which dents into the paper's surface forming a valley.

Mountain-fold—Relative to the displayed view of the paper being folded, a mountain-fold is always folded behind the project's surface. If you were to unfold a mountain-fold you would see a mountain-crease, which rises up from the paper's surface forming a mountain ridge.

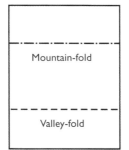

Mountain-fold

Valley-fold

Results

Standard Symbols

Mountain-fold

Valley-fold

Directional Arrows

In Front

Behind

Turn Model Over

Insert/Apply Pressure

Repeat

Enlarged View

Various types of arrows help make the folding instructions even clearer. These arrows are easy to understand with a quick study of the illustrated key. Whenever you see the repeat arrow in a diagram, you must apply the demonstrated folding procedure to all indicated parts of the project.

TRIANGLE BOX

This unusual box has interesting features: first, the top perimeter of the lid is slightly raised above the lid surface. This is possible because you can vary the dimensions of the perimeter fold segments. Second, when designing decorative paper inserts for any lid, you may choose to develop shapes from the edges or from the corners of the lid's shape.

Design Tips

- Use sharp scissors or a pointed razor knife with a fresh blade to cut out the paper pieces. This will give you cleaner edges and a better-looking box.

- When removing paper pieces, cut from the back side of the paper provided. Cut just inside the outlines and fold exactly on the indicated crease lines.

- It will not be necessary to glue the ornamental lid elements to the top of the lid. This will enable you to switch the patterns whenever you wish.

- Use white paste instead of liquid glue for this project. Use only the smaller amount to prevent warping.

YOU WILL NEED

- **Triangle Box paper elements**
- **Scissors and/or X-acto knife**
- **Paste or glue stick**
- **Brush for applying paste**

HOW TO BUILD A TRIANGLE BOX

The triangle shape is not the most economical form for a box to contain most gift objects. However, you will find that nothing presents a very small and special item so well as the equilateral triangle. It is very pleasing to the eye and makes a change from the traditional cube form.

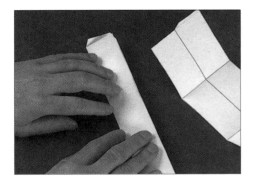

1 *Valley-fold the short lines of the base wall; then carefully align the opposing long edges and fold in half so that the colored side of the paper shows. Repeat with the other base wall elements. Make the folded edges sharp and clean by running the side of your thumbnail along the folded paper.*

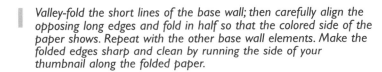

2 *Apply paste to the outside of the exposed tab and bring the two short ends of the base wall element together.*

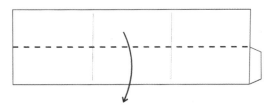

3 *Tuck the pasted tab in between the folded layers of the end of the paper and press firmly to make a good fit. This forms the walls of the base of the box. The top of this triangular form has a folded edge and the bottom has an open, double edge of paper. Make the floor of the box by folding the tabs to stand vertically around the triangular edge of the base bottom. Apply paste to both sided of each tab, then attach the floor to the wall by carefully fitting the tabs of the floor into the open edges of the base wall elements.*

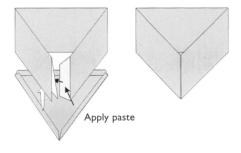

Apply paste

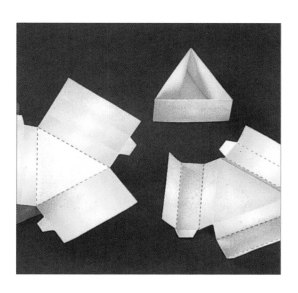

4 Carefully fold the edges of the lid. Begin with the underside (the side of the lid paper with the white triangle) and valley-fold the innermost creases. Unfold and turn the paper over. Make valley-folds indicated and crease them to close at right angles to the top of the lid.

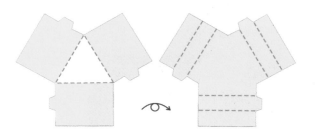

5 Apply paste to one or both side of each tab. Tuck each pasted tab into its adjacent open lid-wall edge. Press firmly to seal. Allow the lid to dry on the box base.

6 There are two possible lid patterns included here. The equilateral triangle inserts make a striped pattern, the three right-angle inserts make a three-cornered pattern. Begin by folding the tabs on the indicated crease lines of all color inserts. Square the folded tabs so that they are at right angles to the face edge of the paper form. For the equilateral triangle set of inserts, lay the small shape over the large shape. Tuck the tabs into the open edges in the perimeter of the box lid so that the result is a three-colored stripe pattern across the top of the box.

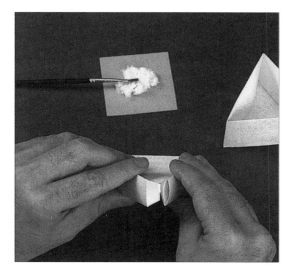

151

7 For the three-colored, right angle set of inserts, arrange the pieces in a centered, overlapping manner by tucking the pointed end of the triangle under the wide end of the next one. Square the folded tabs so that they are at right angles to the face edge of the paper form. You should end up with the three colors evident in identical four-sided shapes.

8 Tuck the tabs into the open edges in the perimeter of the box lid. This is an example of pattern development from the edges of the lid shape.

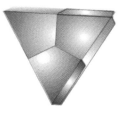

9 The finished triangle box. How many other ornamental lid insert designs can you come up with?

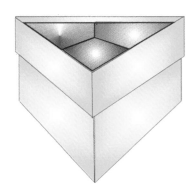

TRIANGLE BOX GALLERY

You can scale this canister set to any size, for an attractive storage system. Use heavy paper to make large sets.

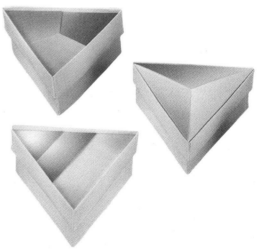

Tri-colored lids form modular elements. There are many possible arrangements for these elements. Feel free to experiment with them. This model is stackable and would make an attractive small organizer set.

Here the modular elements have patterns and curves cut into them.

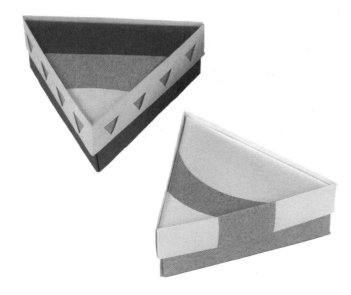

CUBE BOX

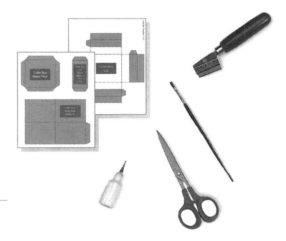

These perfectly square containers combine utility with simplicity and beauty. Make several cube boxes to "nest" or stack together or use paper in primary colors to make a set with different color tops and bottoms. They are ideal for storage, but can also be used to contain gifts.

Design Tips

- Use a straightedge and a razor to cut neat edges for the decorative lid elements.

- It is not necessary to glue the ornamental lid elements into the top of the lid. This will enable you to switch the patterns whenever you wish.

- Allow extra distance between the inside of the fold lines of the decorative lid elements if you make boxes from heavier paper.

- To make a nesting set, photocopy the pattern on a copier with a zoom function. Reduce or enlarge by 15% for a perfect fit.

YOU WILL NEED

- **Cube Box paper elements**
- **Scissors and/or X-acto knife**
- **Paste or glue stick**
- **Brush for applying paste**

HOW TO BUILD A CUBE BOX

If you prefer patterned to plain papers, use simple, bold designs to highlight the perfect geometry of the cube. Pair textured and glossy papers for a subtle contrast between boxes and lids of the same color. You can weave two solid colors together to give the lid an attractive checkerboard or triangle pattern.

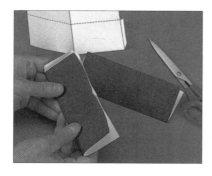

1 *Valley-fold the short lines of the base wall; then carefully align the opposing long edges and fold in half so that the colored side of the paper shows. Repeat with the other base wall element. Make the folded edges sharp and clean by running the side of your thumbnail along the folded paper.*

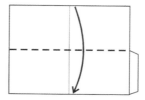 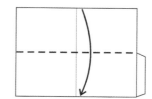

2 *Apply paste to the outside of one of the tabs. The outside of a tab is on the same side as the colored side of the paper. Connect the two base wall elements together, end to end, by inserting the pasted tab of one between the folded layers of the other. The pasted tab should stick to only one inside surface of the base wall element.*

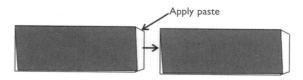

Apply paste

3 *Apply paste to the outside of the exposed tab and bring the two ends of the base wall elements together. Tuck the pasted tab between the folded layers of the end of the paper and press firmly to make a good fit.*

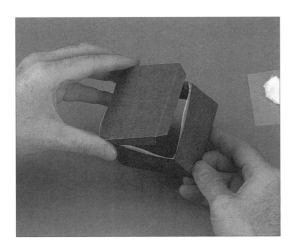

4 *Make the cube even by adjusting the creases. This is the base wall of the box: The top edge is folded; the bottom is an open, double edge paper. The tabs of the floor will be pasted between the open edges of the paper. Fold the tabs of the box floor, as shown, apply pastes and carefully insert into the base wall.*

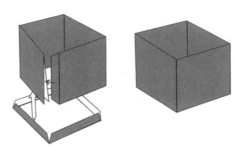

5 *Carefully fold the edges of the lid. Begin with the underside and valley-fold the innermost creases. Unfold and turn the paper over. Make the valley-folds indicated and crease them to close at right angles to the top of the lid. Apply paste to one or both sides of each tab.*

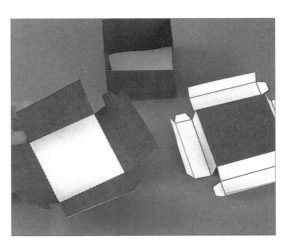

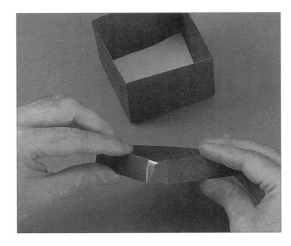

6 *Tuck each pasted tab into its adjacent open lid-wall edge. Press firmly to seal. Allow the lid to dry on the box base.*

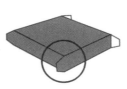

7 Fold the tab edge on each of the lid elements. Make this fold very sharp and clean. Weave the four elements, alternating the colors and fold tab edges at right angles to the finished checkerboard top.

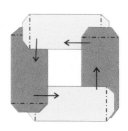

8 Insert tab edge (with or without paste at first) into the open edges of the perimeter of the box lid.

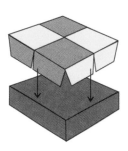

9 The finished puzzle box. You may further divide the colored strips and re-weave for smaller and more numerous checks.

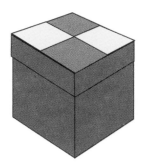

CUBE BOX GALLERY

These checkerboards are created by cutting narrower strips and basket-weaving the top of the lid. Be sure to make strips that are even and clean-cut.

Each of these colorful nesting boxes is fifteen percent smaller than the size before it. Use the zoom function on a photocopier to reduce or enlarge the pattern for different sizes.

Simple, bold patterns are very effective for this project. The woven triangle pattern was created by cutting out four triangle-shaped elements, with tabs. Each triangle is the size of one-quarter of the lid, when a line is drawn diagonally from one corner to an opposite corner.

FRAME BOX

This box is the perfect container for treasures, keepsakes, or souvenirs. A cutout in the lid lets you frame photographs or scrapbook items such as invitations, theater tickets, newspaper clippings, wedding or birth announcements, or any other mementos you hold dear.

Design Tips

- This is a good box to make from heavier materials such as textures, cover-weight paper. Use a ruler and letter opener or similar tools to pre-score such materials to make folding easier.
- If you pre-score the folding edges of the inside of the frame opening, you will get neater and more accurate results.
- Allow a little more distance between the inside of the fold lines of the frame if you make boxes from heavier paper.
- You should glue the frame elements to the top of the lid, but it is not necessary to apply glue to items under the frame.

YOU WILL NEED

- **Frame Box paper elements**
- **Scissors and/or X-acto knife**
- **Paste or glue stick**
- **Brush for applying paste**
- **Ruler or other straightedge**
- **Scoring tool (such as a letter opener)**

HOW TO BUILD A FRAME BOX

Frame a baby picture and keep a lock of hair or first tooth in the box. Send a gardener friend a box of seeds with the seed packet framed on the lid. The frame box is wonderfully adaptable for all sorts of little gifts and special occasions. The recipient will really appreciate the personal touch that this kind of box has.

1   *Valley-fold the short lines of the base wall; then carefully align the opposing edges and fold in half so that the colored side of the paper shows. Repeat with the other base wall elements. Make the folded edges sharp and clean by running the side of your thumbnail along the folded paper.*

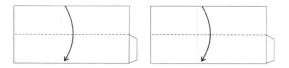

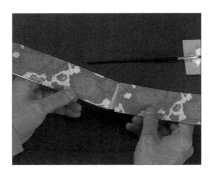

2   *Apply paste to the outside of one of the tabs. The outside of a tab is on the same side as the colored side of the paper. Connect the two base wall elements together, end to end, by inserting the pasted tab of one between the folded layers of the other. The pasted tab should adhere to only one inside surface of the base wall element.*

Apply Paste

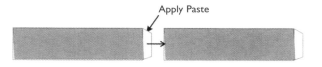

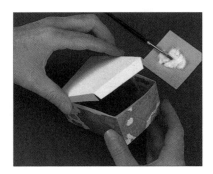

3   *Apply paste to the outside of the remaining exposed tab and bring the two short ends of the base wall element together. Tuck the pasted tab between the folded layers of the end of the paper and press firmly to make a good fit. Make the rectangle even by adjusting the segment creases. You now have the base wall of the box. The top edge is folded and the bottom of the rectangle is an open, double edge of paper. The tabs of the floor of the box will be pasted between these open edges of paper. Prepare the floor of the box by folding the tabs to stand vertically around the edge. Apply paste to both sides of each tab. Carefully fit the tabs into the bottom, open edges of the base wall.*

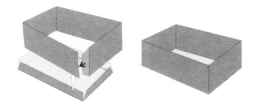

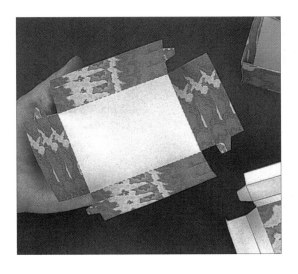

4 *Fold the edges of the lid. Begin with the underside and valley-fold the innermost creases. Unfold and turn the paper over. Make the valley-folds indicated and crease them to close at right angles. Apply paste to each tab.*

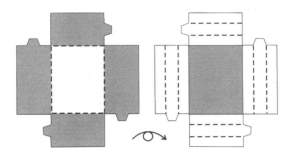

5 *Tuck each pasted tab into its adjacent open lid-wall edge. Press firmly to seal. Allow to dry on the box base.*

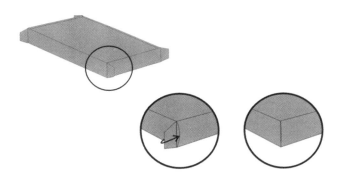

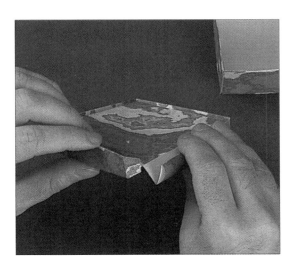

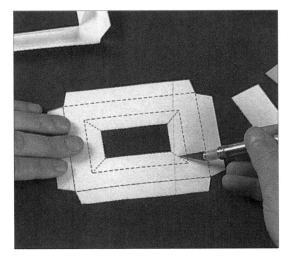

6 *With an X-acto knife, cut out the rectangular center, indicated by the innermost dotted line, then cut on the four angled, dotted lines (a). This opens the center of the frame. Valley-fold the cut edges outward and tab edges inward (b). Turn the frame over and set the tab edges at right-angles to the face of the frame (c).*

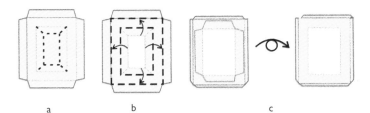

a   b   c

7 Insert the frame tabs into the open edges at the perimeter of the box lid. You may use glue or paste for permanence.

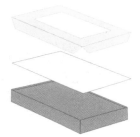

8 A photo or decorative paper may be placed between the lid and the frame before assembly. You may also experiment with other shapes for the cutout center of the frame element.

9 The finished frame box. This example shows off the colorful box paper.

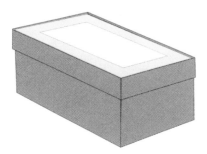

FRAME BOX GALLERY

A photograph inserted in this handsome box gives added meaning to a gift, especially if it reflects the contents of the box.

Any design that fits on the cube box lid can be adapted to the frame box lid. Here, we have borrowed the woven triangle pattern.

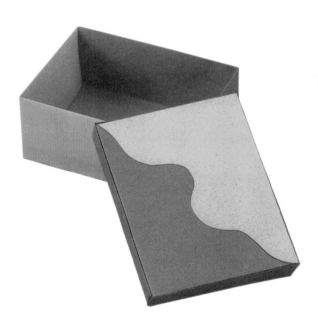

Create amusing and colorful boxes by cutting out shaped elements and arranging them in various ways. You can use decorative lid ideas from any of the other projects in this chapter.

MAGICIAN'S BOX

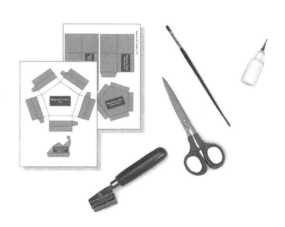

This unusual box is very versatile, and its shape is intriguing even without decoration added. Children love the paper crown and mysterious-looking cutout on the lid. Metallic papers add more "magic" to this box; try foil gift wraps or even kitchen foil.

Design Tips

- Use an X-acto knife to cut out the curved details of the decorative lid elements. You may change the shape of the circles, which are at the end of each lid element, or make them larger or smaller.

- Trace the base wall elements end-to-end on a long piece of paper. This way you will have one less glued joint for the box base.

- You may find it desirable to trim the base floor tabs at a sharper angle before assembly. This is an especially good idea when working with lightweight paper.

YOU WILL NEED

- **Magician's Box paper elements**
- **Scissors and/or X-acto knife**
- **Paste or glue stick**
- **Brush for applying paste**

HOW TO BUILD A MAGICIAN'S BOX

To make lightweight foils sturdier, paste a sheet of paper and attach it as a backing. Changing the circle elements will change the "theme" of the box: moons, stars, hearts, and diamond shapes all work well. Sure to be one of your favorite folded boxes, the magician's box may even become your personal gift-giving hallmark.

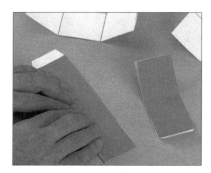

1 *Valley-fold the short lines of the base wall; then carefully align the opposing long edges and fold in half so that the colored side of the paper shows. Repeat with the other base wall element. Make the folded edges sharp and clean by running the side of your thumbnail along the folded paper.*

 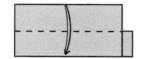

2 *Apply paste to the outside of one of the tabs. The outside of a tab is on the same side as the colored side of the paper. Connect the two base wall elements together, end-to-end, by inserting the pasted tab of one between the folded layers of the other. The pasted tab should stick to only one inside surface of the base wall element.*

Apply paste to outside of tab

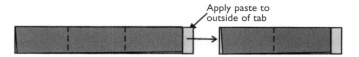

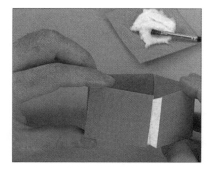

3 *Apply paste to the outside of the exposed tab and bring the two ends of the base wall element together. Tuck the pasted tab between the folded layers of the end of the paper and press firmly to make a good fit.*

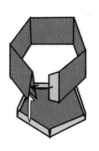 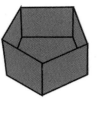

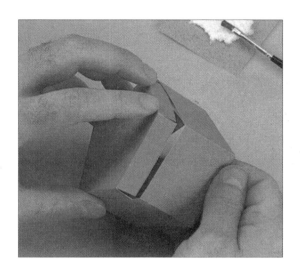

4 Make the shape even by adjusting the segments crease. You now have the base wall of the box. The top edge is folded, the bottom is an open, double edge of paper. The tabs of the floor of the box will be pasted between the open edges of paper. Prepare the floor of the box by folding the tabs to stand vertically around the edge. Apply paste to both sides of each tab. Carefully fit the tabs into the bottom, open edges of the base wall.

5 Carefully fold the edges of the lid. Begin with the underside and valley-fold the innermost creases. Unfold and turn the paper over. Make the valley-folds indicated and crease them to close at right angles to the top of the lid. Apply paste to each tab.

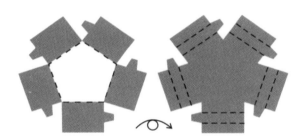

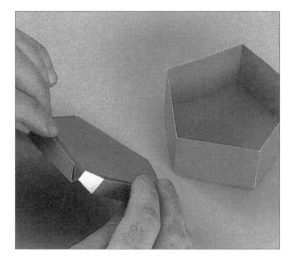

6 Tuck each pasted tab into its adjacent open lid-wall edge. Press firmly to seal. Allow the lid to dry on the box base.

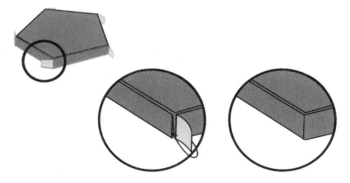

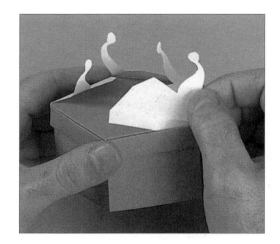

7 With a razor knife, cut out each of the five decorative lid elements. Fold sharply along the dotted line and set at an oblique angle.

8 Insert the tabs end of the decorative elements into the open edges of the lid. Arrange then so that each element overlaps the next. Gently curve the slender extensions upward and give them a slight twist.

9 The finished magicians box.

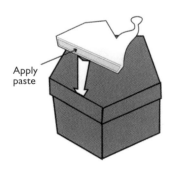

Apply paste

MAGICIAN'S BOX GALLERY

Apple blossom shapes are made from the pattern and method used in the heart box project on an earlier page. The colors of the flowers can complement or contrast with the colors of the box.

Here is an idea borrowed from the frame box project. It is elegant in black and gold: use special papers for special occasions.

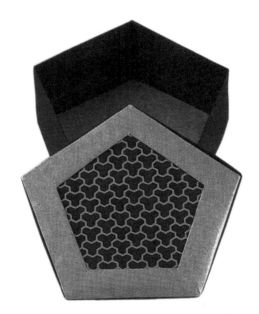

Cut and layered silver foil wrapping paper adds magic to this box. Silver foil paper was pasted to the box material before the window was cut. The star cutout is framed by an overlay.

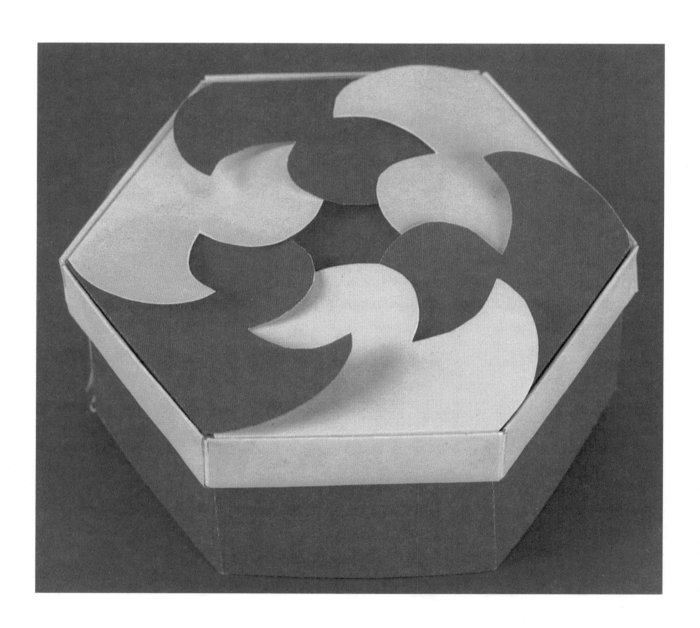

PUZZLE BOX

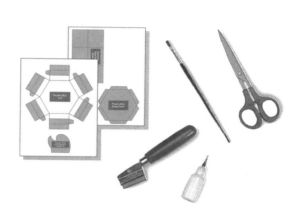

The puzzle box adds wonderful possibilities to the art of presentation. The ornamental lid segments may be created from any paper—in one, two, three, or even six colors.

Design Tips

- Use sharp scissors or a pointed razor knife with a fresh blade to cut out the paper pieces. This will give you cleaner edges and a better looking box.

- When removing paper pieces, cut from the back side of the paper provided. Cut just inside the outlines.

- When mountain-folds are shown in the diagram steps for folding the lid, there are valley-fold dashed lines on the other side of the paper. This way, fold lines will not show on the outside of the finished model.

- If you make more boxes from heavier paper, pre-crease all fold lines by scoring with a straightedge and scoring tool.

- Ordinary white paste or convenient glue sticks, are preferable to liquid glues for this project. Use only the smallest amount of glue to prevent warping.

YOU WILL NEED

- **Puzzle Box paper elements**
- **Scissors and/or X-acto knife**
- **Paste or glue stick**
- **Brush for applying paste**

HOW TO BUILD A PUZZLE BOX

Design your own segment shapes to create an infinite combination of lid patterns, or omit the puzzle pieces to make a distinguished hexagonal box. It is easy to scale these boxes to any dimensions you require, due to the simple geometry involved.

The pattern is adaptable to many materials other than paper. If you want to go for a different effect, try using colored aluminum craft foils or paper-backed fabric. The basic shape of this box is very versatile indeed.

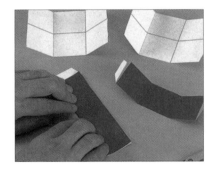

1 *Valley-fold the short lines of the base wall; then carefully align the opposing long edges and fold half so that the colored side of the paper shows. Repeat with the other base wall element. Make the folded edges sharp and clean by running the side of your thumbnail along the folded paper.*

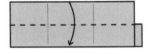 

2 *Apply paste to the outside of one of the tabs. The outside of a tab is on the same side as the colored side of the paper. Connect the two base wall elements together, end-to-end, by inserted the pasted tab of one between the folded layers of the other. The pasted tab should stick to only one inside surface of the base wall element.*

Apply paste to outside of tab

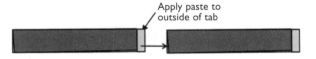

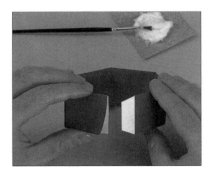

3 *Apply paste to the outside of the exposed tab and bring the two ends of the base wall element together. Tuck the pasted tab between the folded layers of the end of the paper and press firmly to make a good fit.*

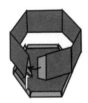

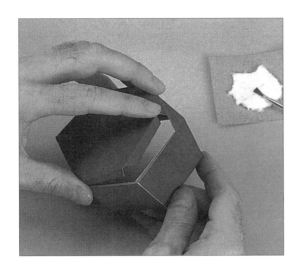

4 Sharpen and adjust the segment creases to create an evenly shaped hexagonal ring. This ring forms the walls of the base of the box. The top of the ring is a folded edge and the bottom of the ring is an open, double edge of paper. The tabs of the floor of the box are pasted between these open edges of paper. Prepare the floor of the box by folding the tabs to stand vertically around the hexagonal edge of the piece. Apply paste to both sides of each tab. Carefully fit the tabs into the bottom, open edges of the base wall assembly.

5 Carefully fold the edges of the lid. Begin with the underside and valley-fold the innermost creases. Unfold and turn the paper over. Make the valley-folds indicated and crease them to close the right angles to the top of the lid. You should now have a lid with a blue top and yellow sides.

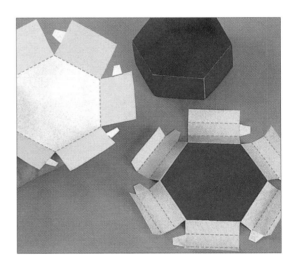

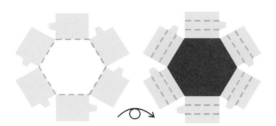

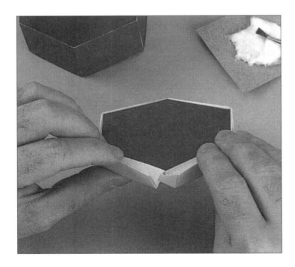

6 Apply paste to the tabs and tuck each pasted tab into its adjacent open lid-wall edge. Press firmly to seal. Allow the lid to dry on the box base.

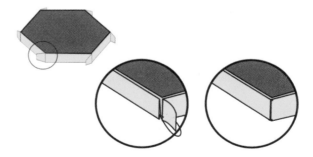

7 Fold the tab edges of each of the six puzzle elements. Make this fold very sharp and clean.

8 Insert the tab ends of the puzzle elements into the edges of the box lid. Alternate the colors and make sure that the pointed end of each shape is visible. The result will be a wonderful pattern. You can experiment with the other ways to arrange the papers in the lid, or design other shapes of your own.

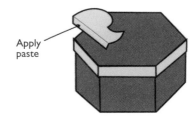

Apply paste

9 The finished puzzle box.

PUZZLE BOX GALLERY

There are endless possibilities with modular lid elements. Some element shapes can be installed in more than one way. The even number of box sides allow for many color possibilities.

You can keep the construction simple by using ornate papers or get fancy by applying delicate cutout shapes to make these decorative flower themes.

Here are coordinated desktop accessories: a pencil holder and a paper clip box. The pencil holder can be weighted with uncooked rice and dried beans to prevent tipping and support pencils in the cup.

HEART BOX

A gift to the one you love is even more thoughtful and personal when presented in this beautiful handmade token of affection. But don't wait until Valentine's Day to transform your favorite paper into a lovely keepsake with this heart box pattern.

Design Tips

- Make all of the flat folds first and organize the paper elements in groups; one for the lid and one for the base. This is especially important for this project, since the box lid and floor look the same and are only slightly different in size.

- Use the edge of the table or ruler to curve rounded elements. Do so in a gentle way with several passes. Heavy-handed curling will cause the edges to become misaligned.

- Apply glue a few dabs at a time when going around the curves. You will have better control and will be less likely to get glue on the visible surfaces of your project.

- Use a white craft glue to attach the flowers to the lid of the box. Use paste to assemble the tab elements.

YOU WILL NEED

- **Heart Box paper elements**
- **Scissors and/or X-acto knife**
- **Paste or glue stick**
- **White craft glue**
- **Brush for applying paste**

HOW TO BUILD A HEART BOX

Not only is this an attractive box, but it is also incredibly easy to make. From cutting to final assembly, this project can be completed in less than half an hour. The heart-shaped top of the lid may be decorated as simply or elaborately as desired, or not at all. Rubber stamps, cutouts, colorful stickers, and colored markers can all be employed to personalize this classic gift box.

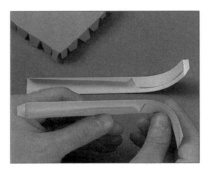

I   *Cut out all elements for the lid and keep them separate from the box bottom elements. Valley-fold the wide area of the lid rim elements first, then valley-fold the narrow areas to overlap. The narrow areas must remain visible. It is this lower paper edge that will support the heart-shaped top of the box lid. Valley-fold the tabs of the heart-shaped lid. Turn the lid over so that the tabs point downward.*

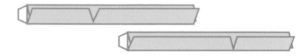

2   *Each lid-rim paper has a V-notch that divides its length. Gently curve the short end of each lid rim paper. Keep the notch on the inside of the curve.*

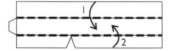

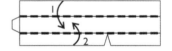

3   *Apply paste to both sides of the tabs of the lid top paper. You may paste and tuck as you go along. Assemble the lid by inserting the tabs of the heart-shaped top into the open edges of the rim papers. Tuck the end tab of each rim into the open end of the other rim.*

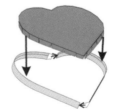

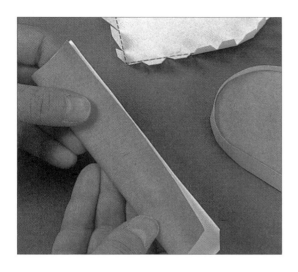

4 Valley-fold the base rim elements and the tabs of the base floor.

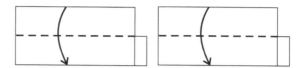

5 Gently curve one end of each of the base walls, then apply paste to both sides of the tabs of the base floor paper. Assemble the base by inserting the tabs of the heart-shaped floor between the open edges of the base wall papers. Tuck the end tab of each rim into the open end of the other rim.

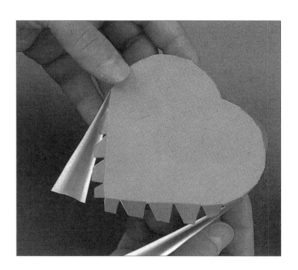

6 Shape the leaves by first folding them in half lengthwise, then tightly fan-folding them from one end to the other. Open the leaf out and shape it.

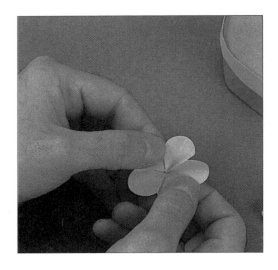

7 Shape the blossoms by mountain- and valley-folding them between each of the five petals in a radial pattern from the center. Gently curl each petal for a softer shape. Glue the smaller petal set into the center of the larger one.

8 Arrange and assemble the leaves and the blossom. Secure them with glue.

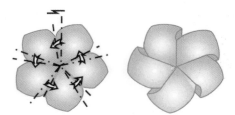

9 The finished heart box.

HEART BOX GALLERY

Pierced patterns are very effective on heart lids. Trace a pattern on the back of the lid and cut it with an X-acto knife. Back the pierced pattern with white or a contrasting color of paper.

The heart box may be adorned with a simple bow. This package bow was adapted from the lotus box lid ornament and folded from gold foil gift wrap.

The classic Valentine's Day presentation, filled with tempting sweets.

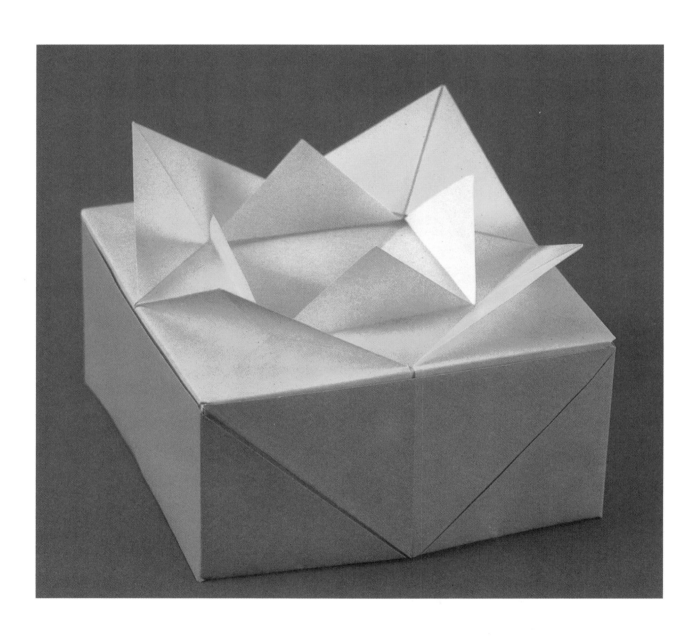

LOTUS BOX

The lotus symbolizes creation, and this lotus can be created anywhere there is paper. Because of its simplicity, this is an ideal project to teach children, who will then have great fun teaching their friends.

This origami box requires no glue or scissors to make: it is constructed by folding square paper.

Design Tips

- Be sure that the papers are cut perfectly square and to the proper size.
- Sharpen all creases with the side of your thumbnail to make them look neat and help them keep their shape longer.
- Cut up colorful old magazines for material. The weight and size of magazine paper is ideal for this project.

YOU WILL NEED

- **Two sheets of 8 x 8 in. (20 x 20 cm) paper, one green and one yellow**
- **One 7½ x 7½ in. (19 x 19 cm) sheet of green paper**

HOW TO BUILD A LOTUS BOX

To make paper square, simply fold the short edge of any paper rectangle against the long edge. Trim away the remnant and unfold the paper. You now have a square sheet of paper. Easy to do anywhere, use lightweight paper for best results.

1 *The folding of the lid and the base are identical. The base paper is one-eighth smaller than the lid paper, so it will fit inside the finished lid. Begin with the largest green paper—with the white side up. (a) Valley-fold paper in half, corner to corner, both ways. Unfold the paper to see that the two fold lines will cross in the middle of the square.*

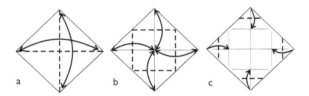

2 *(b) Valley-fold the four corners to the center of the square. Unfold the paper. (c) Valley fold the four corners of the square to the center of the fold lines created in the previous step. (d) Valley-fold the green folded edges in, along the crease lines already made. (e) The models will now look like the illustration shown. Turn the models over. (f) (Magnification). Valley-fold the opposite sides edges to the vertical center line of the square. Unfold.*

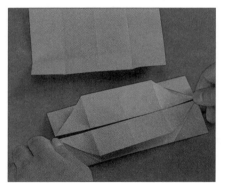

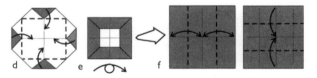

3 *(g) Valley-fold the top and bottom edges to the horizontal center line. (h) Flip up the lower flap to the top of the model to reveal the white side of the paper. (i) Valley-fold the lower green corners to the square angled crease lines. (j) Return the flap to its original position. Repeat steps (g), (h) and (i) on the other side of the paper.*

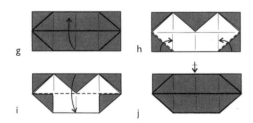

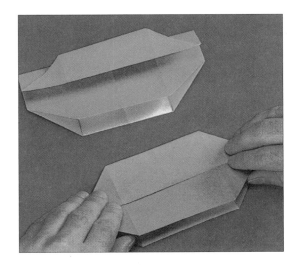

4 *(k) The model should now look like this. Open the model from the center. (l) Push the corners and square the four box walls. (m) Follow steps (a-l) to fold the smaller green paper (for the lid). Both the lid and the base should match the drawing and one should fit inside the other.*

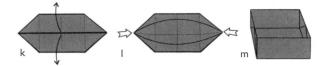

k   l   m

5 *Use the yellow square for lotus top. (a) Begin with the white side up. Fold the square in half, edge to edge, both ways. (b) Unfold to reveal the white paper again. (c) Fold the four corners of the square to the center of the paper. (d) Fold the four new corners to the center. The model will look like the illustration and will have two layers of four yellow "petals" on this side.*

a   b   c   d

6 *(e) (Magnification). Fold the four petal corners of the first layer to the center of their outer edge. (f) Model will look like the illustration. (g) Fold the petal corners of the second (inner) layer to the framed corners of the model. (h) Model will look like the illustration. Turn the model over.*

e   f   g   h

7 *(i) Fold the corners of this square to the center. (j) Unfold and set at right angles to square base. These are the base points. (k) Turn the model over. (l) Slightly elevate the eight petal points marked by dots in the drawing. This is the lotus form.*

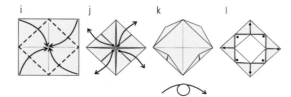

8 *Insert the four base corners into the open edges of the box lid.*

9 *The finished lotus box.*

LOTUS BOX GALLERY

Fold several smaller lotus elements and insert them into the opening of the main lotus. You can experiment with colors and make more petals with a few scissor cuts.

Here the lotus box is used as a photo frame. Unfold the lotus and insert a photo or a slip of contrasting colored paper, then re-fold with the element enclosed.

Standard origami papers come in a wide variety of colors and patterns. All can be used for the lotus box.

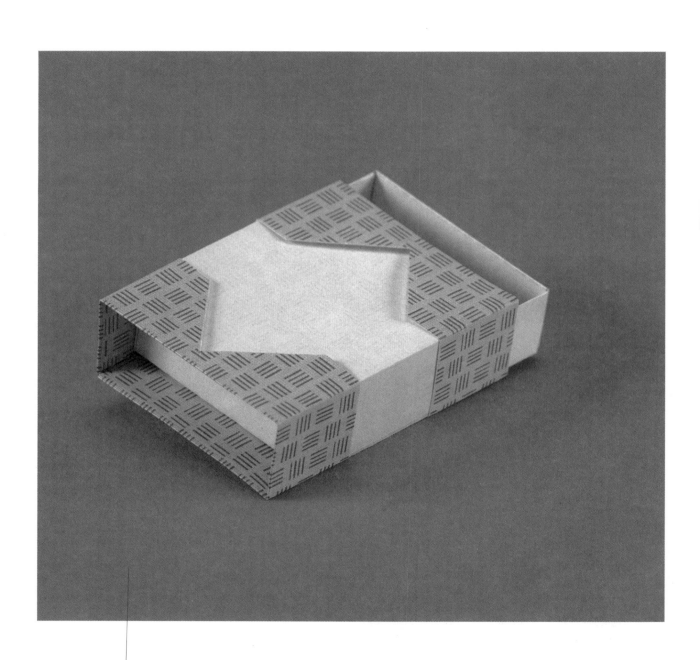

MATCH BOX

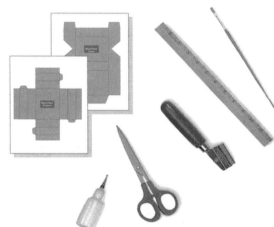

Match boxes are ideal for craft projects and for storing small items. They are the perfect size for organizing small collections; whether sea shells, minerals, beads, or buttons. Of course, you can use real match boxes if you like and decorate them, or you can follow this design and make the box from scratch.

Design Tips

- Pre-score all creases for accuracy and neatness. The boxes fit together better when they are folded neatly.
- Use paste sparingly, and let pasted pieces dry completely before inserting the box drawer into the sliding cover. This will keep the drawer from becoming accidentally glued shut.
- If you want to show parallel bands on the match box cover, skip cutting the notches for the diamond frame. You may also cut other shapes: Circles, ovals, rectangles, etc. Experiment by changing the margin widths, too.
- You can alter the scale of this box to create larger containers. Use heavyweight paper for very large boxes. Try building a nesting set of several match boxes.

YOU WILL NEED

- **Match Box paper elements**
- **Scissors and/or X-acto knife**
- **Ruler or other straightedge**
- **Paste or glue stick**
- **White craft glue**

HOW TO BUILD A MATCH BOX

For the hobbyist, match boxes are a great way to store and display supplies and small tools. Although they won't be emblazed with the name of the latest restaurant or club, making your own match boxes has great advantages: you don't have to get rid of any matches before you can use the box, you can customize the match box size to your purpose, and you can choose the color of the box. Just about any type of paper works well for this project, so you can experiment with confidence.

Colorful and patterned papers can be made into very attractive boxes for small gifts. The simplicity of this design makes it easy to customize and personalize match boxes to suit any occasion.

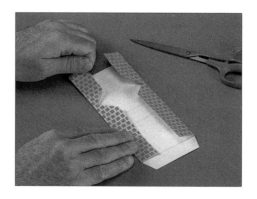

1 Make the slide cover first. Valley-fold the notched edges of the paper inward. You will notice that the notched edges form an open diamond-shape over a contrasting field of color. Turn the paper over.

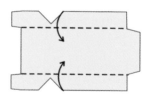

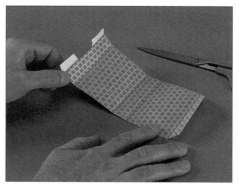

2 Valley-fold on indicated creases as shown, to form separate wall sections for the slide cover. You may wish to pre-score these valley-creases with a ruler and a ball-point pen.

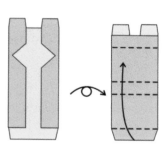

3 Tuck the single, wide tab into the opposite end of the paper form. You may use paste but it is not necessary.

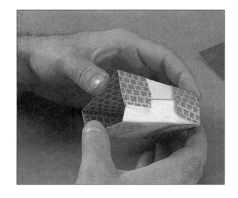

4 Tuck the two, smaller tabs under the square-ended open layers. Secure the layers with paste. Square-up the box form to evenly align the walls: make the creases neat. Turn the model over to display the diamond-framed side.

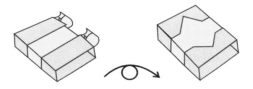

5 Valley-fold on the indicated dashed lines to create the floor of the box drawer. Turn the paper over.

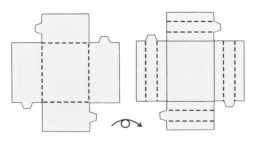

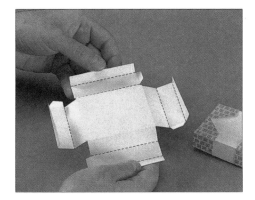

6 Valley-fold on the indicated dashed lines to make the four walls of the box drawer. On the same side of the paper, valley-fold the tabs inward.

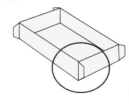

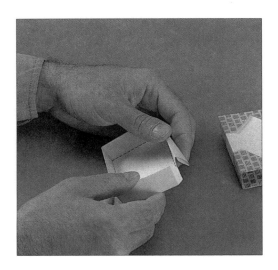

7 *Fold closed the four walls of the box drawer and tuck the corner tabs into their respective corner pockets as shown. The corner pockets are formed by the multiple layers of the box walls. Use paste to secure the corner tabs.*

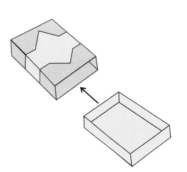

8 *Slide the match box drawer into its cover.*

9 *The finished match box.*

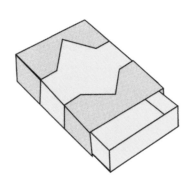

MATCH BOX GALLERY

Color-coded storage boxes are a snap with this simple box project. Insert any color or texture of paper under the folded layers of the slide cover. Makes a colorful desktop accessory.

Personalized match boxes for gift giving. Names can be printed or handwritten in the open frame layer during the first few steps of the project.

Paste several match boxes together to make a chest of drawers. You can assemble boxes in different configurations: Makes a great organizer for small items.

HOW TO MAKE BOX LIDS

Making the lid is the trickiest part of making a paper box. Although each of the ten featured boxes has a different shape, the six step technique outlined below can be applied to any of the box lids in the book. Once you have mastered the basic rules for constructing a lid, you will easily be able to follow the more detailed instructions that accompany each project. Have fun!

1 *Valley-fold on the dashed lines of the underside of the lid paper cutout. Turn the paper over.*

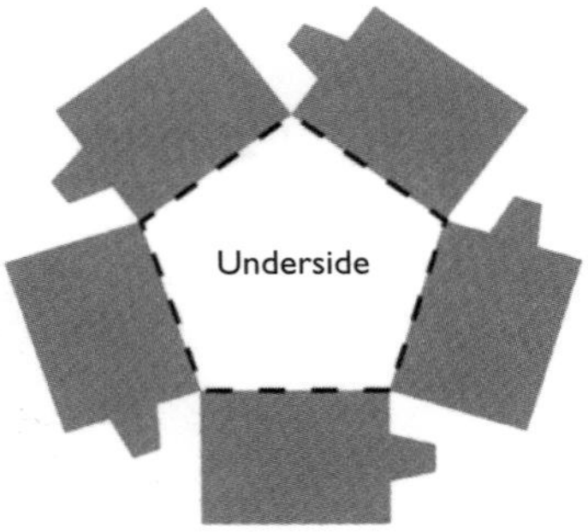

Underside

2 *Valley-fold along the dashed lines. Each rectangular extension is referred to as a lid-rim arm.*

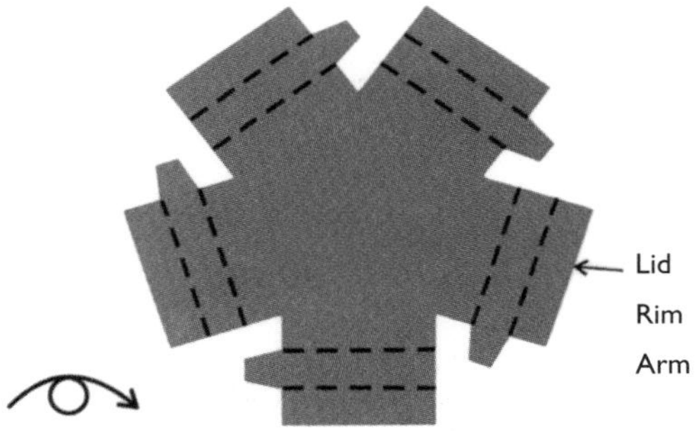

← Lid
Rim
Arm

Topside

Underside

← Lid
Rim
Arm

3 *(Side view of one lid-rim arm.) Valley-fold the outermost segment of the lid-rim arm against the middle segment.*

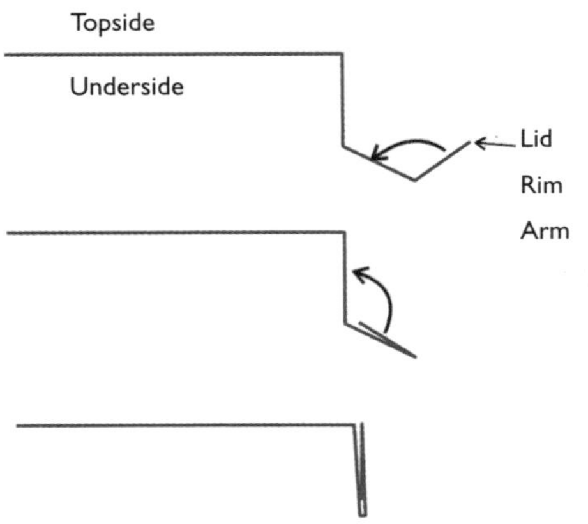

4 Valley-fold this double layer of paper against the innermost segment of the lid-rim arm. Set this three-layer lid-rim at right angles to the top of the lid.

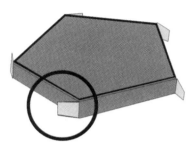

5 Apply paste to the outside of the exposed tabs. Tuck each pasted tab into the adjacent open lid-wall edge. Press firmly to seal. Allow the lid to dry on the box base.

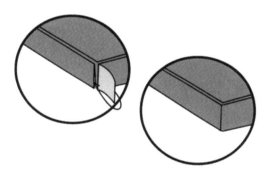

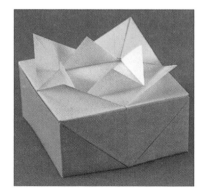
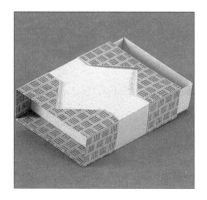
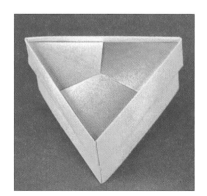

PAPER POP-UPS

INTRODUCTION

What is a pop-up? The best answer is that pop-ups are absolutely the finest greeting cards you can send or receive. They are ingenious and fun, a wonderful mixture of magic and geometry that never fails to bring a smile when an unfamiliar design is opened for the first time. A pop-up is more than just a card; it is an object to be displayed and admired long after other cards have been put away.

The technical definition of just what is and is not a pop-up differs among designers. The construction of pop-up books and greeting cards began in London during the 1850s, but the geometric principles behind them go much farther back. Self-erecting structures have been used for centuries by people as diverse as stage illusionists, cabinet makers, and origami designers, and since the beginning of time by mother nature—just watch how the flowers open. In recent years, pop-up books have become ever-more spectacular as designers try to outdo their rivals to achieve greater sales. Some of the results are truly amazing.

And yet, pop-up techniques are essentially simple. This chapter introduces six of the most versatile techniques with a number of basic—but interesting—projects. Some are explained in step-by-step detail with photographs, while the gallery spreads show photographs or drawings of completed projects. You are also encouraged to change or adapt the projects to your own specifications, rather than just copy the instructions.

GLOSSARY AND KEY

If you have skipped the chapters on making paper flowers, paper animals, and paper boxes and have come straight to this chapter, you may not be aware of the different types of folds you will need to use in order to complete the projects; and even if you have already worked your way through the previous chapters, there is certainly no harm in recapping the techniques required.

Because the photos can show only a segment of a project's folding procedure, it is helpful to know whether the paper is being folded in front or from behind. The origami system of valley-folds and mountain-folds uses two kinds of broken lines (see key diagram) to show when to fold toward the project's surface (valley-fold) and when to fold behind the surface (mountain-fold).

Valley-fold—Relative to the display view of the paper being folded, a valley-fold is always folded in front of the project's surface. If you were to unfold a valley-fold you would see a valley-crease, which dents into the paper's surface forming a valley.

Mountain-fold—Relative to the displayed view of the paper being folded, a mountain-fold is always folded behind the project's surface. If you were to unfold a mountain-fold you would see a mountain-crease, which rises up from the paper's surface forming a mountain ridge.

Gutter crease—This is a valley-fold in the backing sheet that supports the pop-up.

Backing sheet—The mat board that makes the stiff backing for the pop-up.

Covering layer—the paper that covers the mat board.

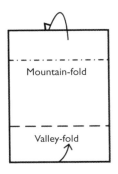

Mountain-fold

Valley-fold

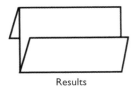

Results

Standard Symbols

Valley-fold — — — — —

Mountain-fold — · — · — · — · —

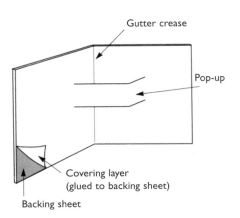

Gutter crease

Pop-up

Covering layer
(glued to backing sheet)

Backing sheet

EQUIPMENT

In the arts and crafts field, a degree of snobbishness often exists among experienced practitioners regarding the best equipment to use. When making pop-ups, however, must of the equipment can he obtained inexpensively from a local stationery store. There is no mythology about who manufactures the sharpest utility knife or the most efficient erasers. The rule is simple: buy the best that you can afford. Even the cheapest equipment will suffice, though you will enjoy using the equipment more if it is of better quality.

The one specialty item recommended is the self-healing cutting mat. These magical mats heal any cut made by a blade, so that the surface never becomes rutted, as wood or thick cardboard would. For the craftsperson who works with a blade, such mats are indispensable; treated well, they will last for many years. Use an adhesive (either a spray adhesive or glue) to attach a cover to a backing sheet or to secure important pieces, such as tabs, of your pop-up design. Apply them carefully and in small amounts, and use a damp cloth to clean up any excess glue.

The only other item of equipment worth mentioning separately is the cutting blade. It is inadvisable to purchase the cheapest types of retractable, snap-off blade knives. They are not very sturdy and not totally safe when cutting heavier cardboards. If you wish to purchase such a knife, buy a sturdy model that securely locks the retractable blade into cutting position. A better buy is an craft-type knife with blades that can be replaced. The blades usually are sharper and make more precise cuts.

BASICS

Papers and Cardboards

The range of papers and cardboards available to you depends on two factors; where you live, and how much time and energy you are prepared to invest. Cities, larger towns, and shopping centers have art, craft, and office supply stores, which usually stock a wide range of quality papers and cardboards in attractive colors. The choice will be more limited at smaller stores away from major centers, but this selection will be wholly adequate for must pop-up projects. In truth, being able to find only a very limited range of basic white paper and cardboard is sufficient, particularly if you are prepared to decorate it to add color and texture.

With a little more time and effort, a wider range of papers and cardboards can be obtained from other sources. Many wholesale paper suppliers sell (or even give away!) sample pads of papers and cardboards from their range, which are extremely useful if you are reluctant to buy a large sheet from a store, only to use a small piece of it. Small printers frequently have scraps or larger sheets of paper that they will sell to you at a very low cost.

If you are unable to purchase papers and cardboards, consider recycling. Use old cereal boxes, record album covers, chocolate boxes, wrapping paper, junk mail, magazine pages, scrap photocopies, old computer printouts, typing paper, and so on. The list is endless. These seemingly unlikely materials are a wonderful, virtually free source of colorful images and textures to make inspiring pop-ups.

An important consideration when selecting a paper or cardboard is its weight. The backing sheet needs to be stiff; otherwise it will not open completely flat. The pop-up that collapses inside it when the backing sheet is closed shut needs to be made from paper or cardboard strong enough to support itself without flopping when the design is opened, but not so thick that it prevents the backing sheet from closing around it. That said, precise weights are unimportant. All that needs to he remembered is that the medium weight paper, thick paper, or thin cardboard used to make the pop-up must be thinner than the cardboard used to make the backing sheet.

Never store paper or cardboard in a roll. The longer it is kept rolled up, the more difficult it will be to flatten. Instead, lay it flat in a safe place under a bed, between sheets of thick cardboard, in an artist's portfolio or in a large drawer. Larger sheets can be cut into more manageable sizes for easy storage.

DECORATING PAPER IDEAS

The first and most important point to make about decorating papers and cardboards for pop-ups is that they need not be decorated at all! Quality materials left plain will look stunning because the different facets of the pop-ups will create subtle and beautiful patterns of light and shade across the structure. By contrast, overly decorated surfaces flatten the pop-up, because the two-dimensional patterns dominate the three-dimensional form. Thus, a modestly decorated surface will look more 3D than an overly decorated one. The principle then, is to use restraint.

If you are going to decorate, try to use non water-based materials. Water crinkles paper and cardboard, so avoid gouache or watercolor paints, which also frequently crack along the line of a crease to leave an unsightly scar.

It is better to use gentle materials, such as marker pens, felt-tipped pens, colored pens, pastels, or chalks. Pastels or chalks will need a coat of artists fixative spray if they are not to smudge when the pop-up closes (a less expensive alternative is unscented hairspray—it does the job just as well). Or try using other decorating materials. Consider photographs, photocopies, fabric, ribbon, glitter, sequins, flower petals, lipstick, metallic foil, acetate—anything flat! These materials may not be practical to use on commercially mass-produced greeting cards but there is no reason why they cannot be used on handmade cards.

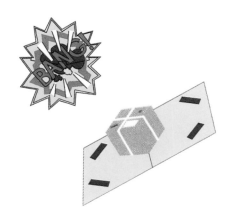

When to Make a Pop-Up

This may seem curious as a basics section, but the many occasions when one could make a pop-up card are not immediately apparent. We all like to receive greeting cards on important occasions, or after an event of personal significance, so someone, somewhere, would love to receive a pop-up from you right now! Here is a list of obvious and not-so-obvious occasions. You can probably think of others.

Birthday	*Sorry*	*Mother's Day*
Wedding	*Valentine's Day*	*Father's Day*
Engagement	*Promotion*	*Anniversary*
Baptism	*New Job*	*Yom Yippur*
New Year	*Birth of Child*	*Christmas*
Halloween	*Retirement*	*Easter*
Graduation	*Moving Away*	
Get Well	*Congratulations*	

PERSONALISING A POP-UP

Embossed paper

The pop-up projects photographed and drawn in the book all have one vital element missing from each design; a written message of personal greeting. When you make your own pop-up cards, don't forget to include it as part of the design. In fact, it is important to personalize a handmade card as much as possible so that it has personal meaning for the recipient.

The pop-ups in the book look, by necessity, a little neutral, so please add, subtract or change anything and everything so that the card you make is unique to you. In a way, the less like a store-bought, mass-produced, commercial card a pop-up card looks, the more it will be appreciated by the person who receives it, even if it looks a little amateurish. Remember, it is the thought that counts, not the slickness of your technique.

MAKE A ROUGH, THEN MAKE IT RIGHT

Pop-ups are geometric structures that must be designed and assembled with precision. Because of this, you are strongly advised to make a rough, or a trial version, before attempting to make a finished design. Not only will the rough reach you a method for designing and assembling the pop-up, but it will also make you aware of how you can successfully deviate from the instructions in the book to make something more personal to you than what is shown.

You may be tempted to skip the rough stage and make a finished pop-up from scratch, but this will probably end in frustration, wasting both time and materials. Use scrap materials to construct the rough, or better still, use the same papers and cardboards as the finished design will be made from so that you can check that all is well with your choice. Making a rough will also give you the opportunity to test any decorative ideas that you may have: Will that green colored pencil stand our on the orange paper? Is the decorative border too dominant? What kind of calligraphic flourish looks best on the backing sheet?

All the necessary tests can be done at this stage; cutting out the pop-up, taping on new pieces, testing decorative ideas, and generally making as much of a mess as you wish. No one will see it! In truth, these roughs can sometimes look better than the finished card if it is designed and decorated in an overly cautious way, so try to transfer some of the energy of the rough into the final version

Here is a rough of the Celebration pop-up next to the finished version. Although some of the ideas tried on the rough are used in the final design, many are rejected. Because a celebration with wine suggests a certain sophistication, the decoration was minimized and the color eliminated to make the card look stylish.

HOW TO MAKE A CREASE

There are three basic ways to make a crease: by hand, by scoring or by indenting. Whichever method you choose will depend on the thickness of the paper or cardboard to be folded, and whether you are making a rough or a finished version. Everyone folds paper by hand, even if it is just to fold a letter in half, it is wise to practice before making a pop-up.

By Hand

This method is possible only with thin or medium weight paper. It is generally very inaccurate and is recommended only for roughs of a pop-up, when speed is important and finesse is not!

1   *Before folding, draw the folds on the paper.*

2   *Make each crease as a mountain-fold. Fold carefully along the drawn line.*

3   *Some of the mountain-folds may need to be folded back on themselves to become valleys.*

Scoring

Scoring is the best-known method for creasing thick paper and cardboard, but it is not entirely recommended. The fold is made by cutting through part of the thickness of the material, thus seriously weakening it. Nevertheless, scoring is useful when making roughs.

1 *With a sharp blade and a steel rule, cut through about half the thickness of the paper or cardboard along the length of the fold on the mountain side.*

2 *Bend the card backward to make a fold. Use care; if the cut is not made to exactly the right depth, the fold will be either too stiff or too floppy.*

Indenting

Indenting is the best method for folding paper or cardboard of any thickness (except for mat board, which needs to be cut). The surface of the material is not cut, but compressed, thus preserving the full strength of the material along the fold.

1 *Turn a blade upside down, so that the blunt tip of the back of the blade is in contact with the paper of cardboard, then compress the material along the fold. Do not break the surface. Do this on the valley side of the crease.*

2 *Bend the card forward to make the fold (the opposite way from when scoring). Compared to the scoring technique. The fold is much stronger.*

HOW TO MAKE A BACKING SHEET

It is essential that any backing sheet on a pop-up is stiff, otherwise the pop-up structure will not fully open when the backing sheet is unfolded. To achieve this, the backing sheet is usually made of mat board, though sometimes a design will be strong enough if the backing sheet is made from thinner cardboard or thick paper.

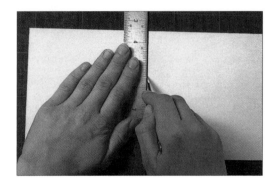

Here then is the method for making a backing sheet from mat board.

1 *Cut out a piece of mat board to the size of the finished pop-up when it is opened flat. Draw a line down the center. Cut the card in two down the center line. Accuracy is important.*

2 *Lay one half over the other and trim off any excess to ensure that they are identical.*

3 *Butt the two halves up against each other and tape them together.*

4 *Turn the mat board over and neatly trim of the excess tape at both ends.*

5 *Turn over again. This is the basic backing sheet. However, it needs covering with a layer of medium weight paper to hide the tape and to coordinate the color of the backing sheet with the pop-up on top of it.*

6 *In a well-ventilated room or outdoors, spray adhesive on the backing sheet. Glue from a tube may also be used, but spray is quicker and better.*

7 *Turn the glued backing sheet upside down and lover it onto the back of the covering layer of medium weight paper.*

8 *Trim off excess covering layer paper by carefully cutting around the edge of the mat board.*

9 *Turn over. Fold the backing sheet and covering layer in half and press firmly to make a sharp gutter crease down the center. This completes the backing sheet.*

SCENERY FLATS POP-UP GALLERY

Speech Bubbles

Each bubble is held away from the backing sheet by its own supporting tab. For extra interest, the bubbles are fixed to the opposite faces of the tabs, so that they face in opposite directions.

Chair

Chairs, sofas and tables make excellent subjects for the student of the scenery flats technique to study, because they are simply a series of linked supporting tabs, each built on a predecessor. Many ingenious designs can be created, some very elaborate. As a variation, try designing the same chair but this time turned sideways against the backing sheet.

Tea Time
Similar to the Celebration project, this design features three flat scenery pieces: a teapot, cup and cake-stand. The teapot is fixed to a supporting tab; the cake-stand is fixed to the teapot at one end and has its own integral tab on the right to fix it to the backing sheet; the cup is fixed directly to the cake-stand at one end and the pot by a tab at the other.

Woodland Glade
Elaborate, multi-layered scenes can be designed with much playfulness once the method for constructing the supporting tab is understood. Note that each piece of scenery is connected to the one behind my means of a tab.

Golfer

A supporting tab always needs fixing at one end to a vertical surface, and at the other end to a horizontal one. A silhouette pop-up stood on a backing sheet meets these requirements and is an excellent way to support a scenery flat (here, the golfer). Other supporting tabs could be fixed to the same silhouette background, perhaps on the other side of the valley.

Cartoon Explosion
The cartoon explosion project illustrates the fan pop-up technique and the drama of its 180° swivel.

Vase of Flowers
In the vase of flowers the pink flower actually propels the "blooming" of the yellow flower.

FAN POP-UPS

Fan pop-ups are among the most dramatic and humorous of all pop-ups. This is primarily because the pop-up shape swivels through 180° as the card is opened, to create movement.

The technique is similar to that of the silhouette pop-up, in that both techniques create a "V" shape that straddles the gutter crease. Fan pop-ups, however, are not flat across the bottom (as are silhouette pop-ups) but are shallow "V" shapes themselves.

This small change of angle creates a dramatic swivelling effect, though the angles themselves need to be calculated with precision if the effect is to work well. So, although fan pop-ups are simple and quick to create, they are subtle and need careful construction.

The two projects provided here show the different effects the fan design affords. Cartoon Explosion has an energetic, jagged outline, but the pop-up mechanism still works in the conventional way. In the Vase of Flowers, notice how the folds on the pink flower provide the power for the yellow flower to open, to create an unusual off-center pop-up effect.

If you want to be even more ambitious, you could try adding a third flower, or even a fourth, each one being powered by the preceding one!

YOU WILL NEED

Cartoon Explosion
• paper elements
• **Thin white cardboard 10 x 6 in. (25 x 15cm) and 8 x 5 in. (20 x 13cm)**

• **Craft knife**
• **Glue**
• **Marker pens**
• **Pencil and eraser**
• **Protractor**
• **Ruler**

Design Tips

• Compare fan pop-ups with silhouette pop-ups. The difference is in the use of angles—in particular, the angle of the "V" across the gutter and the angle across the bottom of the pop-up.

• To learn how changing angles can affect the swivelling of a fan pop-up, spend fifteen minutes making a series of quick studies in which the angle of the "V" across the gutter and the angle across the bottom of the pop-up change in relation to each other.

• Accuracy in measuring angles is key; if your protractor is old and dirty, buy a new one—they are very inexpensive. If you are unfamiliar with how to use one, practice before making a pop-up.

CARTOON EXPLOSION

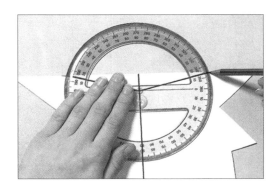

1 On the backing sheet, use the protractor to measure a very shallow "V" shape close to the top edge. The angle to each side of the gutter crease is 76°. The paper elements and templates provide the correct angle for your convenience. Fold and unfold the gutter crease.

2 Glue the paper element tabs along the bottom edge of the pop-up to the line of the shallow "V". Note that the pop-up does not stand upright, but lies almost flat when the sheet is fully open. Fold the backing sheet in half to check that the mechanism works well.

3 With a pencil, draw the explosion. For extra 3D effect, allow "BANG!" to run from the backing sheet onto the pop-up and then right across it. Erase any unwanted lines.

Backing sheet Shapes

This project proves that the gutter crease need not be in the middle of the backing sheet, and the backing sheet need not be rectangular—it can be any shape at all, however bizarre! Think hard about the shape of the backing sheet and where to place the gutter crease. The conventional rectangular backing sheet is often totally adequate, but to use backing sheets in a creative way can transform an ordinary design into something special. For further examples of irregular backing sheets and off-center gutter crease, look at the Locomotive, Car and Photo-frame pop-ups.

4 Colour in the explosion using bright marker pens—the gaudier it is, the better it will look. Use a black marker to outline some of the shapes.

VASE OF FLOWERS

YOU WILL NEED

Vase of Flowers
• **paper elements**
• **Sturdy backing sheet**
  8 x 7 in.
  (20 x 17.5 cm)
• **Covering layer:**
  medium weight, soft
  pink paper
  8 x 7 in.
  (20 x 17.5 cm)
  or larger

• **Craft knife**
• **Glue**
• **Marker pens**
• **Pencil and eraser**
• **Protractor**
• **Ruler**

1 *Cut out and fold the pink flower. Two mountain-folds and one valley-fold (folding from the back of the flower image) enable the flower to fold shut; if you are familiar with origami, this fold pattern will be recognized as a "waterbomb base".*

2 *Similarly, cut out and fold the yellow flower. If using the templates to create your own flowers, use the same medium weight, soft pink paper as on the covering layer. Collapse it shut along the folds. As with the previous flower, the angles between the fold are 45° and 90°. Measure them with a protractor or if you are feeling confident, estimate them by eye.*

3 *Apply glue to the uncolored tab attached to the pink flower paper element. Lower the collapsed yellow flower onto the glue, such that the center point of the yellow flower touches the center fold on the pink one.*

4 Now, collapse the pink flower shut, so that the other half of the glued tab sticks to the top surface of the yellow flower. Check the result against the photograph of the completed project.

5 Make a sturdy backing sheet and covering layer. Draw the artwork, leaving a space where the pop-up flowers will be attached. The design is perhaps best created even before folding the flowers, so that the pop-up flowers and the design on the covering layer are well coordinated.

6 Apply glue to the underside of the pink flower paper element, then glue it to the covering layer as shown. The center point of the flower exactly touches the gutter, leaving angles of 45° above and below it, to the right hand side of the gutter. Then, apply glue to the top surface of the flower. Fold the backing sheet shut, so that it sticks to the glued surface. Unfold to reveal the finished design.

FAN POP-UPS GALLERY

Top Hat

Like the Cartoon Explosion, the opening of the design sees the pop-up hat swivel dramatically into an upright position. Notice how the artwork carefully continues from the hat onto the head, so that the complete drawing is as convincing as possible.

Locomotive

Compare this design with the Car pop-up. Technically, they look very similar. However, creating it as a fan pop-up means that the locomotive leans back a little and is easier to see the Car stand upright. The subtle use of angles can help create exactly the effect that you want.

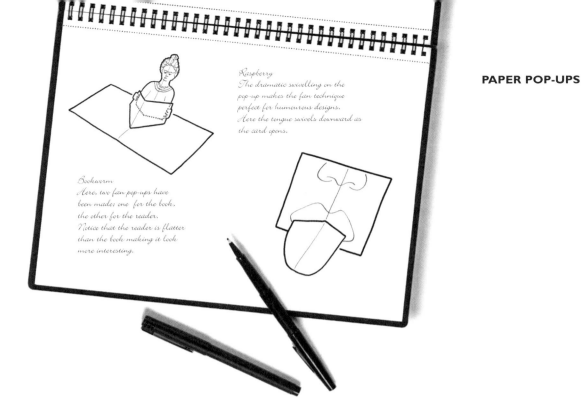

Raspberry
The dramatic swivelling on the
pop-up makes the fan technique
perfect for humourous designs.
Here the tongue swivels downward as
the card opens.

Bookworm
Here, two fan pop-ups have
been made; one for the book,
the other for the reader.
Notice that the reader is flatter
than the book making it look
more interesting.

Songbird

Here, the pop-up has been placed low down on the gutter, so that it does not protrude much above the top edge of the backing sheet. The effect creates a restrained, quiet pop-up helped by the sensitive use of colored pencil.

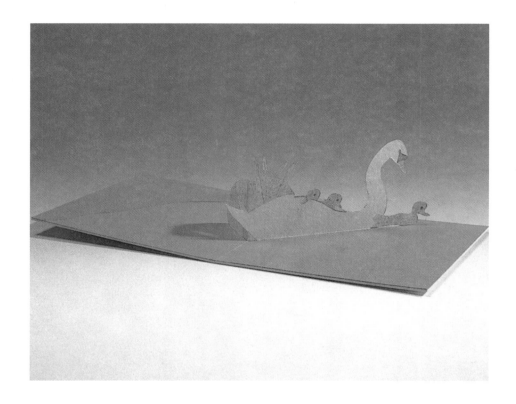

Swan and Cygnets
In Swan and Cygnets, the uncreased tail adds grace to the silhouette.

Monster Jaws
Monster Jaws does not open flat, but its effect is ferocious just the same.

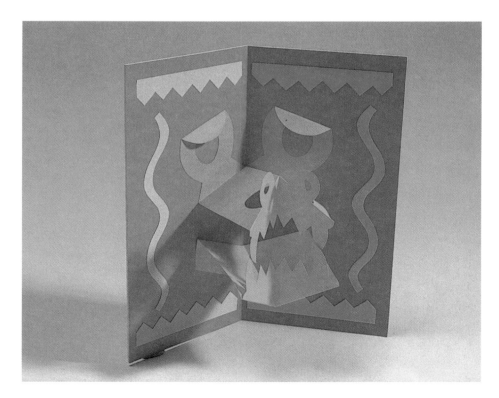

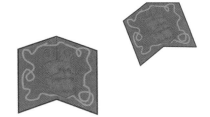

SILHOUETTE POP-UPS

The silhouette technique is probably the simplest and most versatile of all the many pop-up techniques. Constructions can be made with a minimal amount of simple measuring (even none at all, if you have the confidence to work freehand!) and the results can be very impressive.

The pop-up can have any silhouette, however complex, and multiples can be arranged along the same gutter crease, as shown with the Dolphins and Cityscape ideas.

Design Tips

- There are two ways to glue a silhouette pop-up to the backing sheet: cut slits in the backing sheet and tuck the tabs through, as in Swan and Cygnets, or glue the tabs of the paper elements on top of the backing sheet, as in Monster Jaws.
- The versatile silhouette technique lends itself to appealing asymmetric designs when the pop-up stands to one side of the mountain-fold that runs up the middle, as in Swan and Cygnets, Automobile, and Dolphins.
- Try experimenting with the angle of the "V" across the gutter crease. Sometimes the "V" can be flat, sometimes it needs to be tighter. Remember that the tighter it is, the more stable the pop-up will become.

SWANS AND CYGNETS

In Swan and Cygnets, notice how the tail of the swan is unfolded. It projects beyond the vertical fold to complete the graceful outline of the swan. When you design your own silhouette pop-ups, remember this useful device. It adds a lot of finesse.

1 *On the back of the covering layer, use a protractor to measure two 45° lines that meet at the gutter crease. Measure these angles with great care: if they are inaccurate, the pop-up will not close properly.*

2 *Cut out, fold and color the swan and cygnet paper element. If creating a swan and cygnets from the templates, use texture, medium weight white paper. On the "V" lines on the covered layer, draw darker lines that exactly coincide with the position of the tabs on the pop-up.*

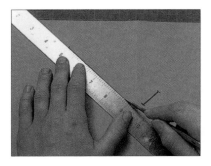

3 *Cut along the dark lines. Note that because this is the back of the covered layer, the long and short lines that represent the position of the tabs are the reverse of how they will appear when the covering layer is turned over and seen from the front. It is annoyingly easy to position the tabs the wrong way—back to front—so think through this step very carefully when designing your own pop-ups.*

YOU WILL NEED

Swan and Cygnets
- **Swan and Cygnets paper elements**
- **Sturdy backing card 11 x 6 in. (27.5 x 15cm) Covering layer: medium weight blue paper 11 x 6 in. (27.5 x 15cm) or larger**

- **Craft knife**
- **Glue**
- **Coloured Pencils**
- **Protractor**
- **Spray Adhesive**
- **Ruler**

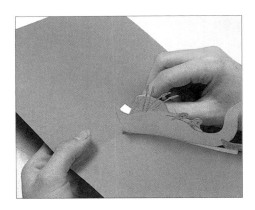

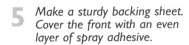 On the front, push the tabs through the slits. Glue or tape them into position on the back. This is the point when you discover if the correct length of slit made in step 3 is on the correct side of the gutter cease. In pop-ups, planning is everything!

5 Make a sturdy backing sheet. Cover the front with an even layer of spray adhesive.

6 Fold the covering layer in half. Lay the gutter crease on the covering layer exactly over the gutter crease on the backing sheet. This is a little awkward to do, but the spray adhesive will allow you to pull the covering layer off and reposition it.

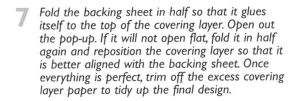

7 Fold the backing sheet in half so that it glues itself to the top of the covering layer. Open out the pop-up. If it will not open flat, fold it in half again and reposition the covering layer so that it is better aligned with the backing sheet. Once everything is perfect, trim off the excess covering layer paper to tidy up the final design.

MONSTER JAWS

The fun design of Monster Jaws really "snaps"! To make it work well, measure all the angles with great care - it helps to make a rough first. The backing sheet is not meant to open completely flat, so don't wrench it open with too much force. This design looks good when displayed, but it's seen at its best when held in the hand and played with.

1 *Make a sturdy backing sheet and covering layer. Trim off excess covering layer. Draw two "V" shapes, 2 in. (5cm) apart, each arm creating an angle of 70° to the gutter crease. Note that this 70° angle is the same as the angle on the two jaw pieces. This parity ensures that the jaws will "snap".*

YOU WILL NEED

Monster Jaws
- **Monster Jaws paper elements**
- **Sturdy backing sheet 7 x 7 in. (17.5 x 17.5 cm)**
- **Covering layer: medium weight blue paper 7 x 7 in. (17.5 x 17.5 cm) or larger**

- **Craft knife**
- **Glue**
- **Coloured Pencils**
- **Protractor**
- **Spray Adhesive**
- **Ruler**

2 *Cut out and fold the upper jaw paper element as shown. If you create the jaw pieces from the templates, use medium weight pink paper for both pieces. Note how the nostrils project above the level of the "V" crease and how the tops of the eyes fold over to create eyebrows. Simple effects such as these add interest to a pop-up, particularly as they are achieved without decorating the paper with felt pens, coloring pencils or crayons.*

3   *Apply glue to the back surface of the eyes, then glue them to the covering layers.*

4   *Fold the backing sheet in half, allowing the jaw to swing forward and upward. When the backing sheet is folded flat in half, press it very hard to reinforce the creases on the jaw piece.*

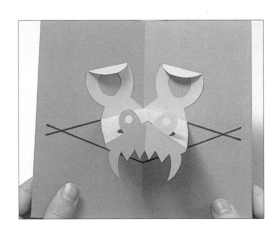

5   *Cut out and fold the lower jaw paper element. Note that it is essentially the same shape as the upper jaw, though simpler. Apply glue to the back of the paper element tabs.*

6   *The lower jaw cannot be glued to the covering layer in the same way as the upper jaw (by pressing flat against the covering layer), because the upper jaw is now in the way. So, although it's awkward, lower one glued tab onto the covering layer as shown, lining up the crease with the line drawn on the backing sheet. Then, begin to fold the backing sheet in half, so that the second glued tab sticks to the opposite half of the covering layer, up against the other side of the gutter crease. The effect is the same as the upper jaw, but upside down.*

SILHOUETTE POP-UP GALLERY

Airliner

The silhouette technique is wonderful for dramatically lifting a pop-up high above the backing sheet. Remember to reinforce the vertical stake by doubling or trebling the thickness of the paper—a single layer will flop to one side.

Automobile

When the pop-up stands to one side of the gutter crease (as the car does here), the backing sheet on the other side of the gutter can seem very large and very empty. The solution is to reduce it in size, so that the gutter becomes off-center.

Cityscape
Layer upon layer of "V" shapes of paper can be laid across the gutter crease to crease to elaborate multi-layered designs. Notice how the layers become taller toward the back.

Puppies
In this design, the "V" recedes rather than advances, so the pop-up is at the front of the card, not at the back. For added visual interest, the small dog bowl points forward.

Entwined Hearts

This spectacular pop-up is actually very easy to make. The "V" of paper that crosses the gutter crease is enclosed across the back to make a box that is technically identical to the Movie Theater project. Here, though, the back hearts slot into the front hearts—no glue is used.

Guitar
The Guitar
uses the basic
tent technique.

Stars
Stars incorporated
an unusual twist,
with the two stars
sharing a fold.

TENT POP-UPS

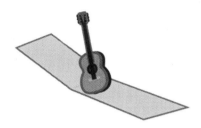

I t could be said that the tent technique is the silhouette technique "turned upright". They are fundamentally similar, yet achieve different pop-up effects. The technique is also a relative of the scenery flats technique, in that both display a flat pop-up shape on the front of a supporting tab.

Design Tips

- The supporting tab behind the main pop-up is best made so that it slots through the covering layer. In this way, its glue tabs are hidden out of sight and the final design looks much tidier.

- Not how some of the projects (Stars) and the gallery pop-ups use the basic tent form as part of the final design, whereas others hide it behind a flat cutout.

- If you are looking for an elegant technical challenge, try making the Guitar and Stars project from a single sheet of stiff cardboard, instead of from separate pieces. The pop-up shapes are cut from the backing sheet, lifted upright along the folds where folds are currently made and glued together over the gutter.

GUITAR

The guitar project shows the basic tent technique. Once learned, it can be used to display any shape with any silhouette or even be turned sideways, as in the Balloon idea at the end of the chapter. Simple, versatile, and particularly good at displaying objects in a seemingly unsupported way, the tent technique creates a feeling of lightness that is unusual in a pop-up.

YOU WILL NEED

- **Guitar**
  paper elements
- **Sturdy backing sheet**
  14 x 3 in.
  (35 x 7.5 cm)
- **Covering layer:**
  wood-grain
  shelf paper
  14 x 3 in.
  (35 x 7.5 cm)
  or larger
- **Support: shelf paper**
  5 x 1 in.
  (12.5 x 2.5 cm)

- **Craft knife**
- **Glue**
- **Coloured Pencils**
- **Pencil and eraser**
- **Pair of compasses**
- **Protractor**
- **Spray Adhesive**
- **Ruler**
- **Gold marker**
  pen (optional)

1 *Fold the covering layer in half. Draw a line 1 in. (2.5 cm) long, three-quarters of 1 in. (2 cm) away from the gutter crease. The length of the line will match the width of the supporting tab. Its distance from the gutter dictates how upright the tab will stand—the closer to the gutter it is, the more vertical the tab will be.*

2 *Cut along the drawn line through both layers. Make sure that the cut is exactly parallel to the gutter crease. Cutting through both layers at once guarantees that the construction will be symmetrical.*

3 *Open the covering layer. Cut out and fold the support from the guitar paper elements. Push the tabs through the slits on the covering layer and glue or tape them in place underneath.*

4   *Make a sturdy backing sheet. Spray the front surface with an even layer of spray adhesive.*

5   *With great care, lower the folding covered layer onto the backing sheet, so that the gutter crease on the covering layer is exactly on top of the crease on the backing sheet. Take as much time as you need to do this perfectly.*

6   *Close the backing sheet onto the other half of the covering layer. Open the pop-up and trim the excess covering layer paper. If the backing sheet will not open flat, this is probably because the covering layer was not positioned accurately at step 5, so reposition it—the spray adhesive allows you to do this.*

7   *Cut out the guitar paper element. If you make the guitar from the template, use thin cardboard. Apply glue to the front of the supporting tab and fix the guitar to it; if the shape is particularly large or spindly, reinforce it with an extra layer of cardboard. Here, the guitar neck has an extra layer glued to it to prevent it from bending backward over a period of time.*

STARS

In the Stars project, the ingenious way in which the two stars are joined by a fold is an unusual but effective use of tent technique. To make more stars, simply continue the joining pattern and make a longer gutter crease.

YOU WILL NEED

- **Stars paper elements**
- **Sturdy backing sheet
  11 x 6 in.
  (28 x 15 cm)**
- **Covering layer:
  medium weight
  red paper
  11 x 6 in.
  (28 x 15 cm)
  or larger**

- **Craft knife**
- **Glue**
- **Coloured Pencils**
- **Pencil and eraser**
- **Pair of compasses**
- **Protractor**
- **Spray Adhesive**
- **Ruler**
- **Gold marker
  pen (optional)**

1 *Cut out the Stars paper elements, or follow the templates and make your own from thin white card rather than paper (so that the stars will be sturdy).*

2 *On a sheet of medium weight red paper, the same size or a little larger than the sturdy backing sheet, draw a central gutter crease. Then, 3 in. (7.5 cm) away from the crease on each side, draw four short lines to coincide with the position of the tabs on the stars' feet. Cut along the four lines. Note that this is the back of the sheet, so position the cuts the reverse of how they would be on the front side.*

3   *Make an 11 x 6 in. (27.5 x 15 cm) sturdy backing sheet, but do not cover the card with paper. Apply glue to the front.*

4   *Make a sturdy backing sheet. Spray the front surface with an even layer of spray adhesive.*

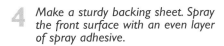

5   *Trim off the excess paper to create a tidy edge to the backing sheet. This can be done without a ruler. The thickness of the card will keep your knife running straight.*

6   *Carefully push the tabs on the stars into the slits made in step 2. This will be made easier if, back in step 3, glue is not applied around the tab areas. When the feet are all securely inserted, fold the whole card in half to finally create the gutter crease through the colored layer.*

TENT POP-UP GALLERY

Balloon

The supporting tab used to support the Guitar may also be used with the backing sheet standing upright, so that a shape (here a balloon) can apparently hang suspended in mid air. Compare this design with the Celebration project—it is technically similar but simpler.

Photo Frame

This is indeed an eccentric design: The pop-up is bigger than the backing sheet. Nevertheless, this simple project is a wonderful way to send an important photograph to someone, so that they may easily display it. A larger backing sheet would make the overall design look clumsy.

The photograph rests on a support similar to that in the Guitar.

Eiffel Tower
This is one of the simplest
pop-ups to make, yet quite
dramatic. Two images of the
Eiffel Tower are glued to the
backing sheet astride the gutter
and glued together at the top.

Campsite
The tent features a conventional
support with an extra triangle
glued across the middle to create
the front flap of the text.
A fold down the center of the
triangle allows it to collapse when
the backing sheet is closed shut.

Clothesline

Cotton thread is a material that is underused
in pop-ups. It has many interesting technical
uses and it creates a satisfying airiness that
contrasts well with conventional solid blocks
of paper cardboard.

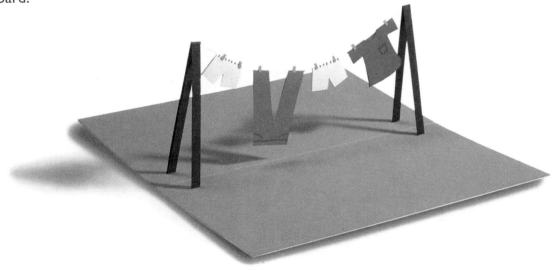

Gift Box
This square-on box pop-up sits directly on the gutter crease.

Movie Theater
Movie Theater uses the diagonal box pop-up structure.

BOX POP-UPS

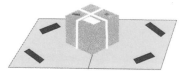

There are two main box pop-up techniques; the "square-on" box, which sits squarely over the gutter crease, and the "diagonal box", which sits at 45° across the gutter. These techniques are popular because they convey a sense of solidarity and completeness. They are also wonderful to watch when the backing sheet is opened and closed. Even the smallest error will mean that a 3D box will not collapse flat, so take as much time as you need to construct a design—it will be very helpful to make an accurate rough.

Design Tips

- The "square-on" box technique is constructed from several pieces, so check and double-check that, where applicable, measurements on different pieces that are meant to be the same are precisely so. Do this before gluing them together.

- Don't let your concentration slip! With both techniques, it is easy to concentrate on the construction of the boxes, and forget about the covering layer. The covering layer must be measured and cut with the same precision as the boxes.

- Try constructing hexagonal boxes, or cylinders, or making a lid for the diagonal box. The box principle is a surprisingly creative one and many elegant forms can be constructed with a little experimentation. Try making other solids too, such as a pyramid.

GIFT BOX

When building the Gift Box, you will find that a completely solid pop-up is a particularly satisfying structure to make, because the way that it erects and flattens as the backing sheet opens and closes is fascinating to watch.

YOU WILL NEED

- **Gift Box paper elements**
- **Sturdy backing sheet 8 x 5 in. (20 x 12.5 cm)**
- **Covering layer: medium weight green paper 8 x 5₁/² in. (20 x 13 cm) or larger Brown wrapping paper: approx 19 x 8 in. (48 x 20 cm)**

- **Craft knife**
- **Glue**
- **Coloured Pencils**
- **Pencil and eraser**
- **Pair of compasses**
- **Protractor**
- **Ruler**
- **Air mail stickers (optional)**
- **Gummed gold and silver stars (optional)**

1 *Make two slits in a sheet of medium weight green paper at least 8 x 5₁/² in. (20 x 13 cm), the size of the sturdy backing sheet. Each slit is 2₁/² in (6 cm) long and 1 in. (2.5 cm) away from the gutter crease.*

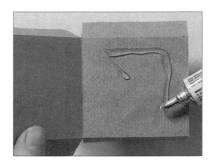

2 *Cut out the Gift Box paper elements. Fold the support as shown on the paper element. Apply glue to one of the large panels, then fold it in half to glue it tight shut. Make sure all the edges and folds align.*

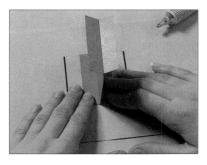

3 *Glue the support to the gutter crease, centered between the two cuts. Fold the support flat against the backing sheet and check that edges of the support line up with the ends of the cuts.*

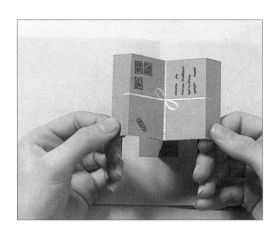

4 Apply glue to the tabs across the top of the support. Lower the lid onto the tabs, being careful to exactly align the fold on the lid with the edge along the top of the support.

5 Fold the paper element that will become the walls of the box. Glue the tab at one end of the strip to the other end, to make a square tube. Push the bottom tabs through the cuts in the backing sheet and secure them beneath with tape and glue.

6 Apply glue to the two tabs on the lid. Glue the tabs to the other side of the box, making sure that they are positioned exactly in line with the top edge.

7 Fold the backing sheet in half. Apply glue to two $5_1/^2$ x 4 in. (13 x 10 cm) rectangles of mat board and glue them to the backing sheet, one on each side of the gutter crease. Trim off the excess colored paper.

MOVIE THEATER

With the Movie Theater, the "diagonal box" version of the Box technique can look somewhat uninteresting just as a square tube, so this design introduces four panels that cross the box in parallel. The result is a design complex in shape but simple in concept.

YOU WILL NEED

- **Movie Theater paper elements**
- **Sturdy backing sheet 13 x 6 in. (33 x 15 cm)**
- **Covering layer: medium weight red paper 13 x 6 in. (33 x 15 cm) or larger**

- **Craft knife**
- **Glue**
- **Coloured Pencils**
- **Pencil and eraser**
- **Pair of compasses**
- **Protractor**
- **Ruler**
- **Air mail stickers (optional)**
- **Gummed gold and silver stars (optional)**

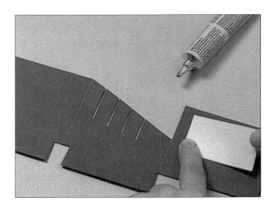

I *Cut out the Movie Theater paper elements. If you're creating your own from the templates, make the theater from thin blue cardboard, the audience from thin grey cardboard and the screen from medium weight paper. Glue the movie screen to the larger theater piece. The example shown here is white, but you may use a still from the real movie. The accurate cutting of this piece is very important, as any inaccuracy will be seen against the dark background.*

2 *Fold the theater piece along all the folds shown on the paper element. Glue the end tab behind the screen to make a square tube. If the tube can squash flat, everything is perfectly aligned; if it will not squash flat, adjust the position of the tabs behind the screen. Remember, if the piece will not flatten, neither will the completed pop-up.*

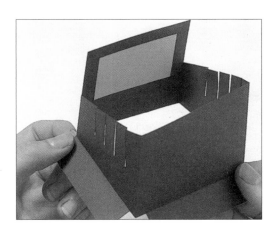

3 *This is the completed theater piece. If it has been incorrectly measured and no amount of repositioning of the end tab will allow it to flatten, you unfortunately have no alternative but to make it again. Before doing so, check the measurement to find the error, so that when it is remade, you will know what to correct.*

4 *On the covering layer, draw two lines at 45° to the gutter crease, which meet about 2.5 in. (6 cm) from the top edge of the covering layer. The angles must be exactly equal, so double-check them with a protractor before proceeding to the next step.*

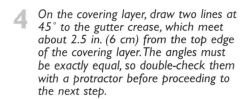

5 *Position the tabs on the large theater piece over the top of the drawn lines. Mark on the lines where the tabs begin and end. Note the small gap across the gutter between the marked lines.*

6 *Cut along both marked lines with a knife. It is probably a good idea to exceed the length of the lines by a fraction. This will ensure that the tabs will have a little slack when inserted. Too much slack, though, will leave an unsightly cut on the covering layer—so lengthen the slit with discretion.*

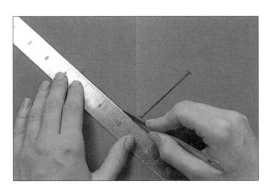

7 Insert the tabs through the slits. If the fit is very tight, lengthen the slits a little rather than risk tearing the covering layer. Slip the tabs in position on the underside of the covering layer, securing with tape or glue.

8 Make a sturdy backing sheet. Cover the front with an even layer of spray adhesive, remembering to do this in a well-ventilated room or outdoors.

9 Fold the covering layer in half, allowing the theater piece to collapse flat inside. Lower the covering layer onto the half of the backing sheet, so that the gutter on the covering layer exactly follows the line of the gutter on the backing sheet. Do this with considerable care. Fold the remaining half of the backing sheet over the top so that it sticks to the top of the covering layer. Unfold to check that everything has worked well, then trim off the excess covering layer paper.

10 *Cut out the four audience panels. Each piece contains two slits exactly 3in (6.5cm) apart and half the height of the panel. Each panel is a different height and equal in height to its position within the theater against the sloping side walls. Thus, each piece needs measuring independently and with care.*

11 *Slot each panel into position. Note that the slits in the theater piece and audience are not the width of a single knife cut, but are wider, made with two slits just a fraction apart. These wide slits help the structure to swivel flat when the backing sheet is closed. Not the stars on the covering layer, added for decoration.*

12 *Test the accuracy of the construction by folding the design in half. The audience panels will swivel flat in an elegant and fascinating way! If the swivelling is a little sticky, check the measurements on the audience panels, particularly the 3in (6.5cm) distance between the slits on each piece and the width of each slit.*

BOX POP-UP GALLERY

Ruined Temple

The same boxes made in the Movie Theater and the Cactus can easily be stretched to become rectangular boxes. Also, the simple outlines of these two boxes can be made very complex. The Ruined Temple is a rectangular box with a complex silhouette.

Tic-Tac-Toe Game

This design may be a little whimsical, but it is nevertheless a very practical idea! The support for the game board is similar to the Gift Box but without the solid faces across the middle—they are unnecessary. All manner of board games could be presented in this way, perhaps on a larger scale.

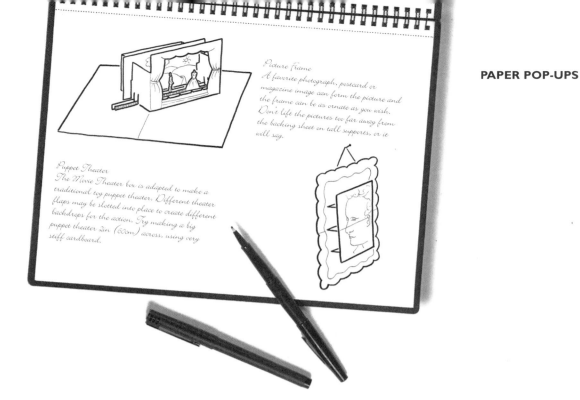

Picture Frame
A favorite photograph, postcard or magazine image can form the picture and the frame can be as ornate as you wish. Don't lift the pictures too far away from the backing sheet on tall supports, or it will sag.

Puppet Theater
The Movie Theater box is adapted to make a traditional toy puppet theater. Different theater flaps may be slotted into place to create different backdrops for the action. Try making a big puppet theater 2in (50cm) across, using very stiff cardboard.

Cactus

The four arms of the cactus are slotted into the four sides of the box that straddles the valley-fold. The box itself is a simplified version of the Movie Theater project. Two pieces of cardboard are slotted together to make a cactus. Thus, although complex, the design uses very little glue.

Coil Heart
The Coil Heart project shows what can be done with a simple application of the coil technique.

Musical Score
The Musical Score is a bit more complex.

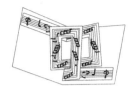

COIL POP-UPS

The coil technique is a curious one: It requires little or no measuring, and no careful construction, and the final result is often apparently non-geometric, even haphazard. The result can appear so random that to the uninitiated, even the simplest coil can seem clever. The only technical subtlety is to know how many revolutions the coil should have: Too few and the backing sheet will not open fully flat; too many and the coil will flop about and not stretch open. As a general rule, between two and three revolutions should be about right, depending upon whether the ends are glued to the backing sheet near to or far from the valley-fold.

Design Tips

- Learn the basic technical difference between the flat, simple one-piece coil used to make the Coil Heart, and the multiple-piece coil used to make the Musical Score. Once the difference is understood, many different pop-ups can be made.
- In the rough, experiment with gluing the coils to different places on the backing sheet. In some positions, the coil will barely open; in others, it will twist awkwardly. Seek the place where it stretches just right and looks balanced.
- Try combining the coil technique with others. For example, use it between a silhouette or a tent pop-up and the backing sheet, or between a scenery flat and the backing sheet. The results can look spectacular and bizarre!

COIL HEART

The Coil Heart, a pleasingly simple and quick-to-make design, is good for beginners because the pop-up mechanism is very reliable and requires no measuring. This is a particularly good card to make for Valentine's Day, but there is no reason why you cannot use it for other occasions.

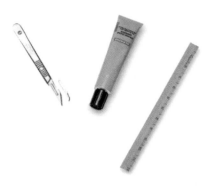

1   *Make an 11 x 5 in. (27.5 x 12.5 cm) sturdy backing sheet.*

YOU WILL NEED

- **Coil Heart paper elements**
- **Sturdy backing sheet 11 x 5 in. (27.5 x 12.5 cm)**
- **Covering layer: medium weight yellow paper 11 x 5 in. (27.5 x 12.5 cm)**

- **Craft knife**
- **Glue**
- **Ruler**
- **Photocopier**

2   *Cut out the blue coil heart paper element, or create one using the templates and medium weight blue paper. Hold it so that the spiral coils counterclockwise from the edge of the center, then glue the end as shown.*

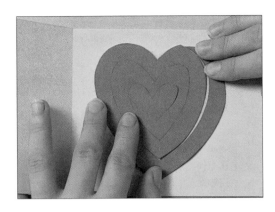

3 *Turn the coil over so that the glue is on the underside. Glue the coil into position on the backing sheet to the right of the gutter.*

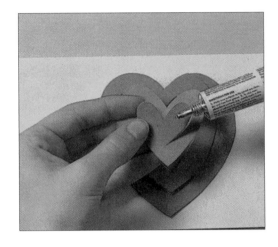

4 *Glue the top surface at the center of the heart. Be careful not to let the glue spread beyond the center.*

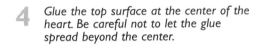

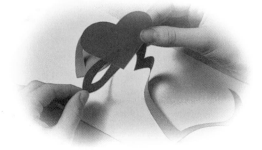

5 *Fold the backing sheet in half, so that the center of the heart glues onto the left-hand half of the backing sheet.*

6 *Open the backing sheet to see the blue heart uncoiled across the gutter. Cut out the red heart paper element—or make one using the template and medium weight red paper—and glue it into the coils, so that it is prominently displayed.*

MUSICAL SCORE

The Musical Score differs from the other step-by-step coil designs in the chapter because the coil does not spiral inward to a point of origin, but remains a constant width, rather like a spiral staircase.

YOU WILL NEED

- **Musical Score paper elements**
- **Sturdy backing sheet 11 x 6 in. (27.5 x 15 cm)**
- **Covering layer: copy paper 11 x 6 in. (27.5 x 15 cm)**
- **Coil: enough photocopies of lines of music to make 14 pieces each 5 x 1¹/² in (12.5 x 4 cm)**

- **Craft knife**
- **Glue**
- **Ruler**
- **Photocopier**

1 *Cut out paper elements. Glue two pieces together as shown, ensuring that the angles between them are exactly 90°. If you are using the paper templates to make this pop-up, make sure you cut out twelve of the beveled shape and two of the rectangle shape.*

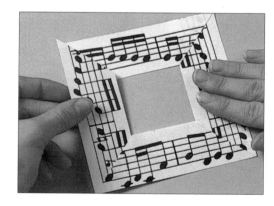

2 *Continue the pattern, gluing the third and fourth pieces into position. Once again, create exact 90° angles at the corners.*

3 *Glue together a total of seven pieces to form this square-section coil. The seventh piece is one of the two rectangular paper elements, used to create a flat end to the coil.*

4 Turn the coil over. Glue the remaining seven units exactly onto the back of the first seven so that the musical score runs along both sides of the coil.

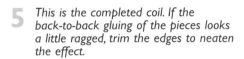

5 This is the completed coil. If the back-to-back gluing of the pieces looks a little ragged, trim the edges to neaten the effect.

6 Make a sturdy backing sheet. For the covering layer, two additional rectangular lines of music have been supplied. Place them an exact distance apart. That distance is the same as the distance between the lines of music along the opposite edges of the square coil.

7 Glue one end of the coil to the backing sheet, so that the music flows uninterrupted across the join. Then glue the top surface of the other end of the coil and close the backing sheet over it, so that the glued end sticks to the backing sheet. If your measurements in step 6 are accurate, the music at the end of the coil will exactly join up with the music on the backing sheet.

COIL POP-UP GALLERY

Fireworks

The three firework rockets are glued to those parts of coils that stand vertically, so that the rockets themselves will also stand vertically, like the Coil Heart. The bright colors were achieved with oil pastel and glitter.

Soccer Kick
Again, this design is essentially the same as the Aerobatic Plane. If soccer isn't an appropriate sport to depict, adapt the image to one that is more relevant.

Rollercoaster
This is essentially the same as the Aerobatic Plane, but with fewer rotations of the coil. Try changing the shape of the coil to achieve a different corkscrew effect.

Aerobatic Plane

A Pop-up design need not always stand up on a horizontal surface such as a desk or shelf. When appropriate to the design, it could hang on a wall! The coil here is similar to the square-sectioned coil used to make the Musical Score, but it's circular and thus requires considerably fewer pieces to make.

Scenery Flats
Scenery flats are a common type of pop-up available commercially; here, the Celebration pop-up derives its movement from the supporting tab (see insert).

SCENERY FLATS POP-UPS

A long with the silhouette technique, the scenery flats technique is probably the most widely used in commercially produced pop-up books and greeting cards. The reason for its continued popularity is not hard to see: it creates any number of seemingly unsupported flat shapes that stand behind or beside each other to make appealingly complex pop-up designs.

Design Tips

- Make the supporting tab exercise suggested on the next spread, then make a few more with different measurements for extra practice. This may seem a little pedantic, but learning the technique well will save time later when you design your own pop-up.
- In the pop-up gallery, the Golfer combines the scenery flats technique with the silhouette technique. Consider also combining the technique with the tent and box techniques—they both make excellent backgrounds for supporting tabs.
- Remember that if scenery flats are designed with too many layers, one behind another connected by supporting tabs, the layers at the front will not be pulled fully upright by the layers behind. As a general rule, four layers is a maximum—any more and the construction may begin to wilt at the front.

HOW TO MAKE A SUPPORTING TAB

Ironically, the most important part of the technique is rarely seen—the supporting tab. The measuring and placement of the tab on the covering layer is critical and must be understood before the scenery flats technique can be used with any fluency. If you are able to make these tabs accurately, all manner of wonderful designs can be created. However, each tab must be measured and constructed with great care.

YOU WILL NEED

- **Craft knife**
- **Glue**
- **Black marker pen**
- **Pencil and eraser**
- **Ruler**

1 *On a covering layer of medium weight paper, approximately 9 x 6 in. (22.5 x 15 cm), draw a central gutter crease. Draw a line to each side of the valley. For this exercise, the two lines are exactly 3 in. (7.5 cm) and 1 1/2 in. (4 cm) upon the design that you are making.*

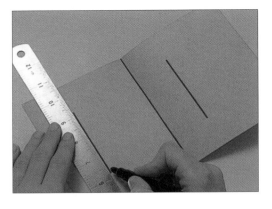

2 *Make a supporting tab from medium weight paper. The distances between the creases must be exactly the same as those measured on the covering layer: 3 in. (7.5 cm) and 1 1/2 in. (4 cm). For this exercise, the width of the tab is 2 in. (5 cm).*

3 *Place the end folds on the supporting tab exactly over the lines drawn on the covering layer. Mark the lines on the covering layer where the edge of the tab crosses them.*

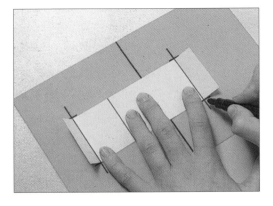

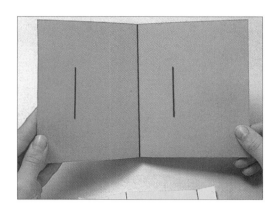

4   *Here are the lines between the marks made in step 3. The length of each line should be the width of the supporting tab.*

5   *Cut each line, checking first that they are exactly parallel to the valley-fold. In fact, you may wish to cut a fraction beyond the ends of each line, in order to help the glue tabs push through in step 6 without risk of tearing the covering layer paper if the fit is too tight.*

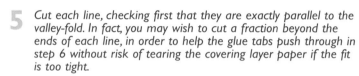

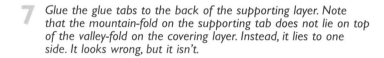

6   *This is the step that can confuse! The glue tabs at the ends of the supporting tabs are pushed through the slits in the covering layer, but which tab goes through which slit? The rule is that the glue tab nearer the mountain-fold on the supporting tab is pushed through the slit further away from the valley-fold. This is the opposite to how you might imagine it.*

7   *Glue the glue tabs to the back of the supporting layer. Note that the mountain-fold on the supporting tab does not lie on top of the valley-fold on the covering layer. Instead, it lies to one side. It looks wrong, but it isn't.*

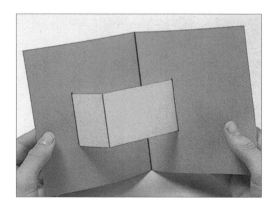

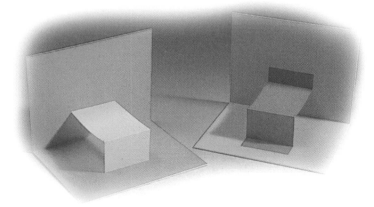

8   *For extra strength, glue the covering layer to a sturdy backing sheet. When designing a rough, instead of carefully making slits to hide the glue tabs, just glue the tabs to the front of the covering layer. The pink and red example show this time-saving alternative.*

CELEBRATION

YOU WILL NEED

- **Celebration paper elements**
- **Sturdy backing sheet 12 x 8in (30 x 20cm)**
- **Covering layer: thick white paper 12 x 8in (30 x 20cm) or larger**
- **Craft knife**
- **Glue**
- **Black marker pen**
- **Pencil and eraser**
- **Ruler**

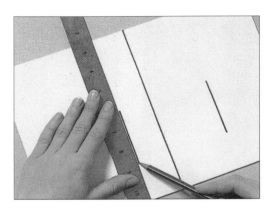

I *Make a sturdy backing sheet, then put a covering layer of thick white paper over it. Draw two lines parallel to the gutter, 2.75in (6.5cm) away from the right, and 1.5in (4cm) from the left.*

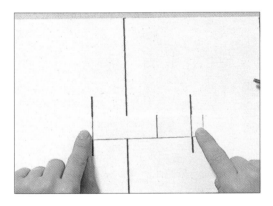

2 *Cut out the strap paper elements, or create them with the templates and thick white paper. Glue the tabs at both ends of the larger strap, then glue the strap flat to the backing sheet, creasing it first. The bottom edge of the strap is 2.5in (4cm) away from the bottom edge of the backing sheet. Note that the mountain-fold is to the right of the gutter crease, not in line with it.*

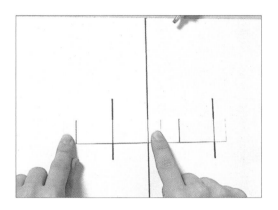

3 *Similarly, fold the small tab, then glue the tabs at both ends. Glue it flat, so that the left tab glues to the backing sheet and the right tab glues onto the large strap. Note that the right-hand fold is in line with it.*

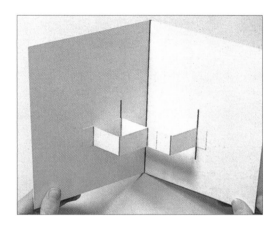

4 *This is the three-dimensional result of steps 1 and 3. Fold the card in half and press it flat to strengthen all the creases. Some of them may move a fraction, but don't worry!*

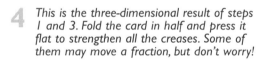

5 *Draw the background illustration on the backing sheet. If your card is to have a greeting or message, add it now.*

6 *Cut out the glass and bottle elements, or create them from thick white paper using the templates. Glue the bottle and glass to the two right-facing straps. Be careful to line up the bottom of the bottle and glass with the bottom edge of the card, so that they appear to stand on the same surface as the card.*

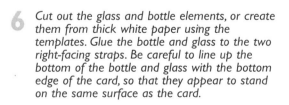

5

PAPER FLOWERS TEMPLATES

Rose Paper Elements—1 of 2
To make two roses

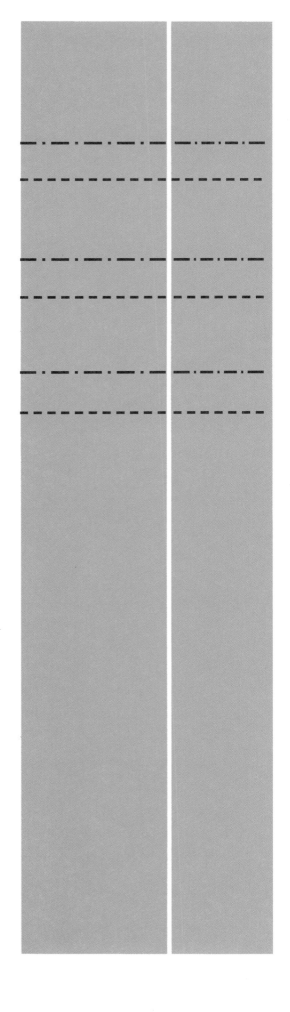

Tulip Paper Elements—I of 2
To make two tulips

Tulip Paper Elements—2 of 2

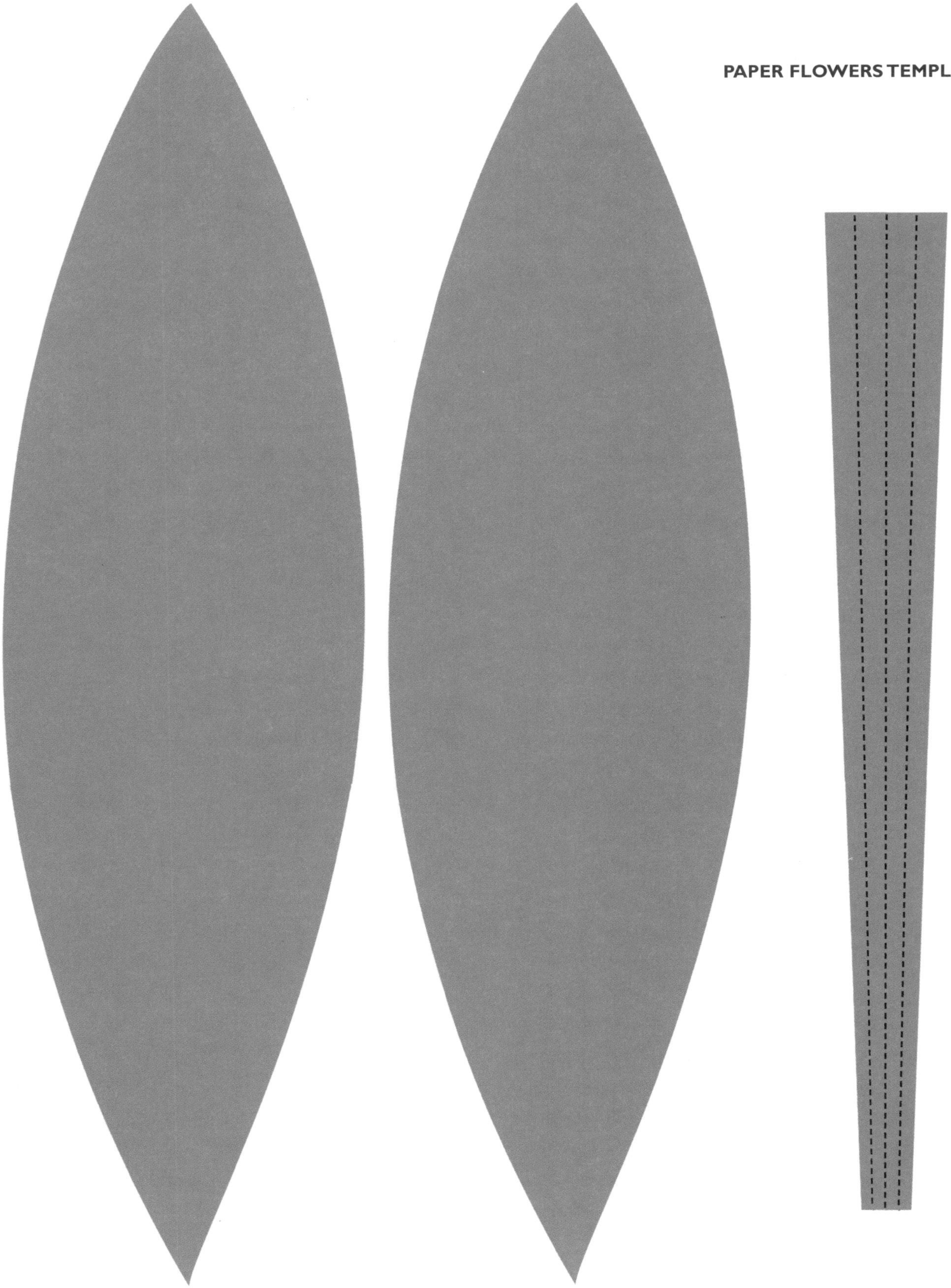

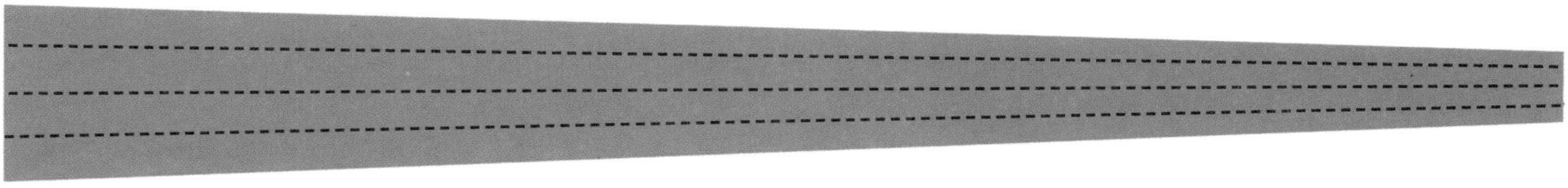

275

Iris Paper Elements—2 of 2

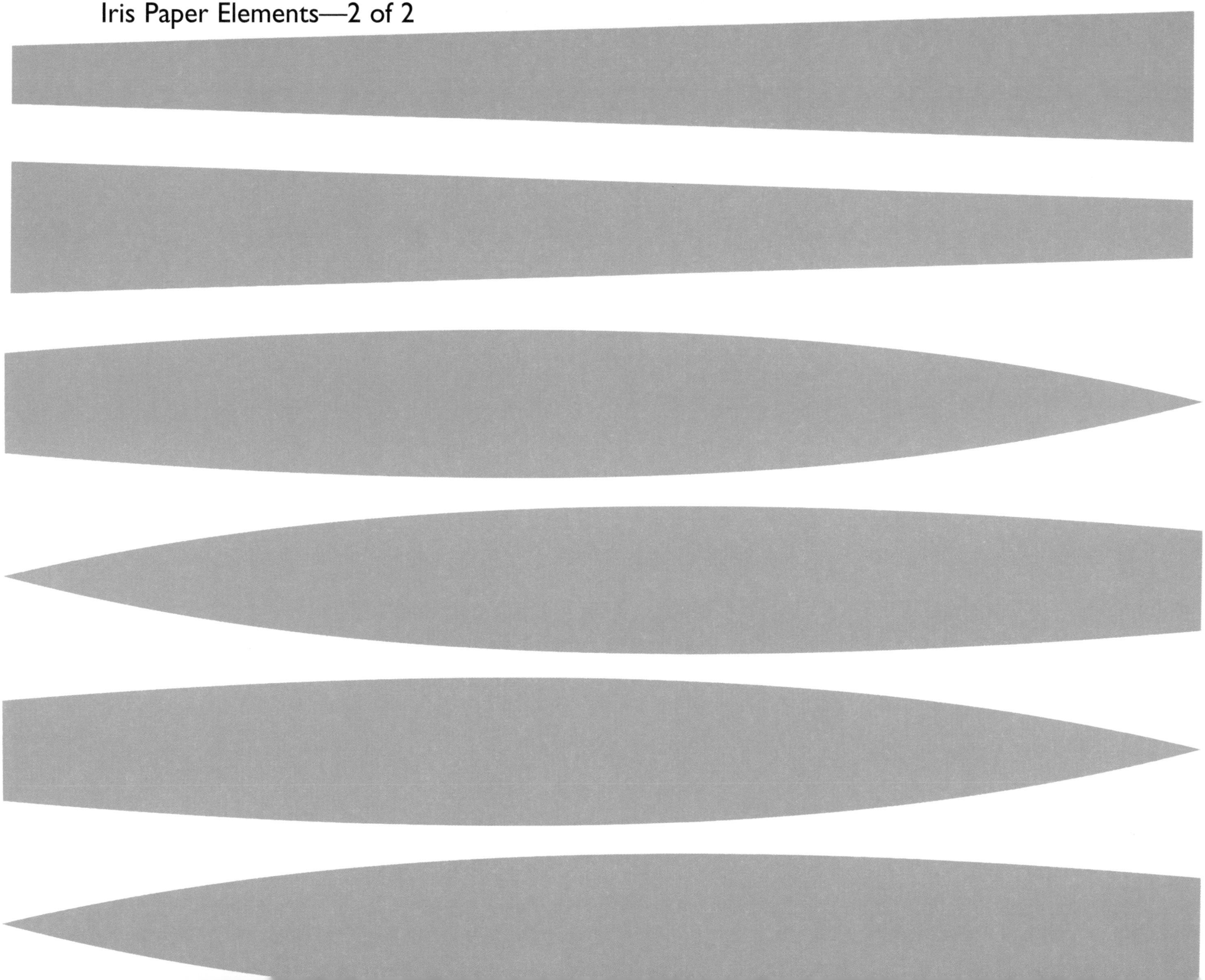

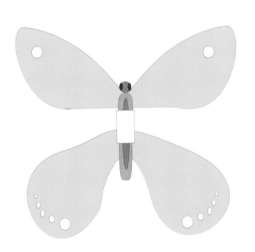

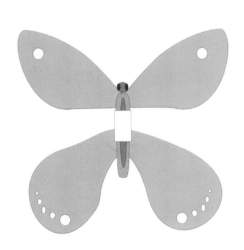

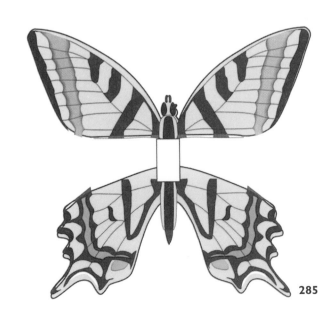

285

Lotus Paper Elements—2 of 2

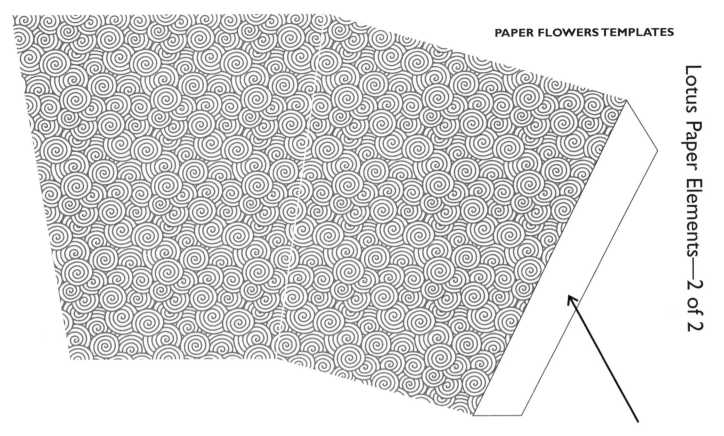

APPLY PASTE

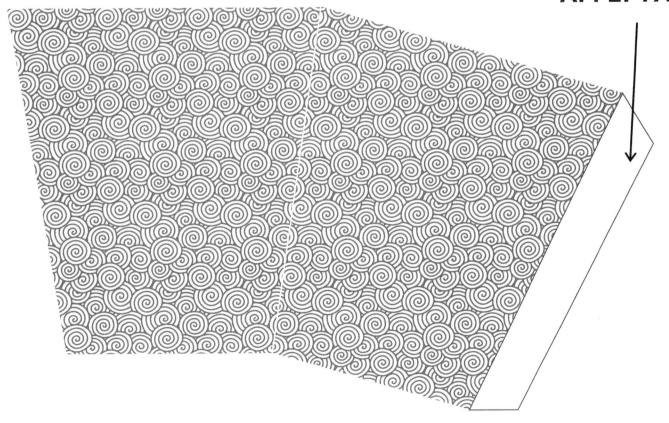

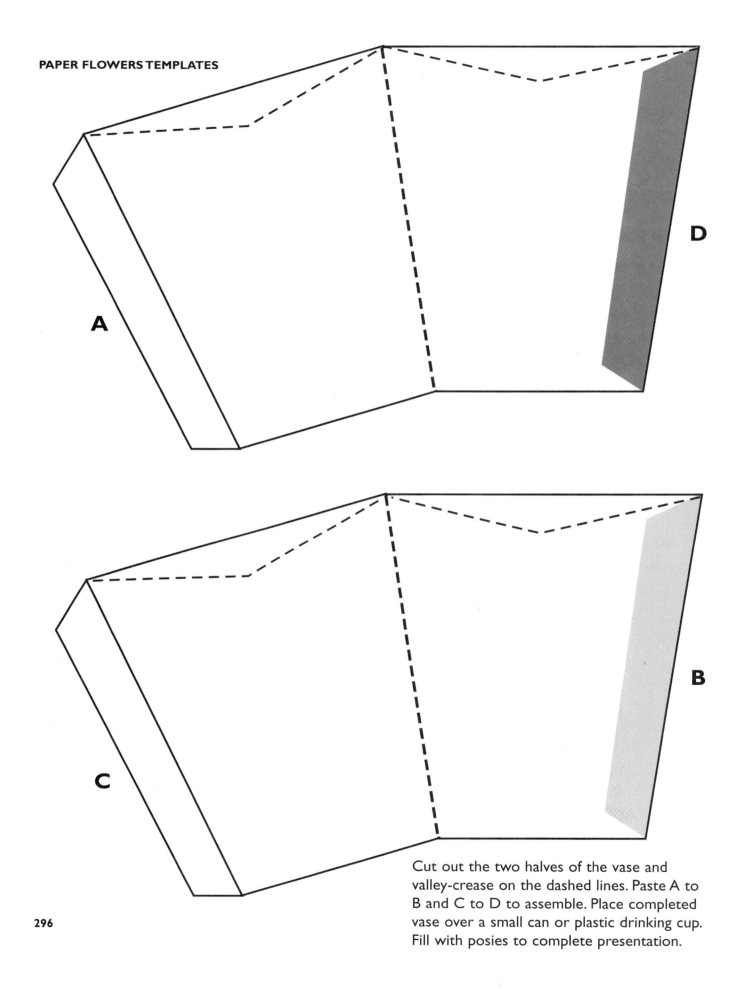

A

D

C

B

296

Cut out the two halves of the vase and
valley-crease on the dashed lines. Paste A to
B and C to D to assemble. Place completed
vase over a small can or plastic drinking cup.
Fill with posies to complete presentation.

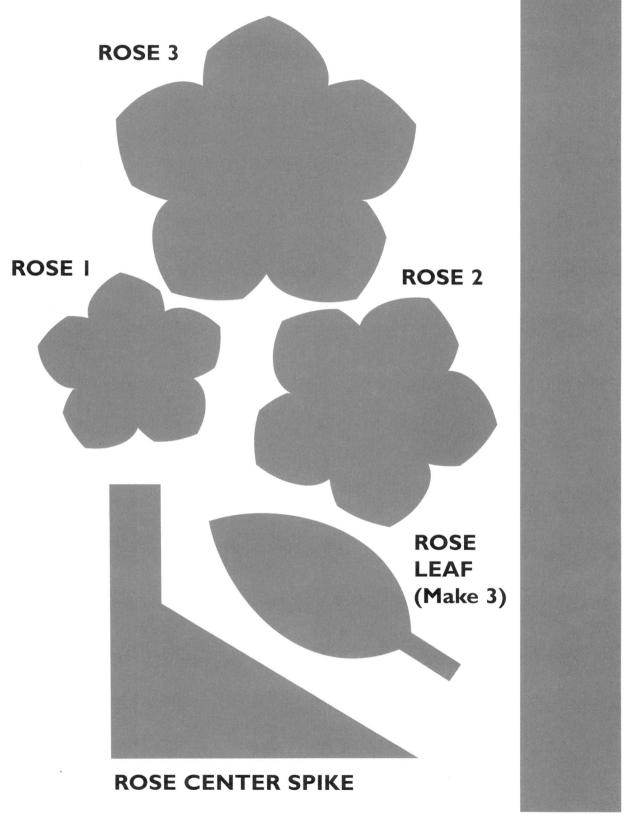

ROSE 3

ROSE 1

ROSE 2

Rose Template

ROSE LEAF (Make 3)

ROSE CENTER SPIKE

ROSE STEM

TULIP FLOWER

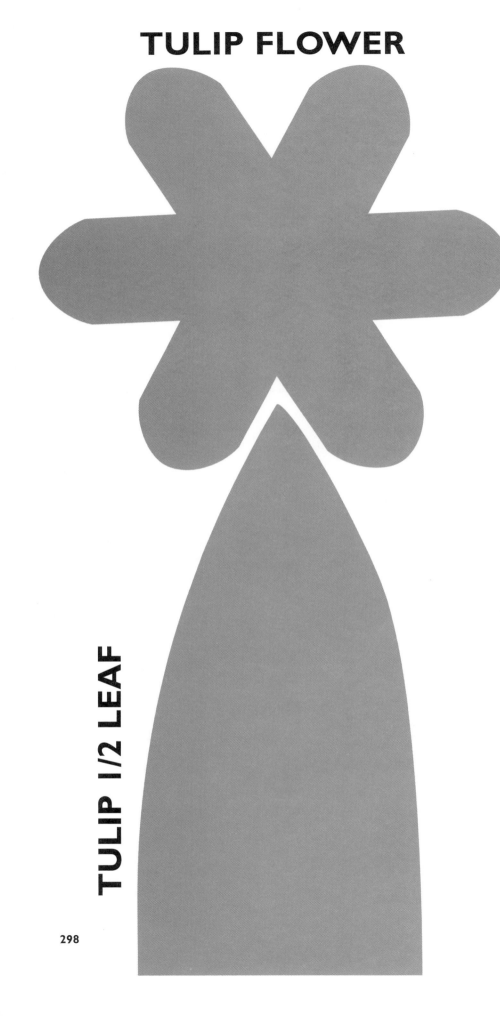

Tulip Template

TULIP 1/2 LEAF

TULIP STEM

298

**DAISY
FLOWER**

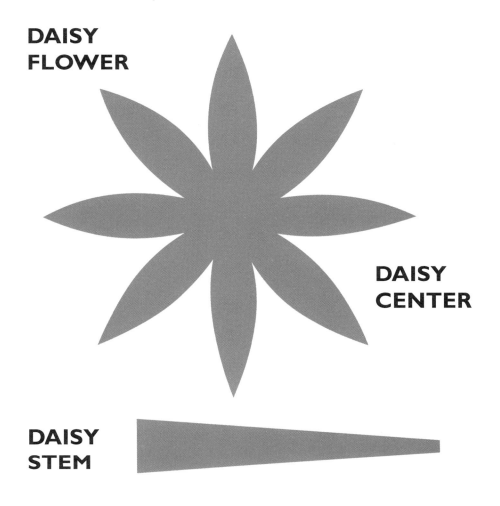

**DAISY
CENTER**

**DAISY
STEM**

DAISY LEAF

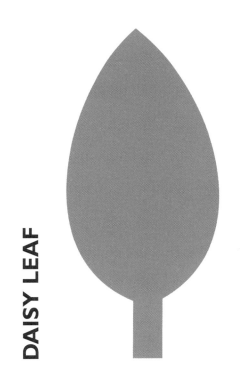

Iris Template

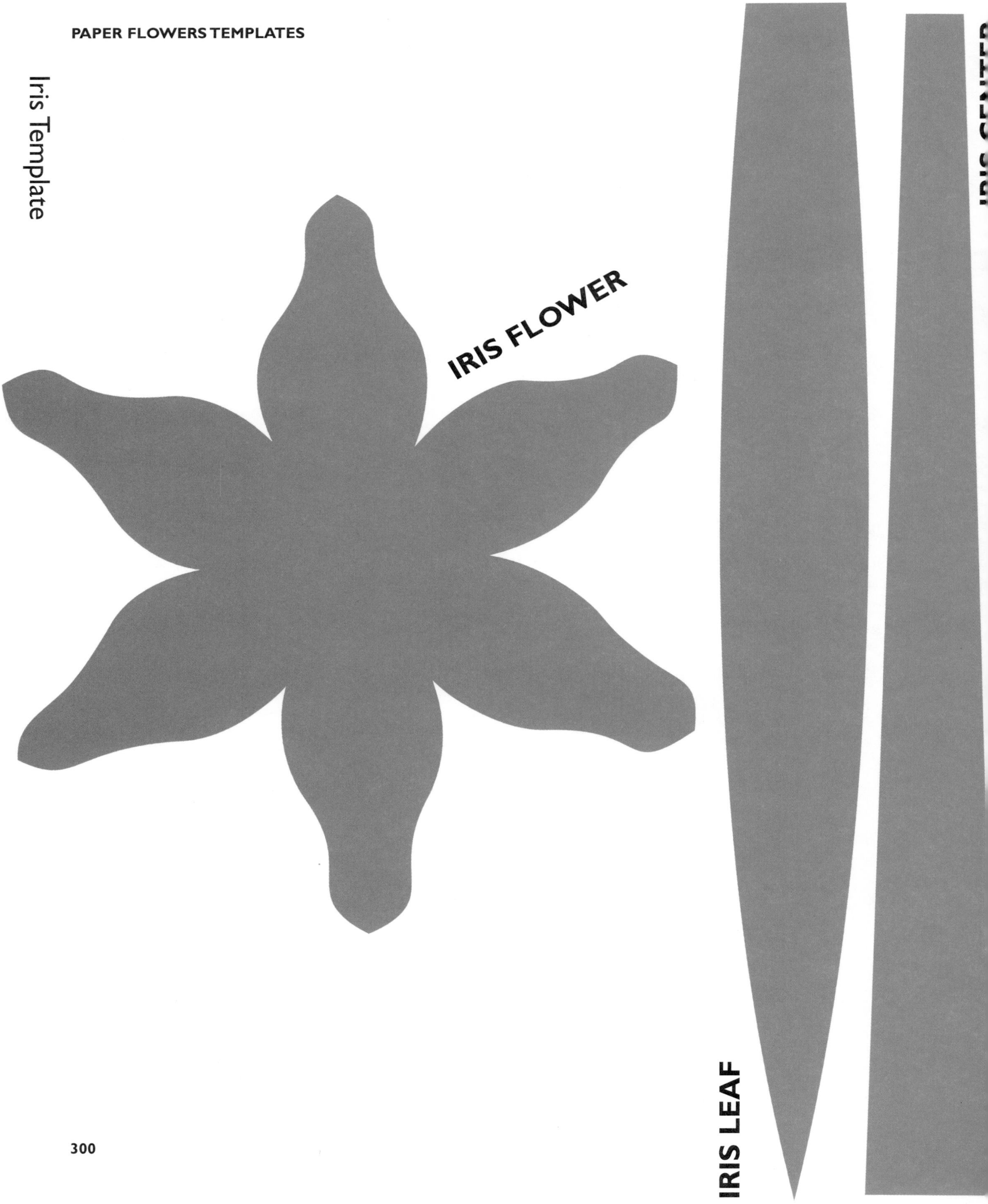

IRIS FLOWER

IRIS LEAF

IRIS CENTER

Daylily Template

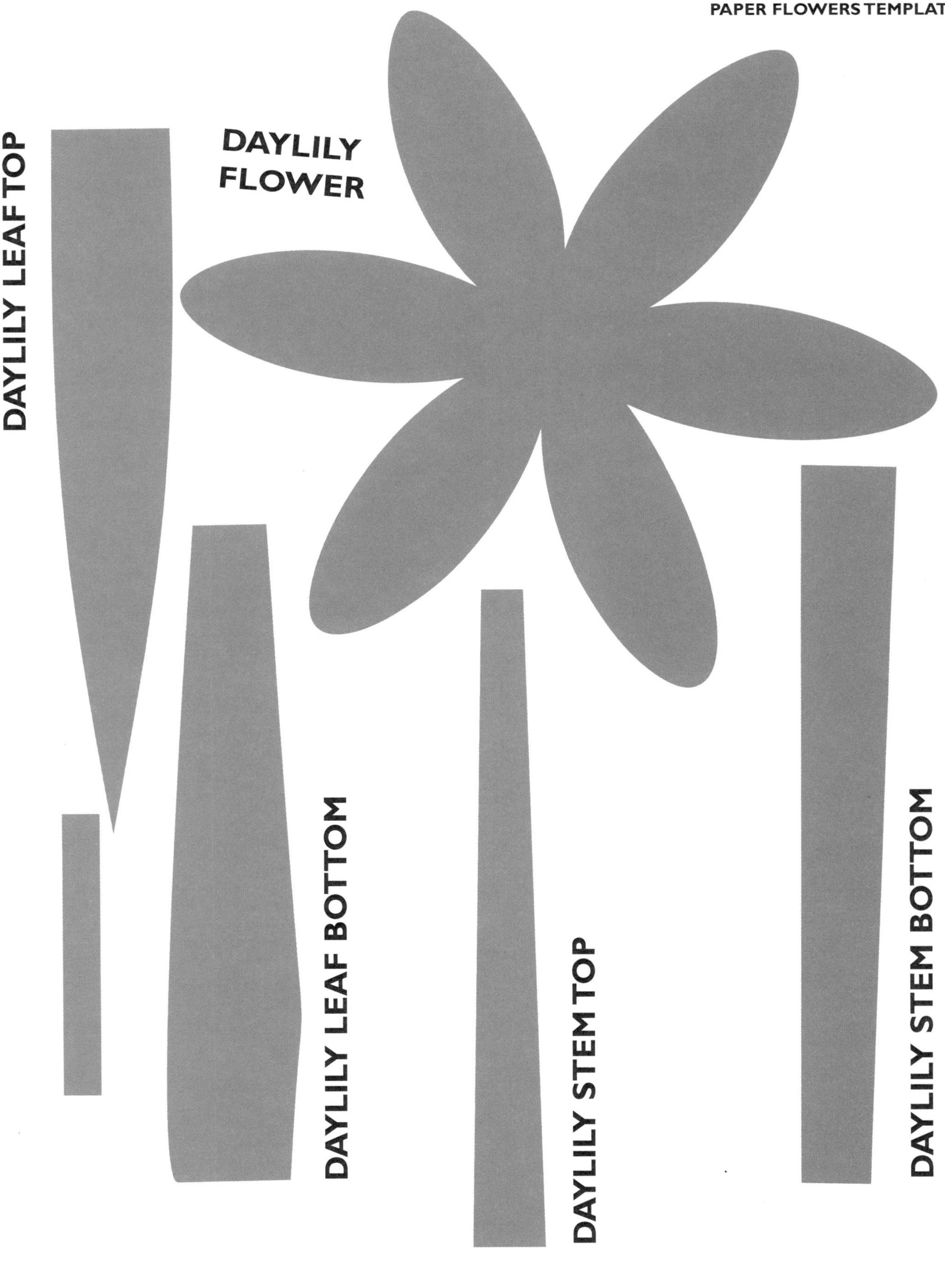
DAYLILY LEAF TOP
DAYLILY FLOWER
DAYLILY LEAF BOTTOM
DAYLILY STEM TOP
DAYLILY STEM BOTTOM

**POSY
DAISY**

Posy Template

**POSY
CUP**

POSY STEM

**SULPHUR
BUTTERFLY**

**SWALLOWTAIL
BUTTERFLY**

LOTUS PETALS

LOTUS CENTER

LILY PAD

CACTUS

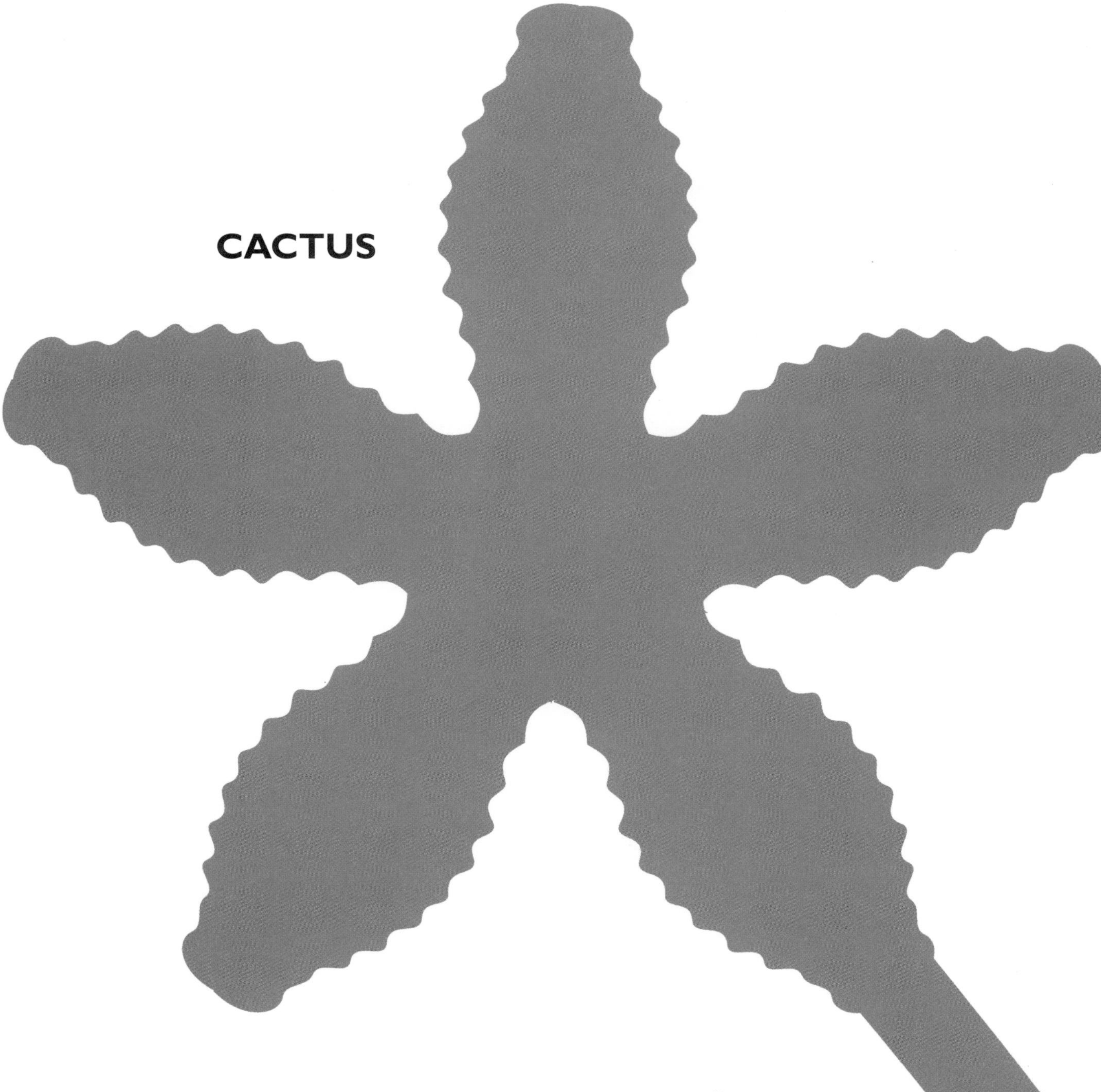

CACTUS FLOWER STEM

CACTUS FLOWER

Vase Template

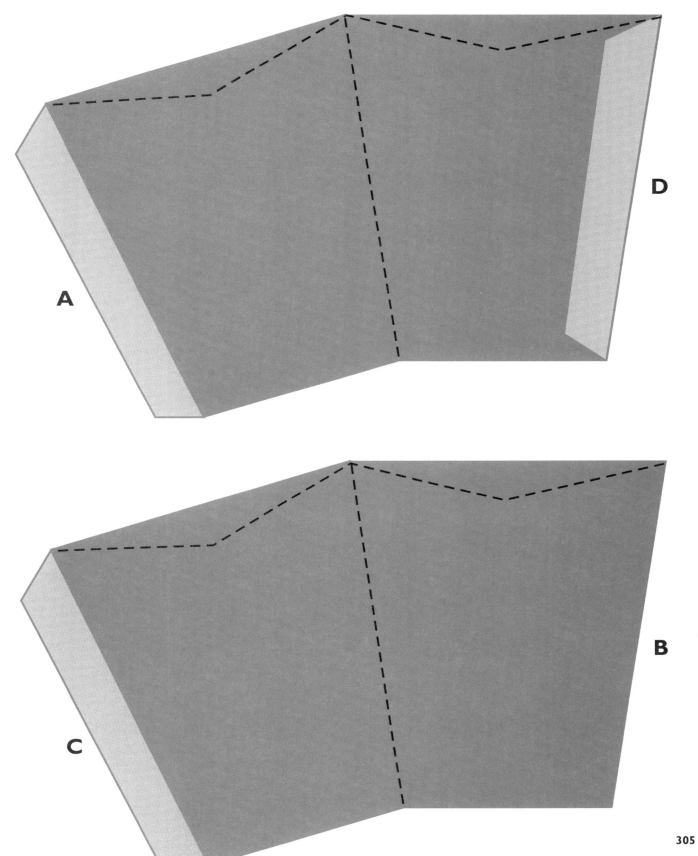

6

PAPER ANIMALS TEMPLATES

Frog Paper Elements—1 of 2

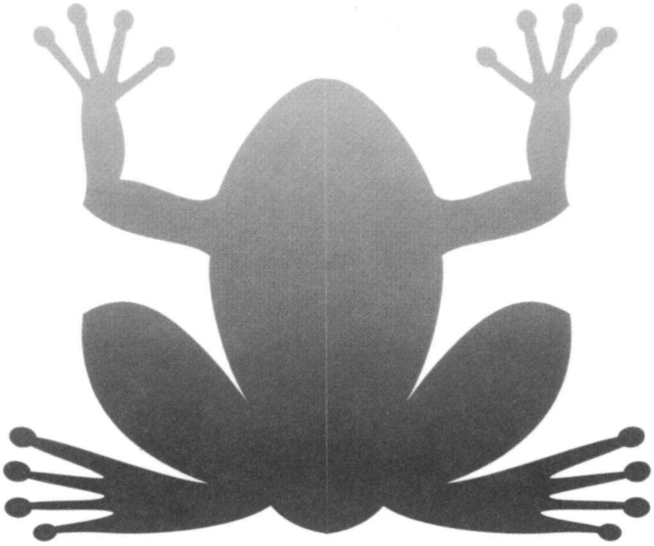

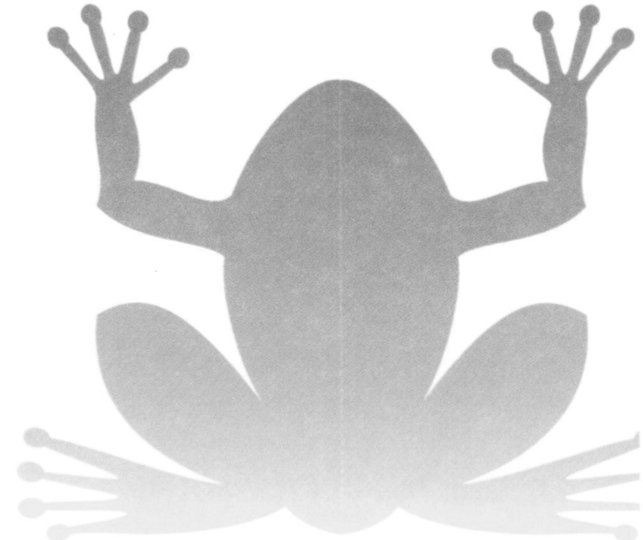

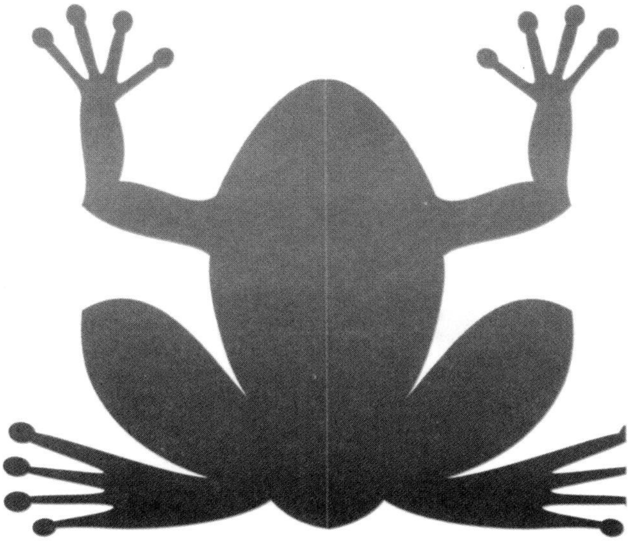

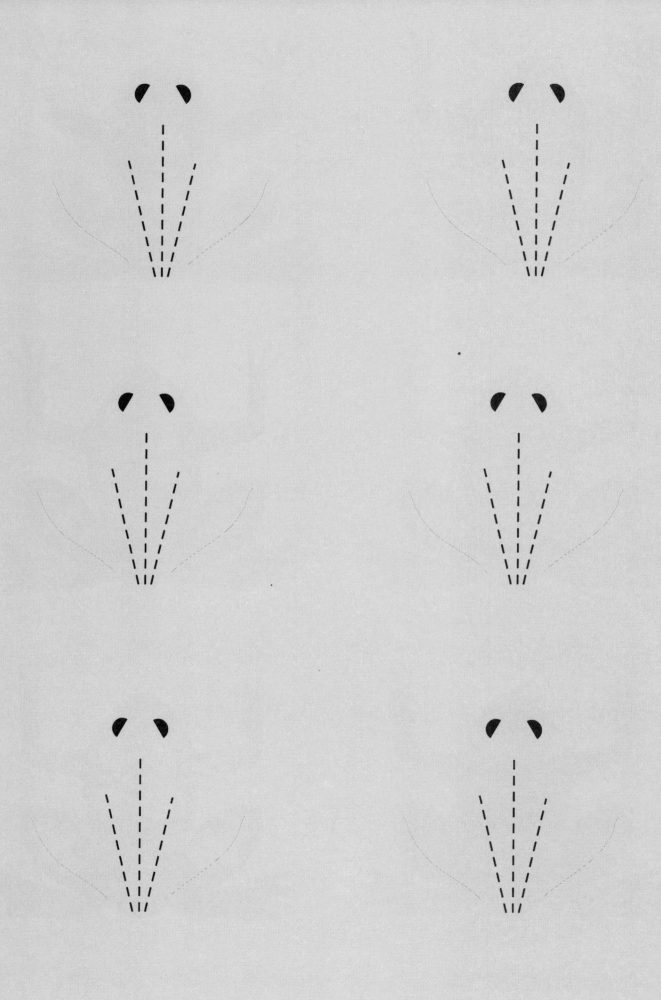

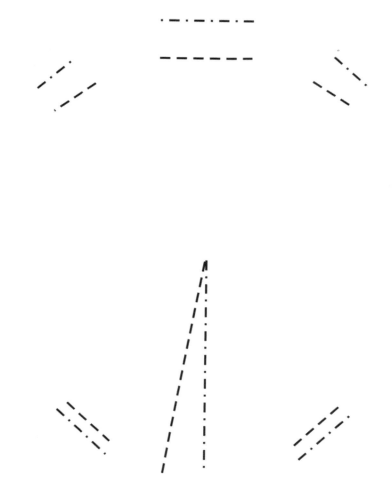

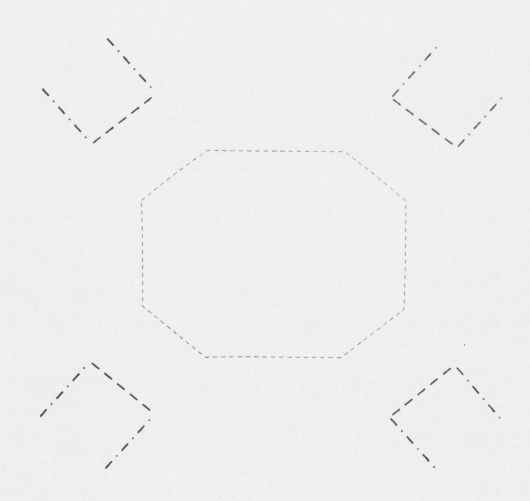

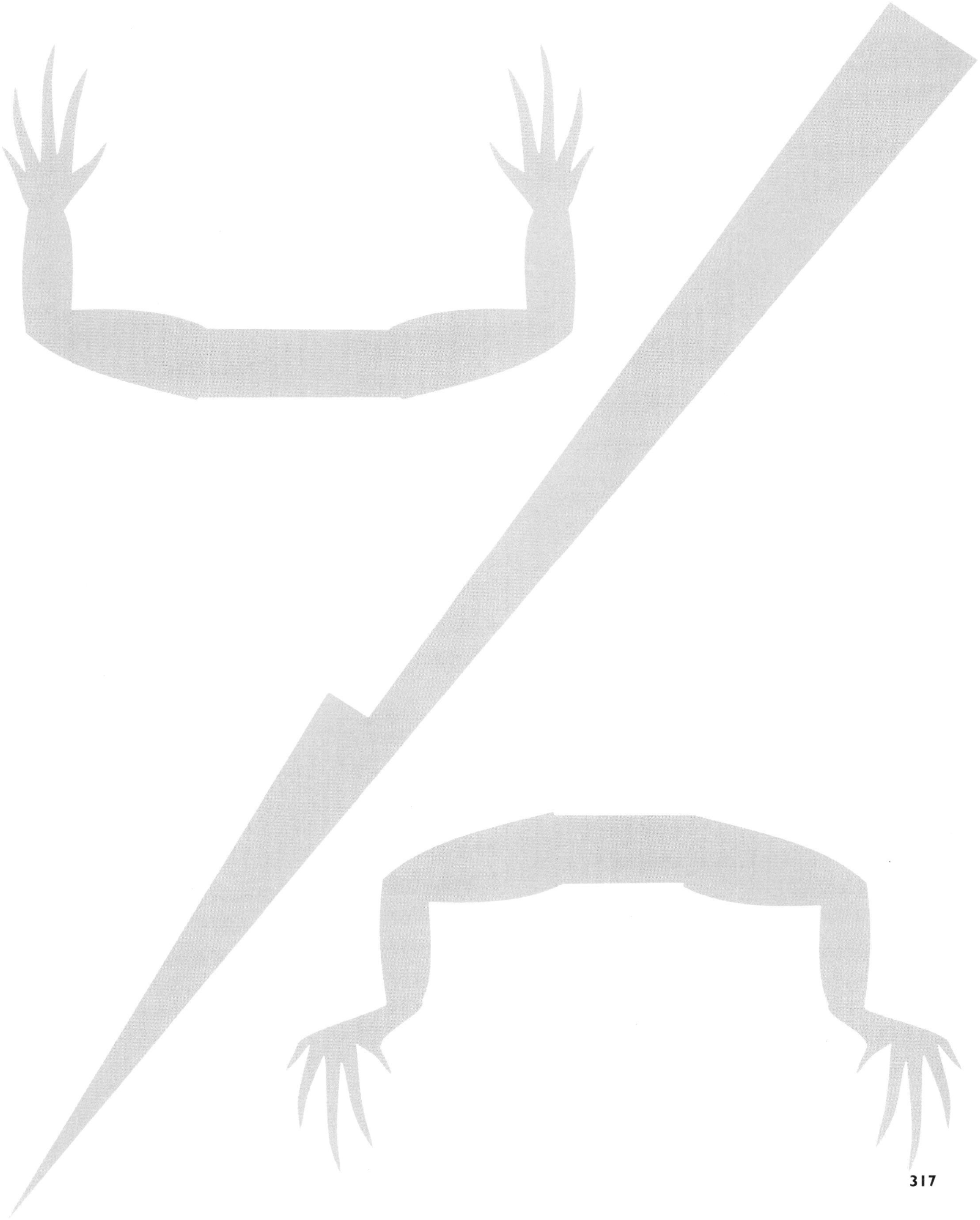

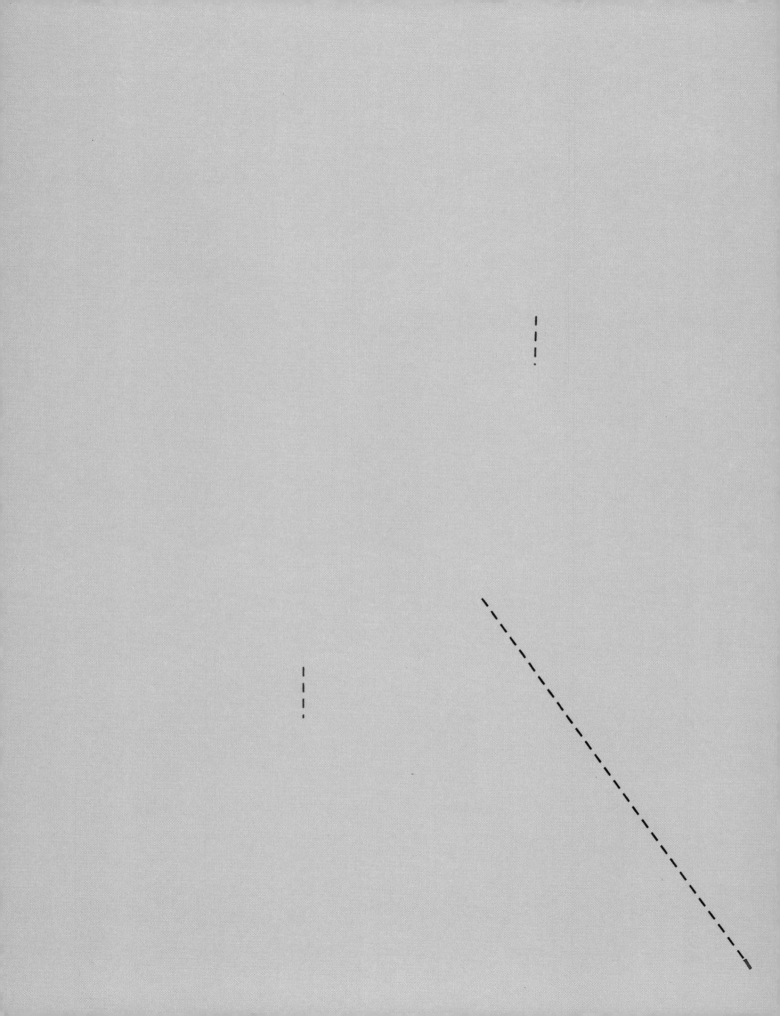

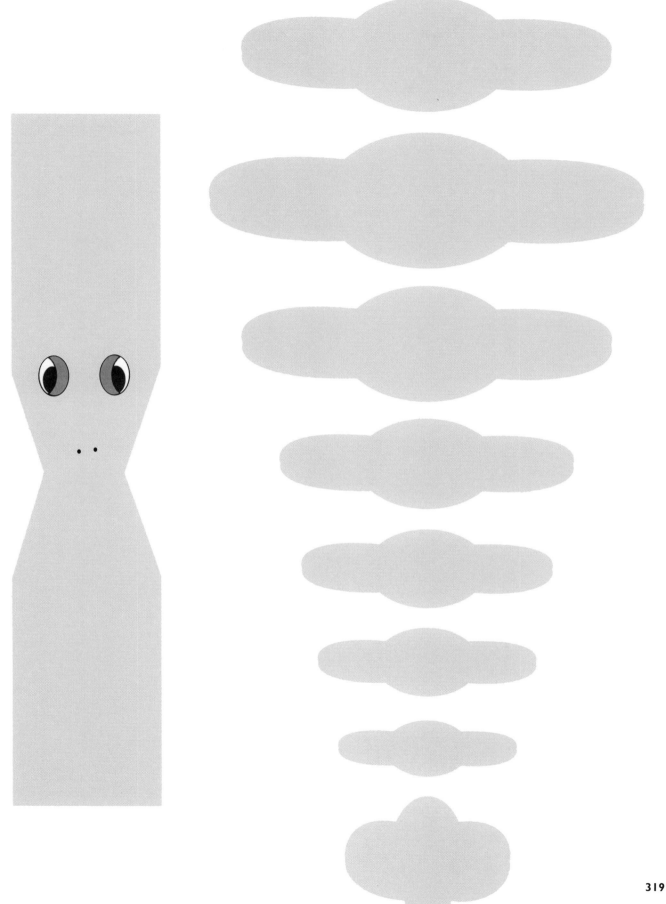

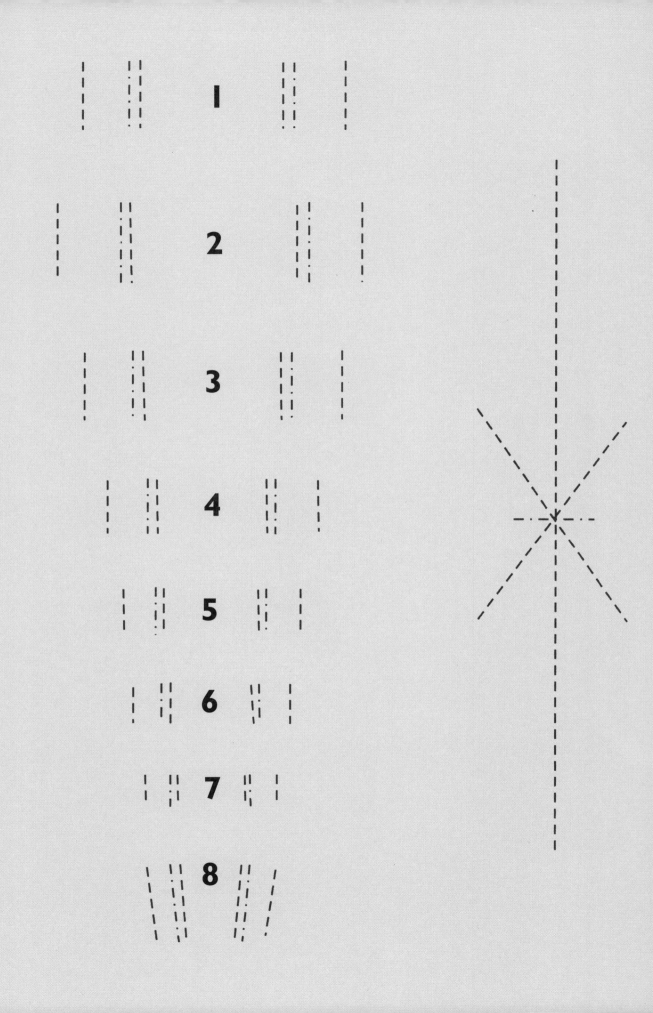

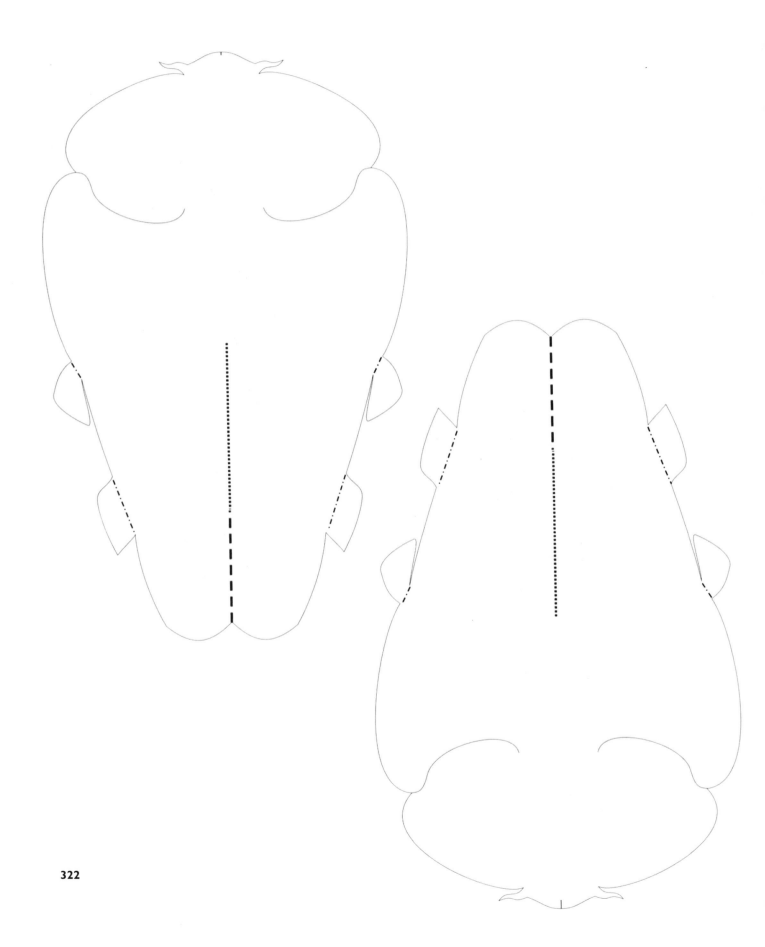

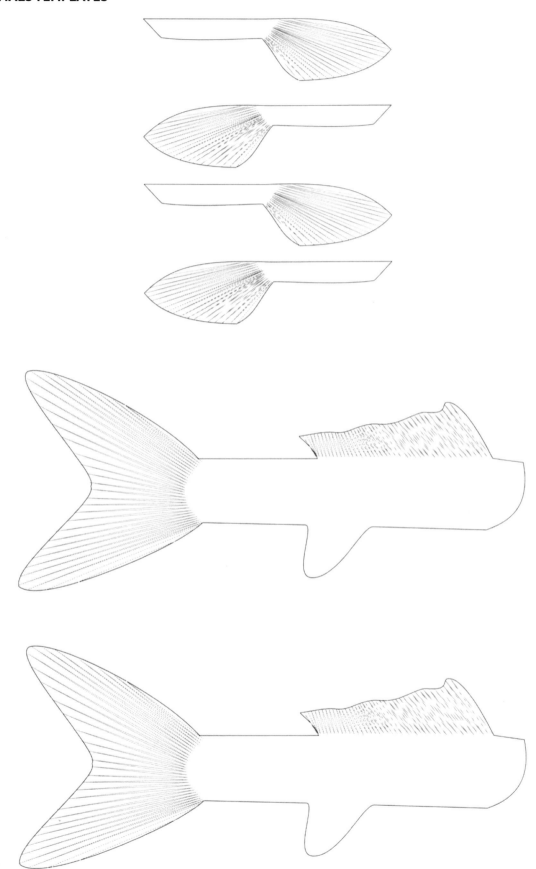

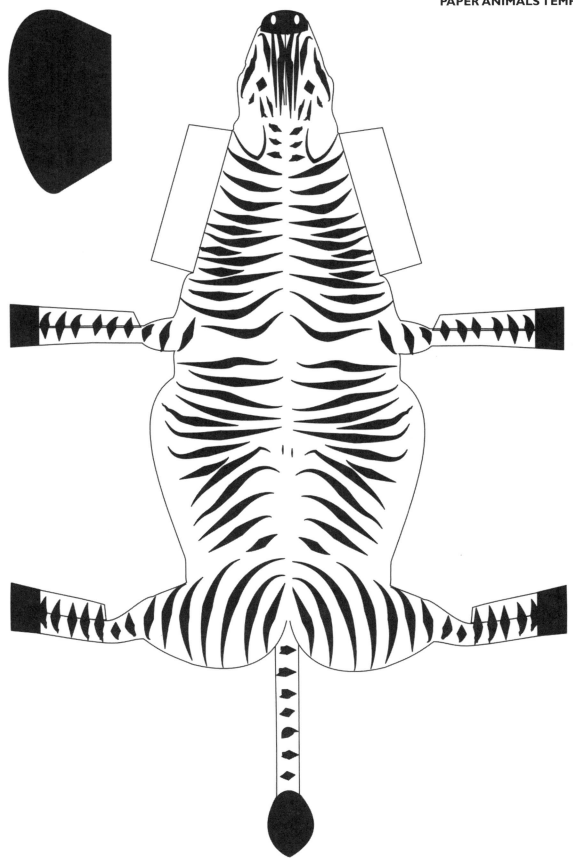

327

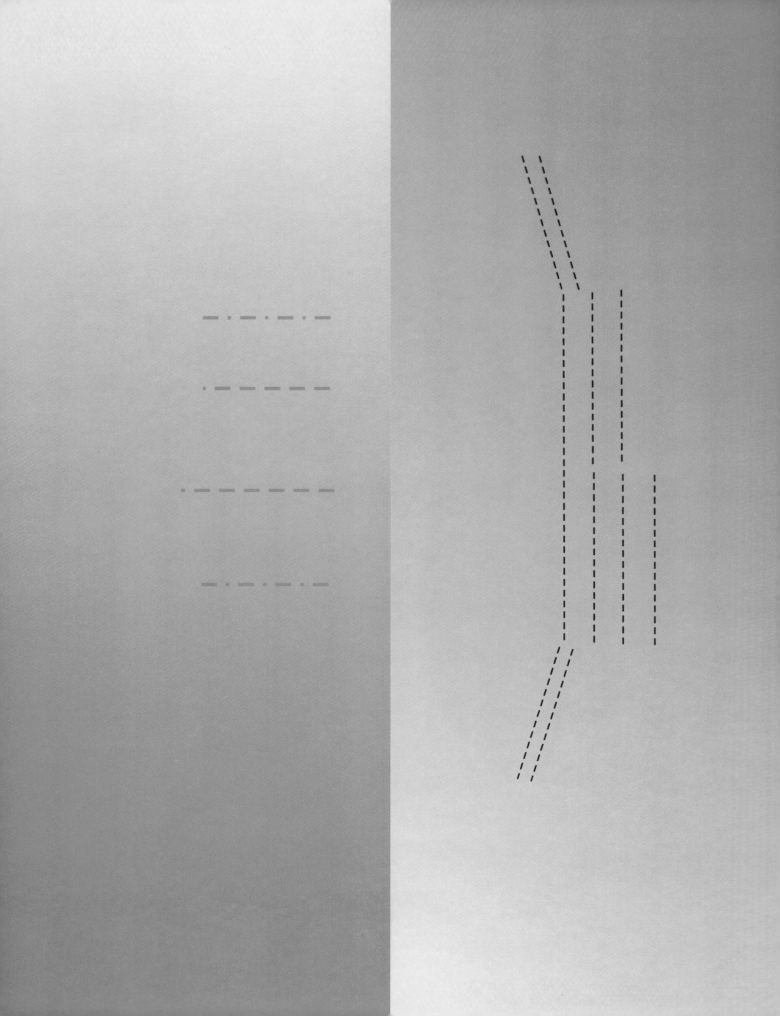

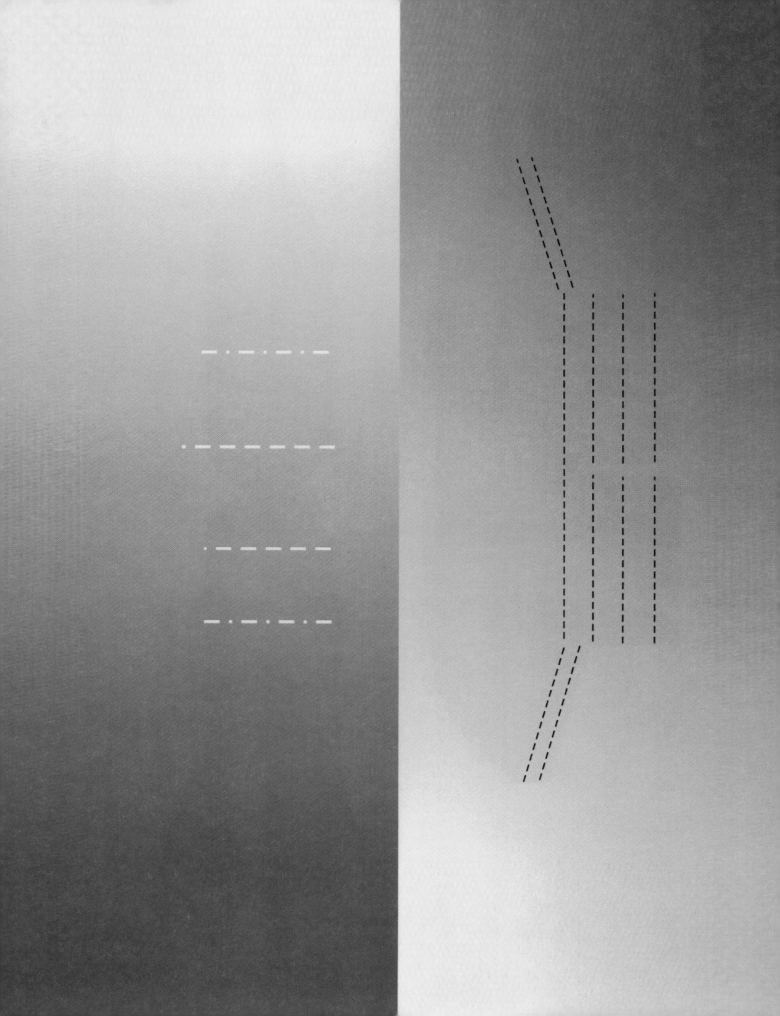

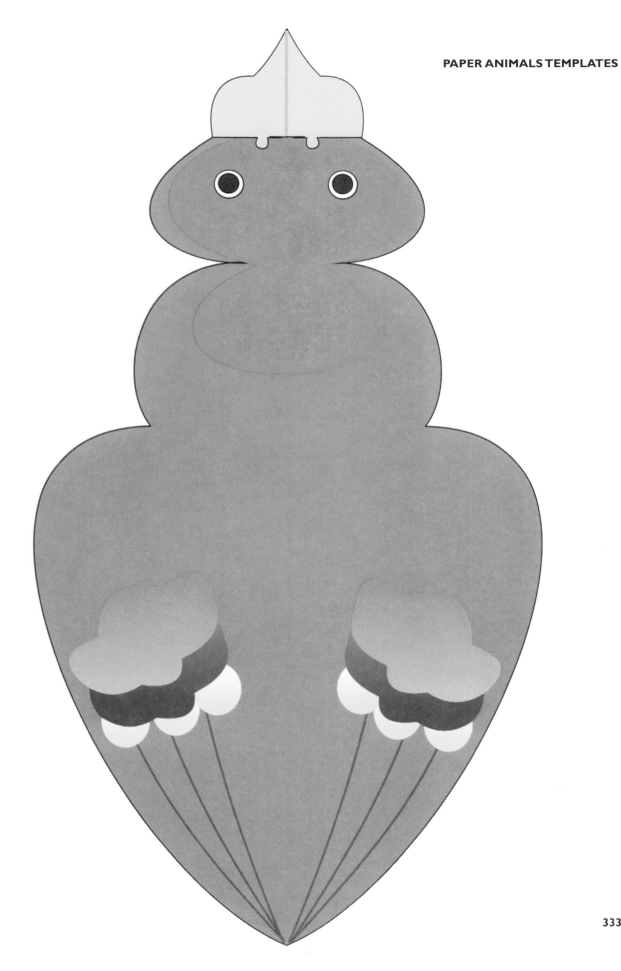

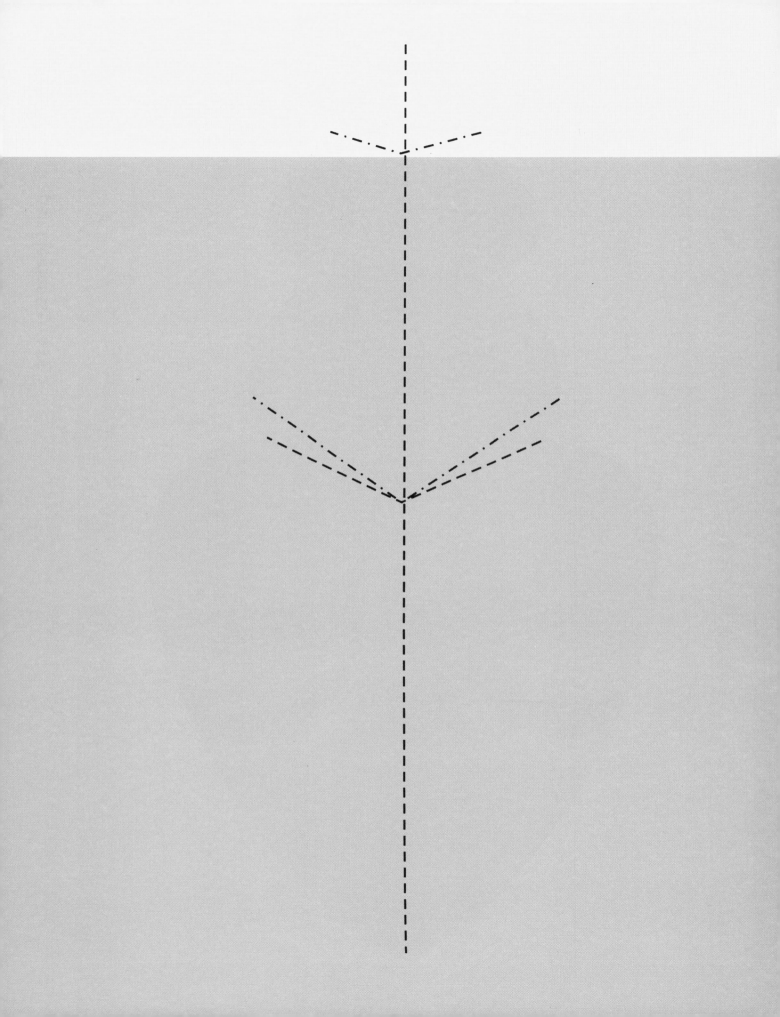

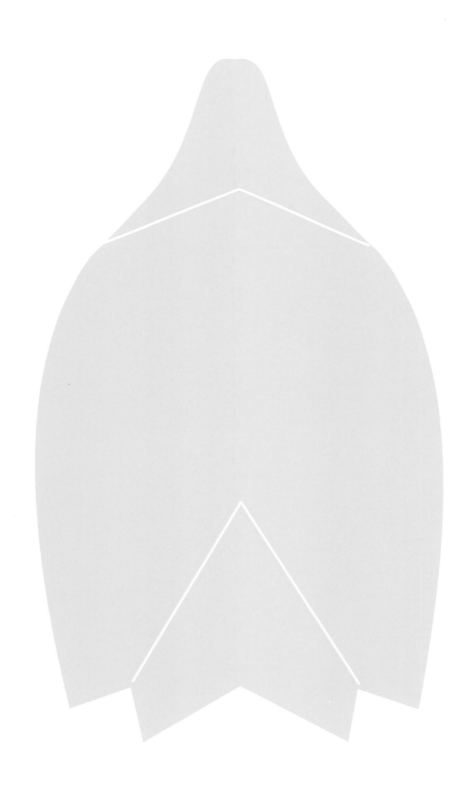

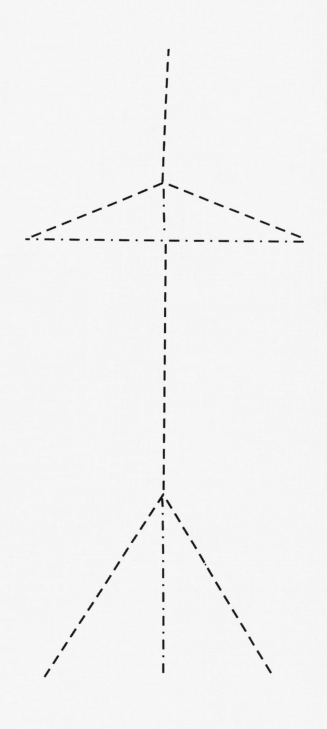

Bat Paper Elements

Frog Template

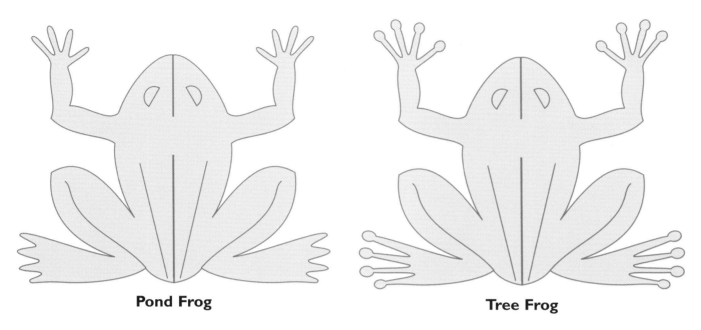

Pond Frog

Tree Frog

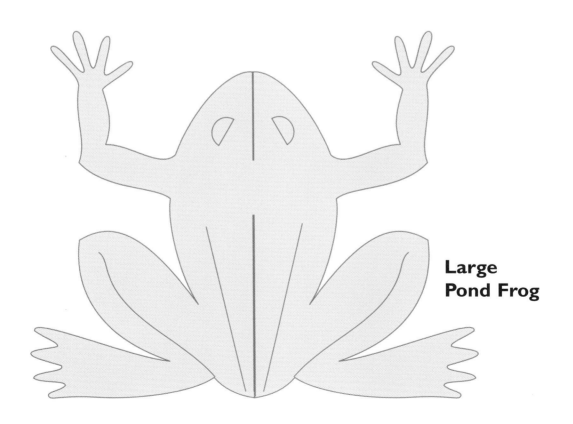

**Large
Pond Frog**

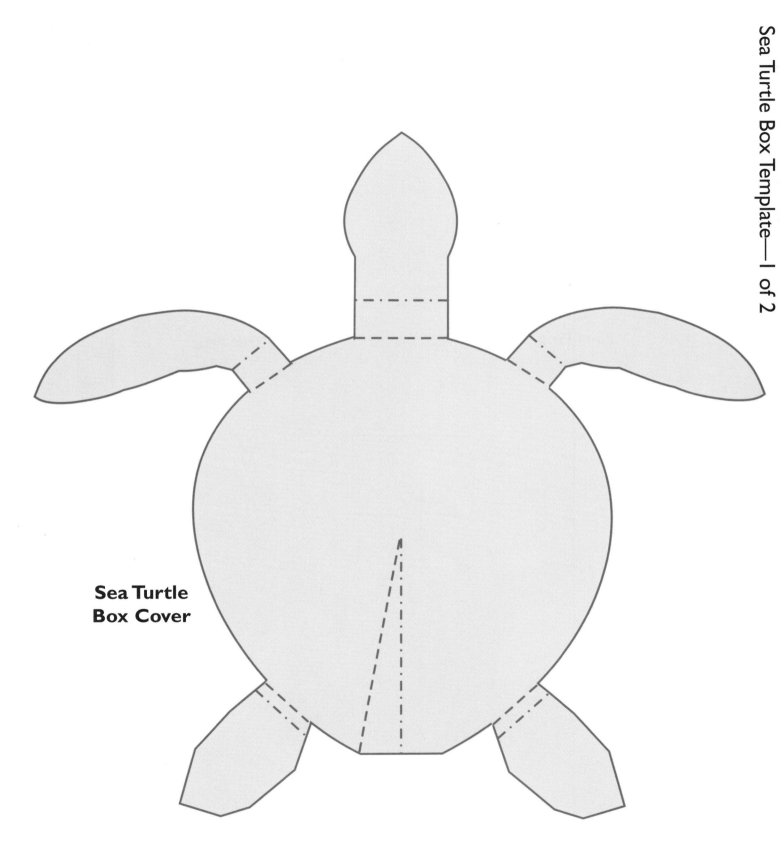

**Sea Turtle
Box Cover**

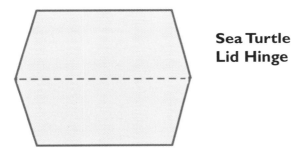

**Sea Turtle
Lid Hinge**

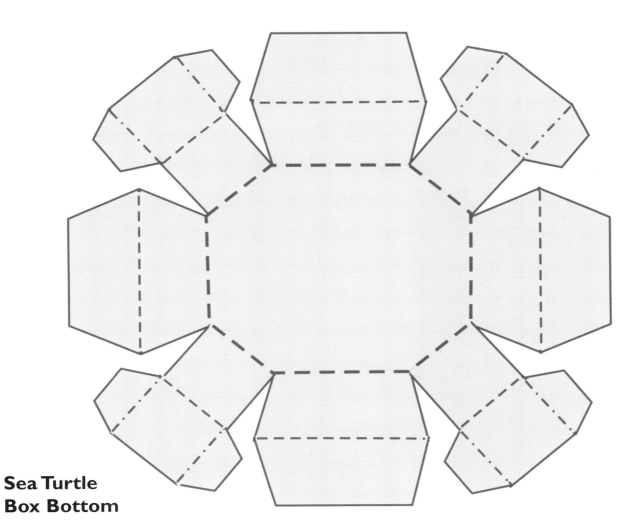

**Sea Turtle
Box Bottom**

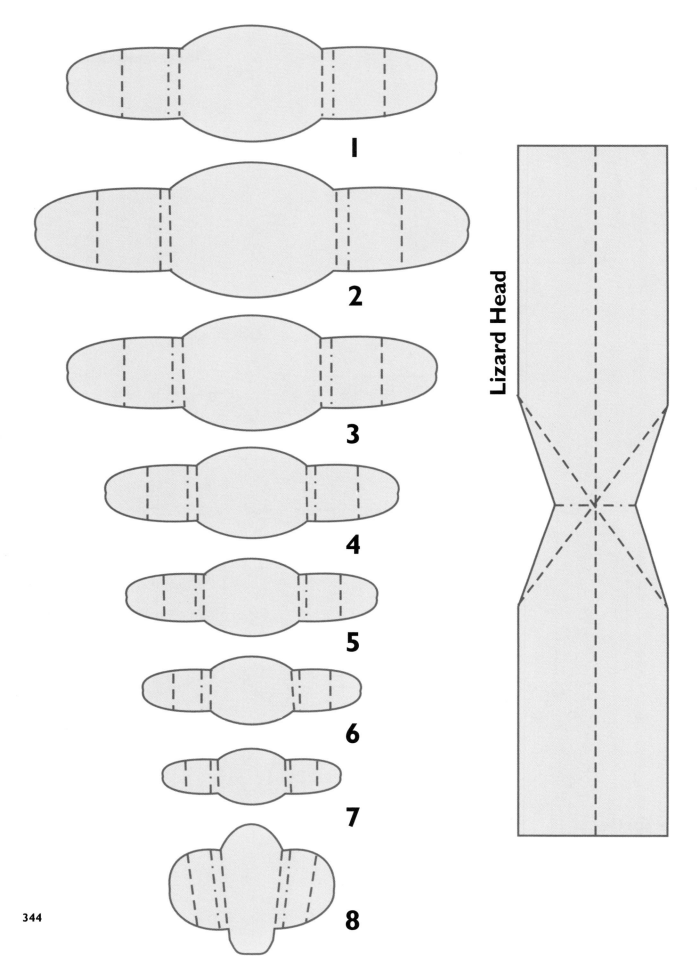

Lizard Head

1

2

3

4

5

6

7

8

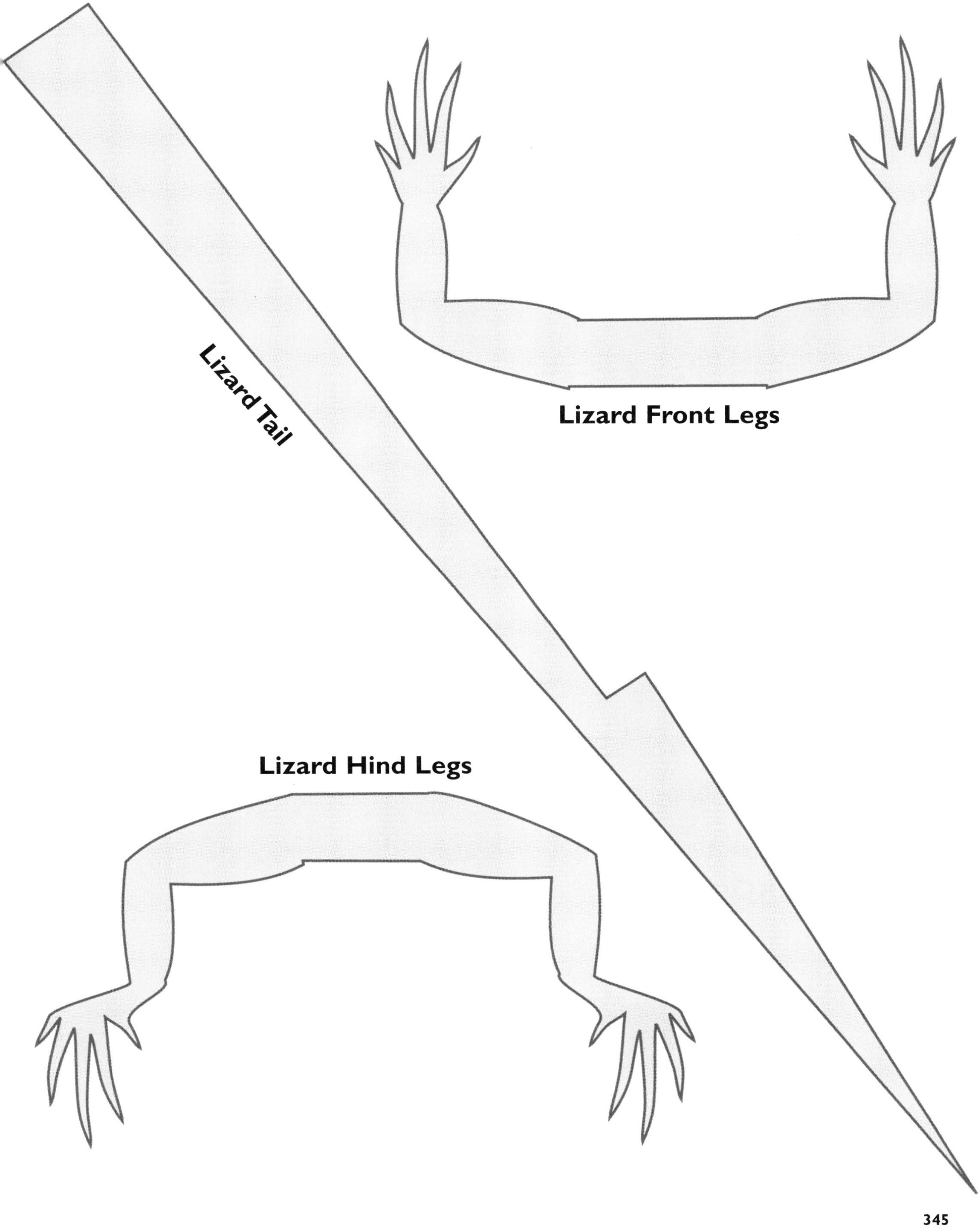

Lizard Front Legs

Lizard Tail

Lizard Hind Legs

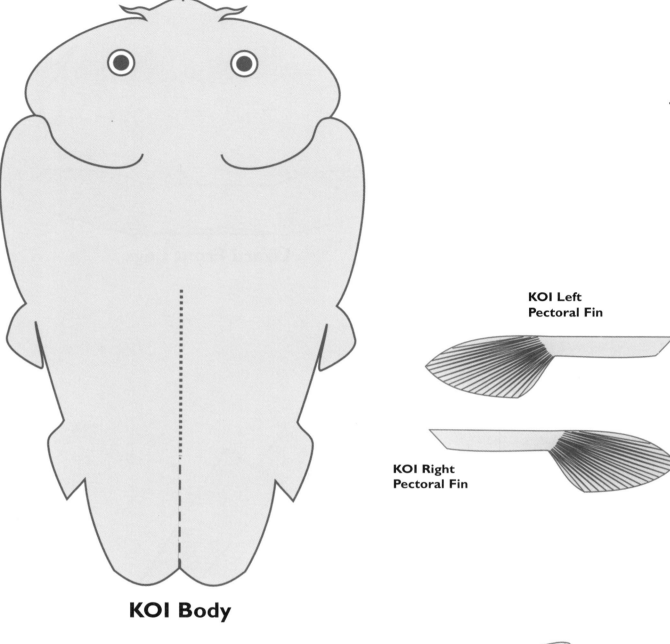

**KOI Left
Pectoral Fin**

**KOI Right
Pectoral Fin**

KOI Body

KOI Centerline Fins

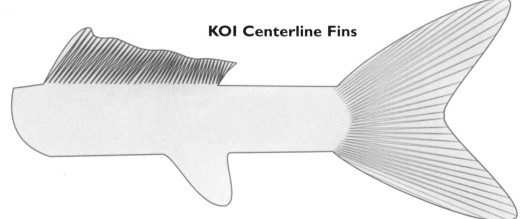

346

Zebra Mane

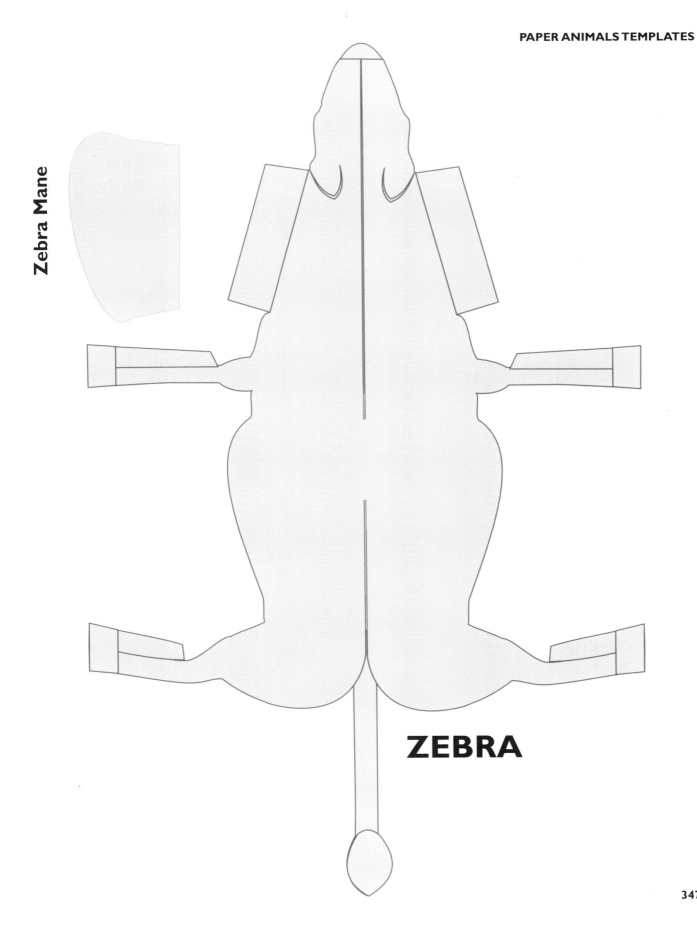

ZEBRA

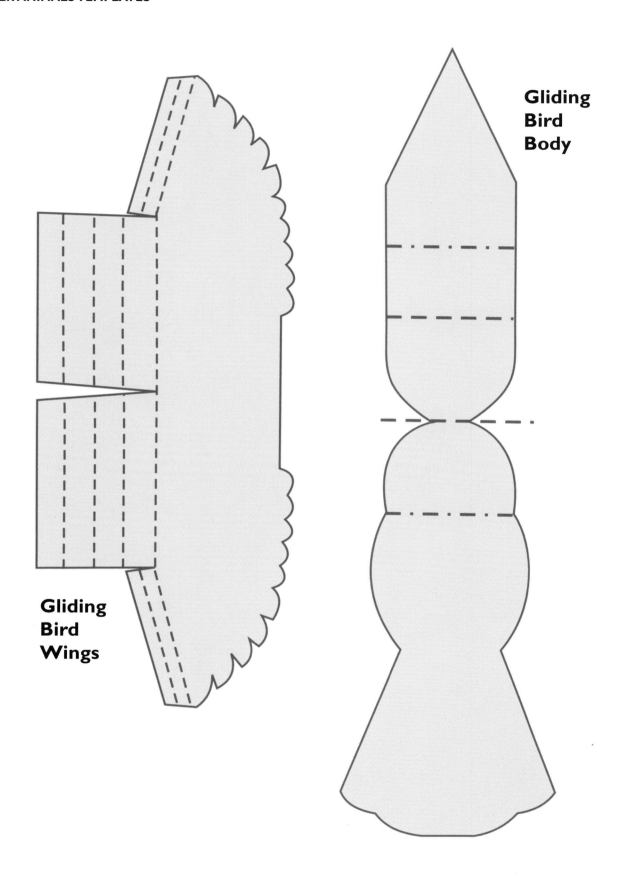

Gliding Bird Template

**Gliding
Bird
Body**

**Gliding
Bird
Wings**

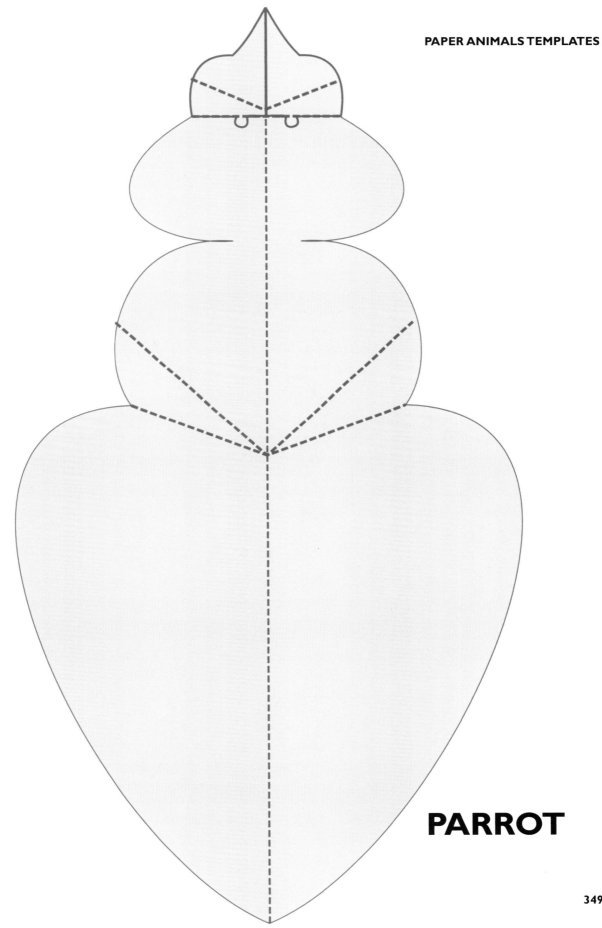

PARROT

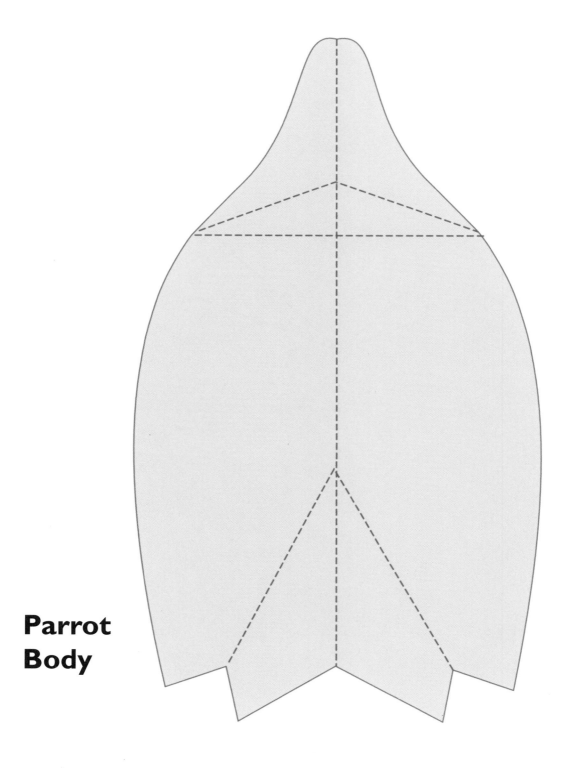

**Parrot
Body**

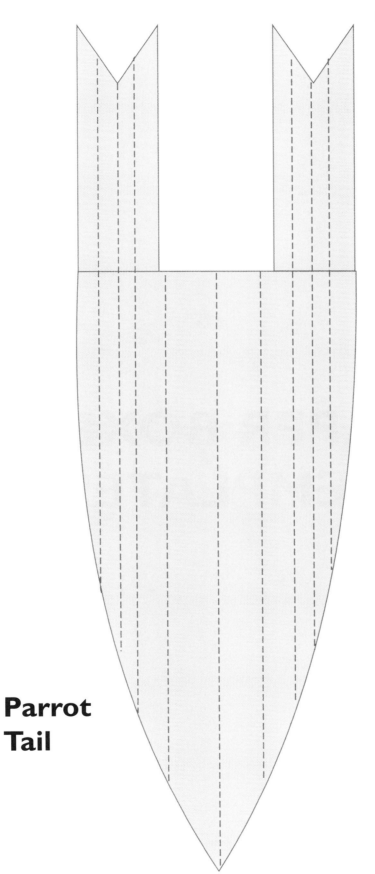

Parrot Tail

7

PAPER BOXES TEMPLATES

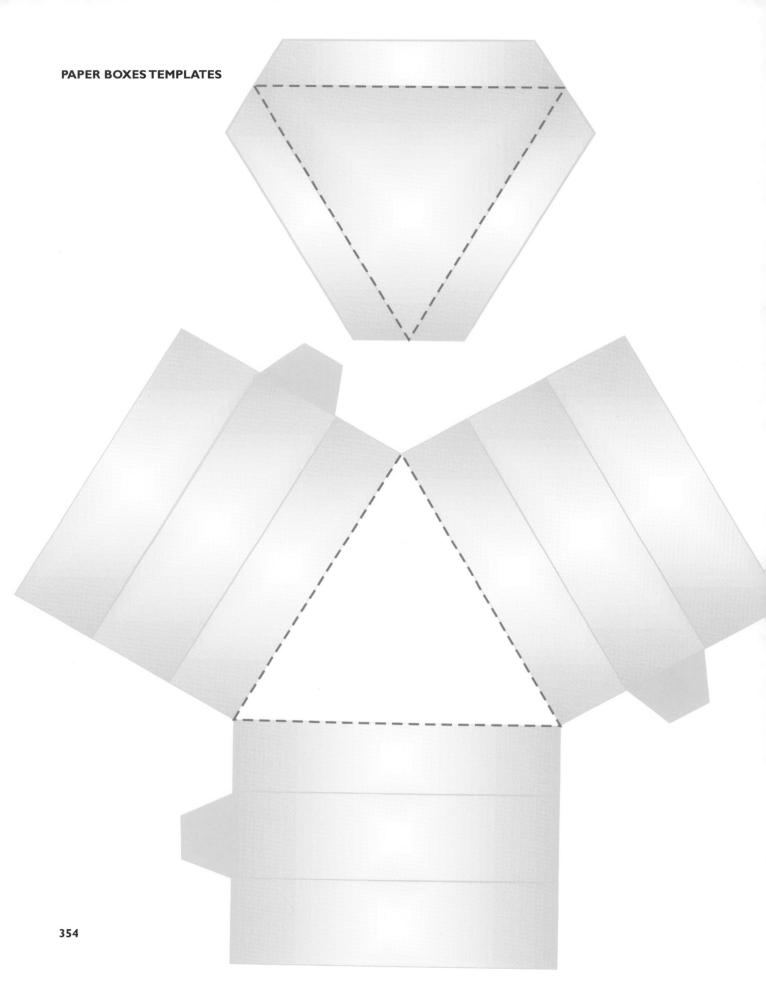

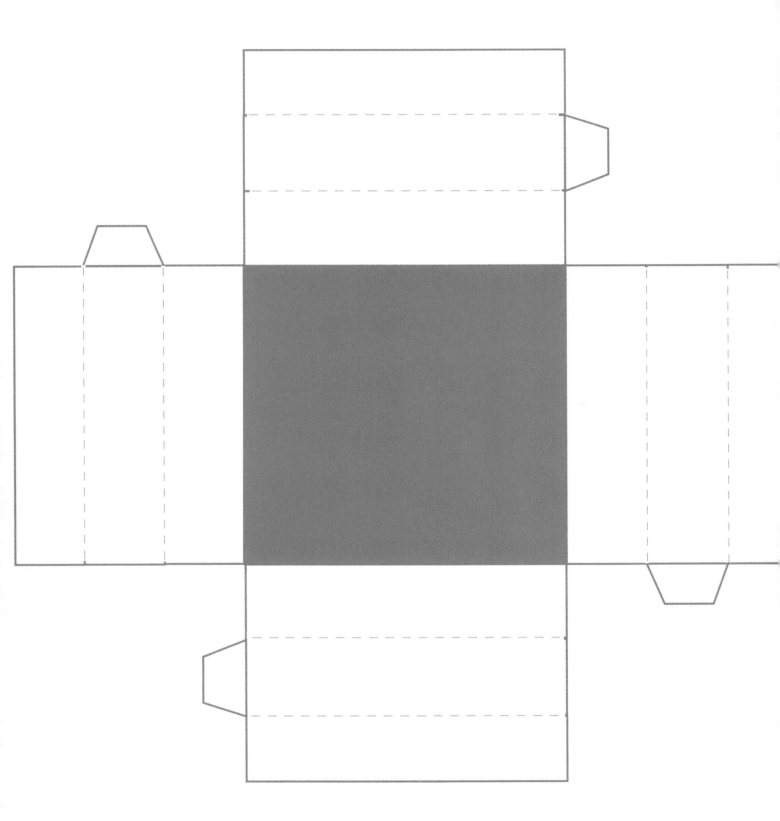

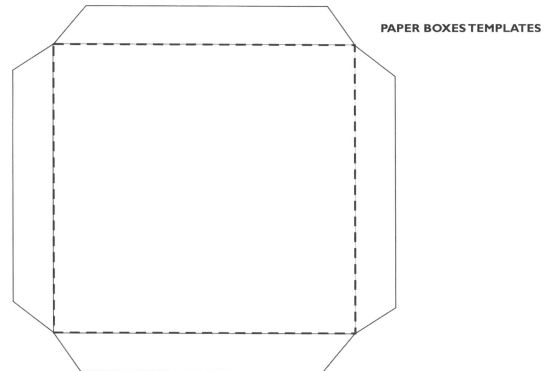

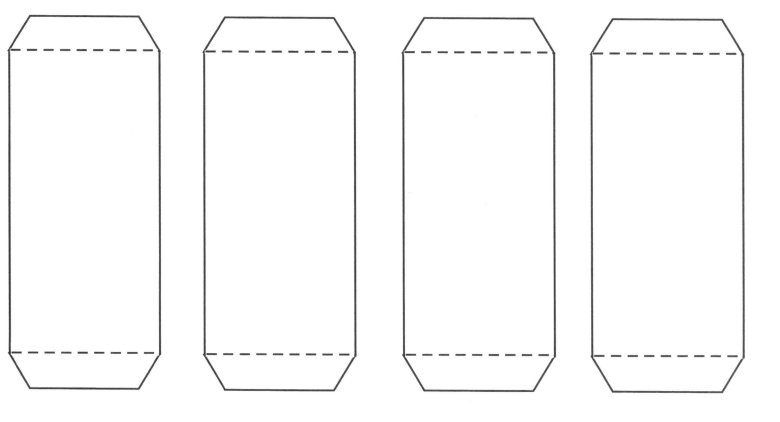

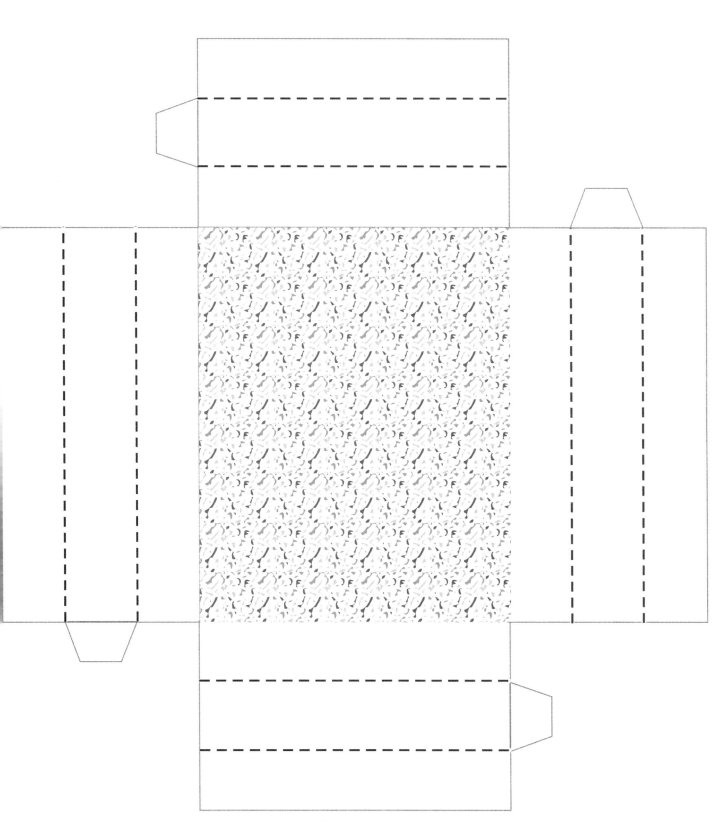

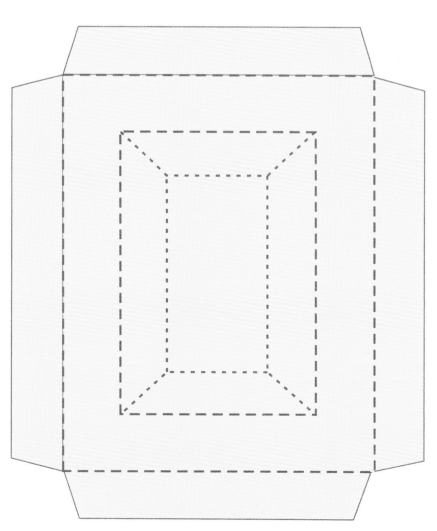

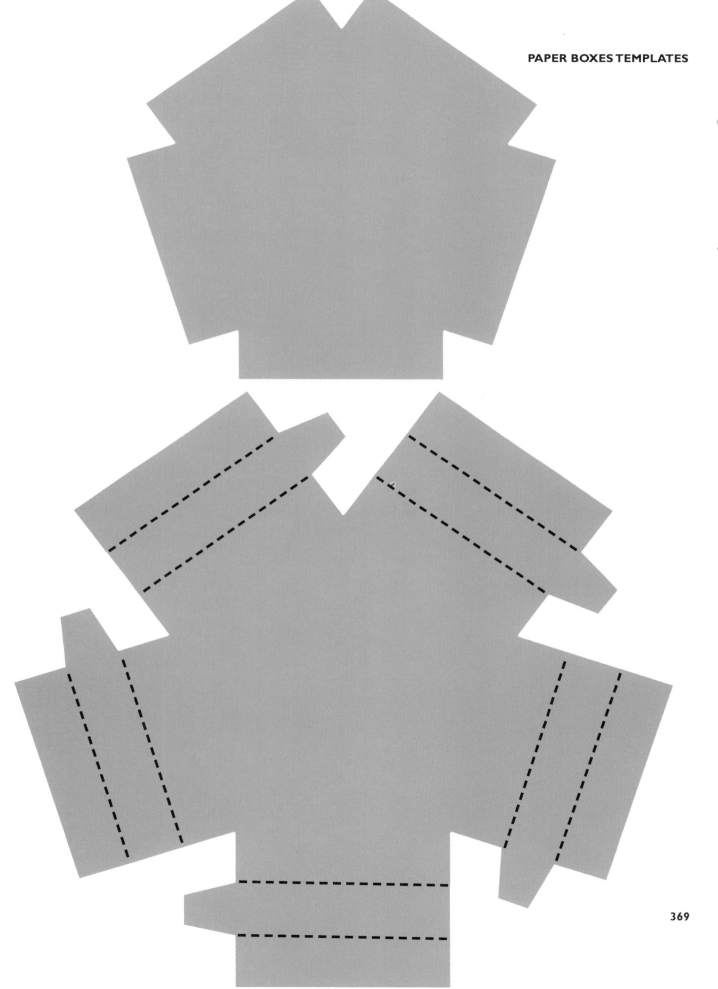

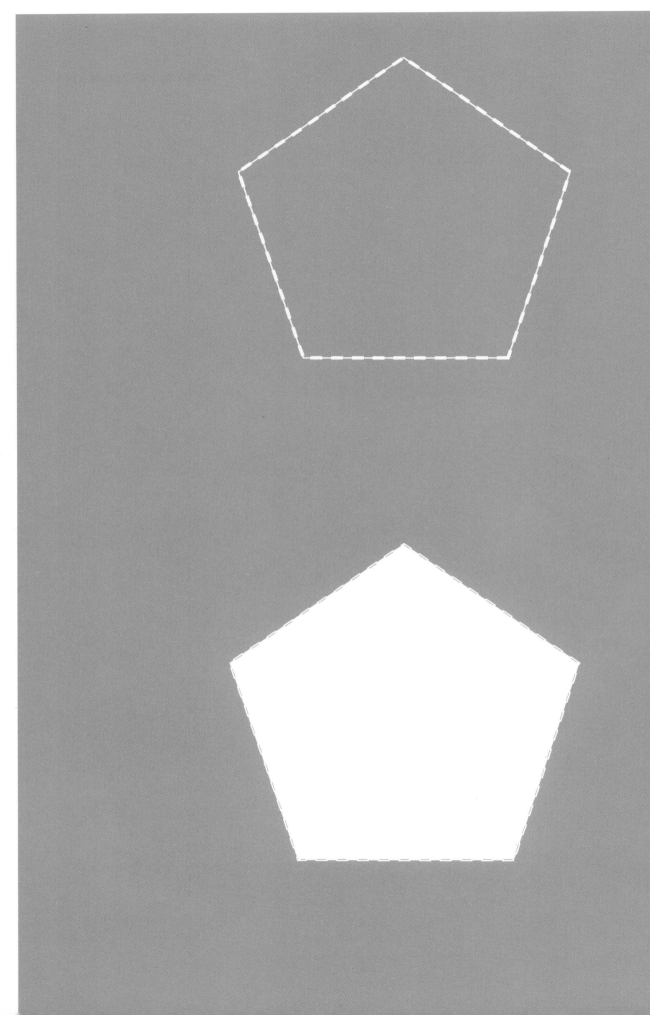

Magician's Box Paper Elements—2 of 2

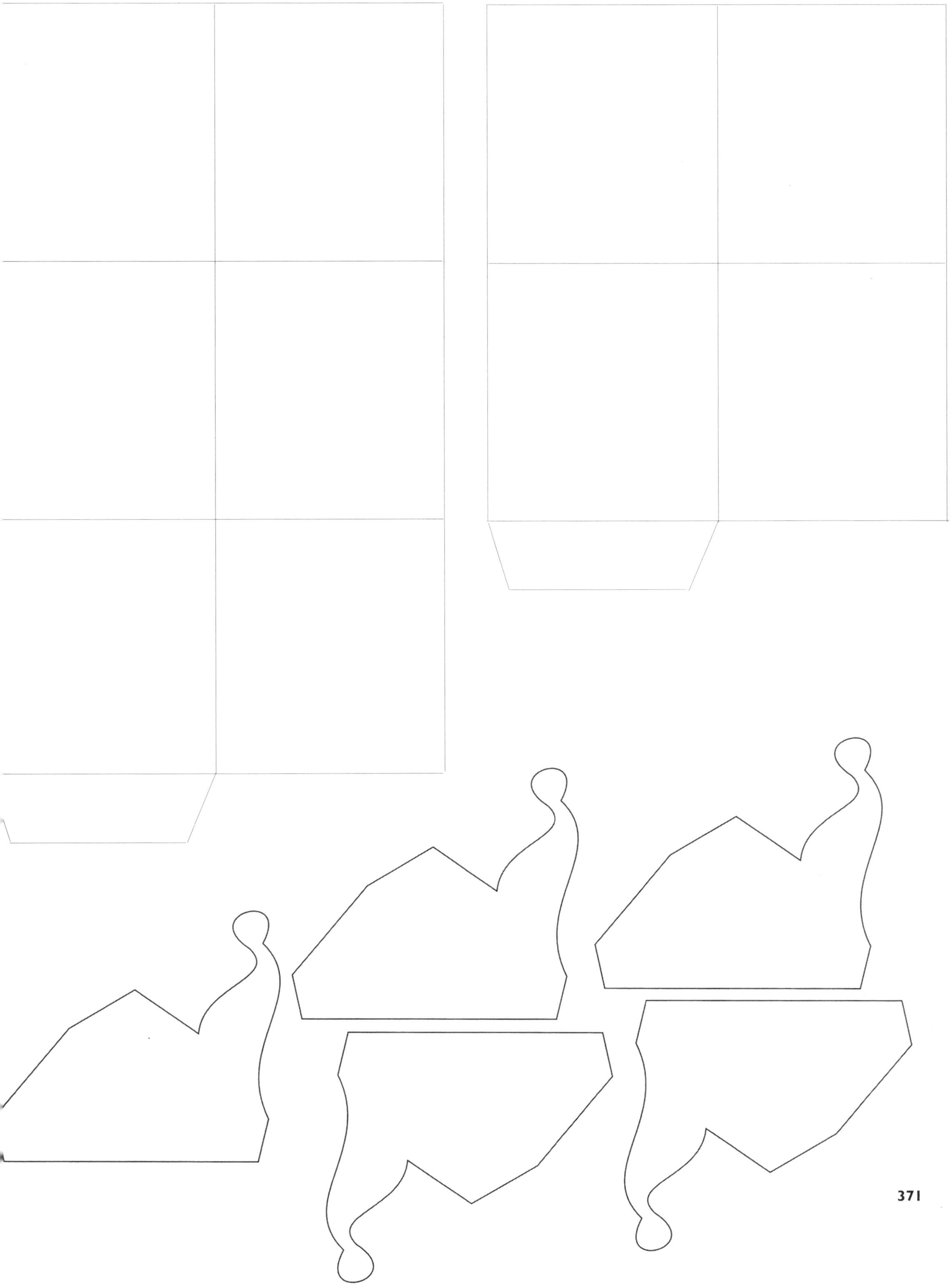

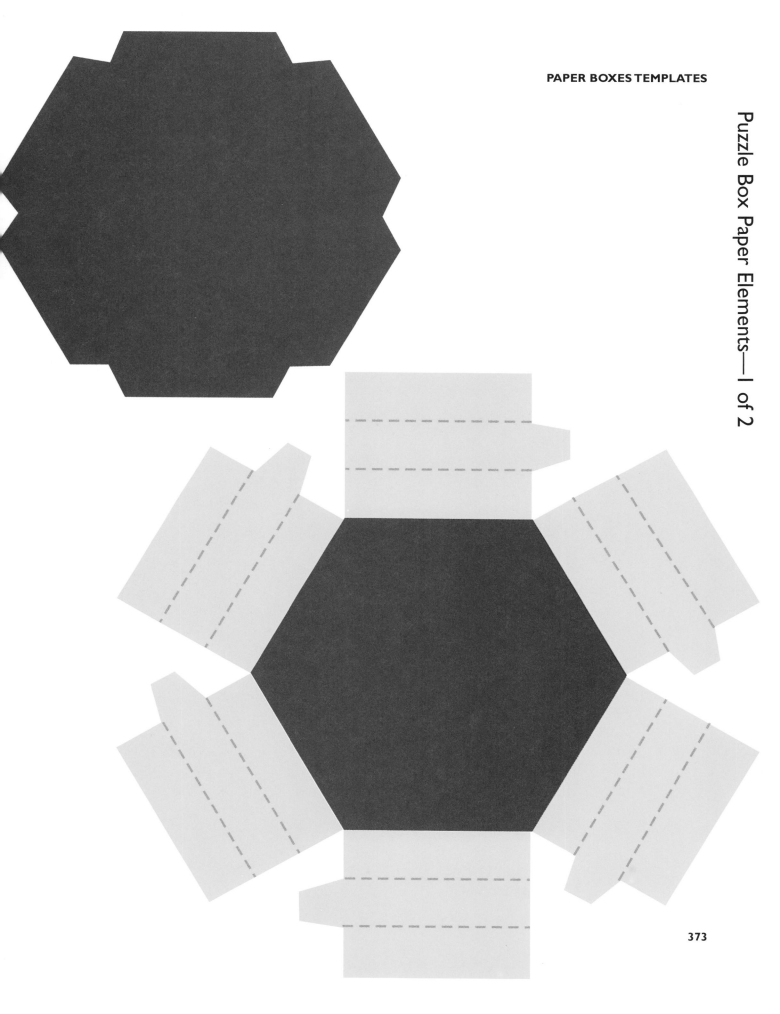

373

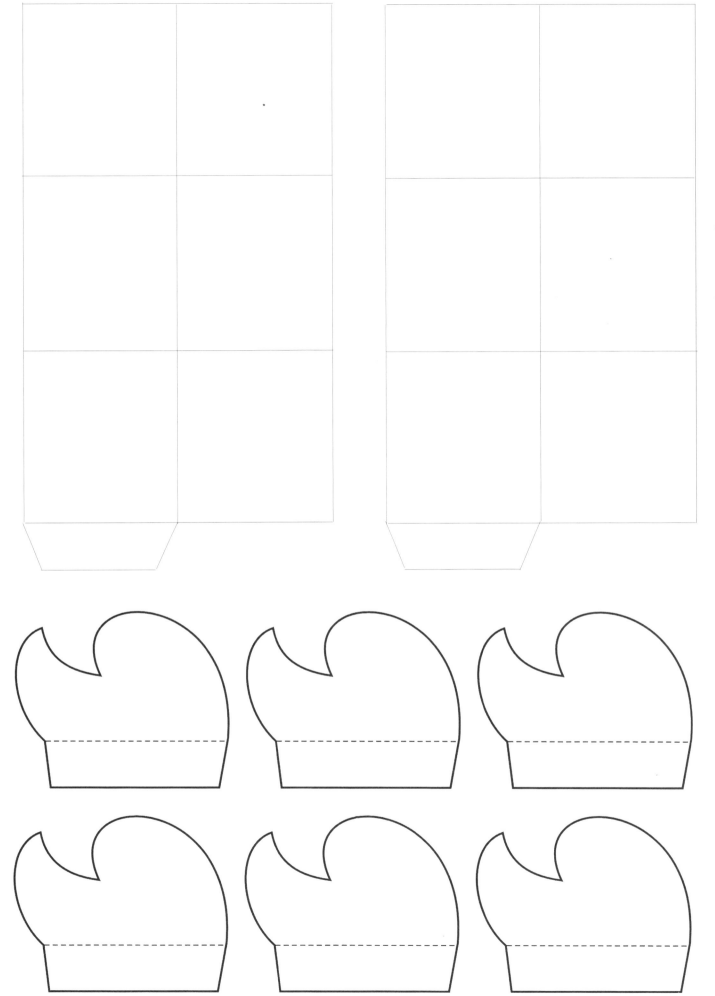

Heart Box Paper Elements—1 of 2

378

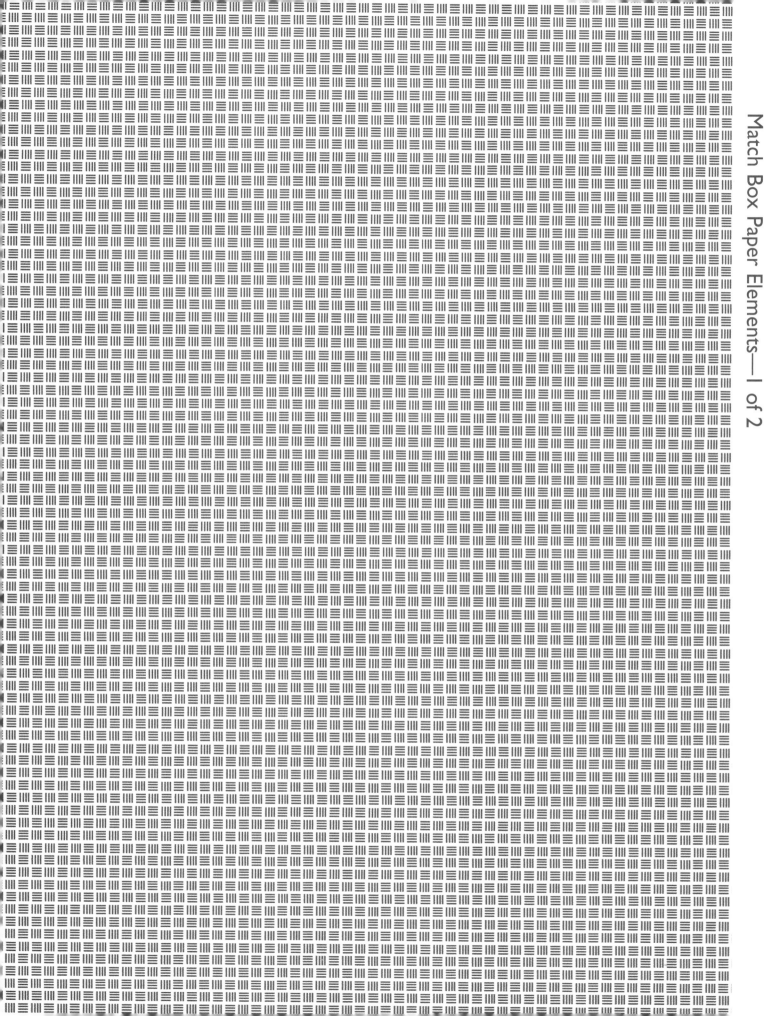

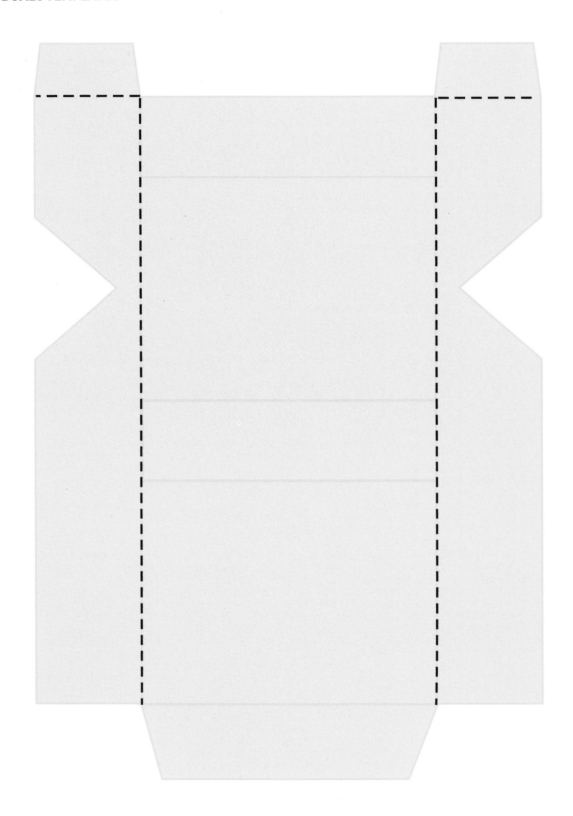

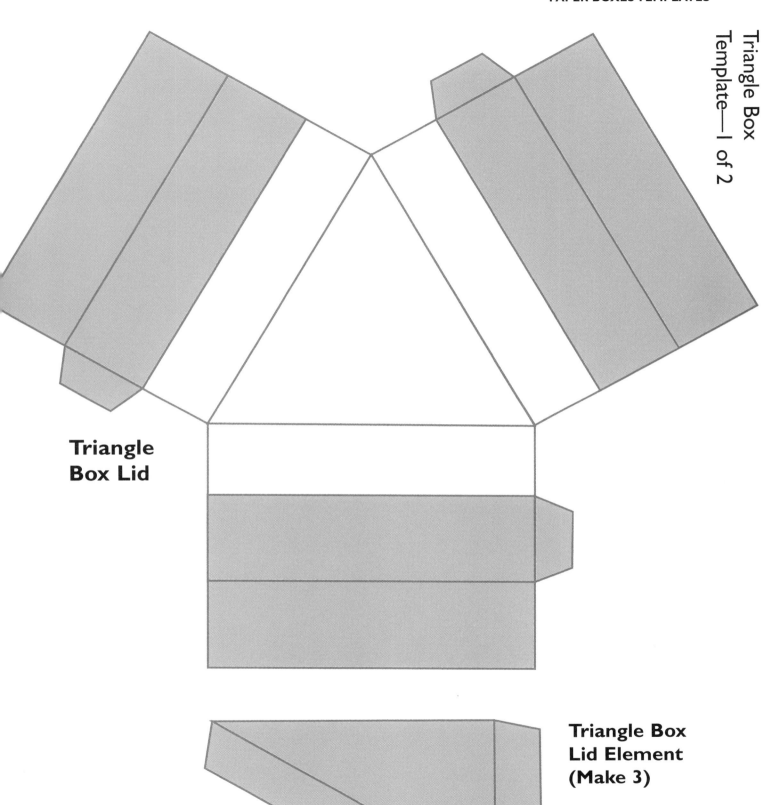

**Triangle
Box Lid**

**Triangle Box
Lid Element
(Make 3)**

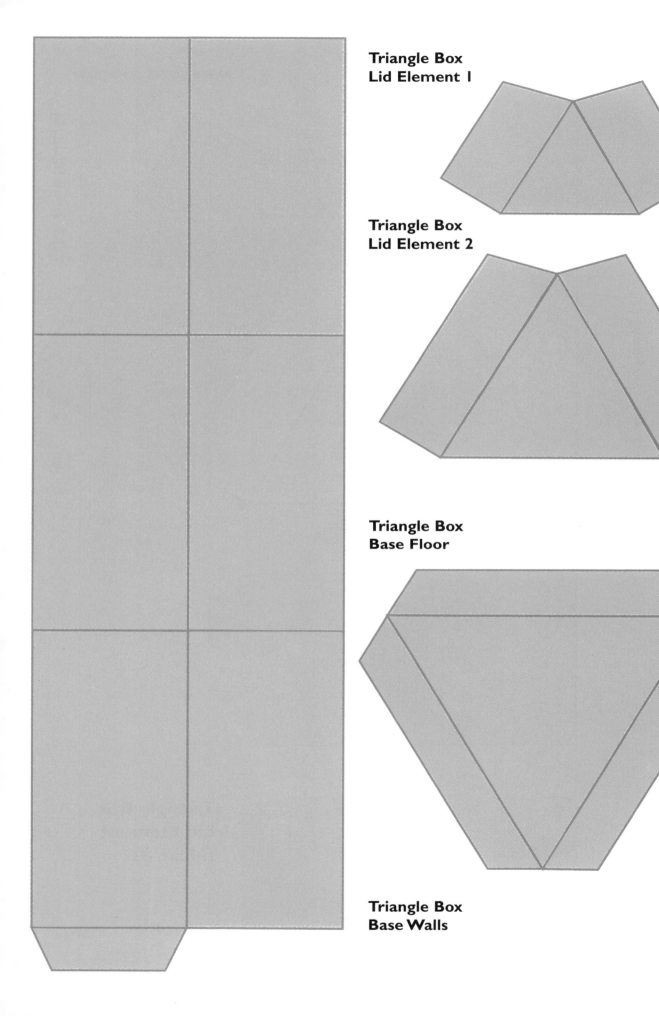

**Triangle Box
Lid Element 1**

**Triangle Box
Lid Element 2**

**Triangle Box
Base Floor**

**Triangle Box
Base Walls**

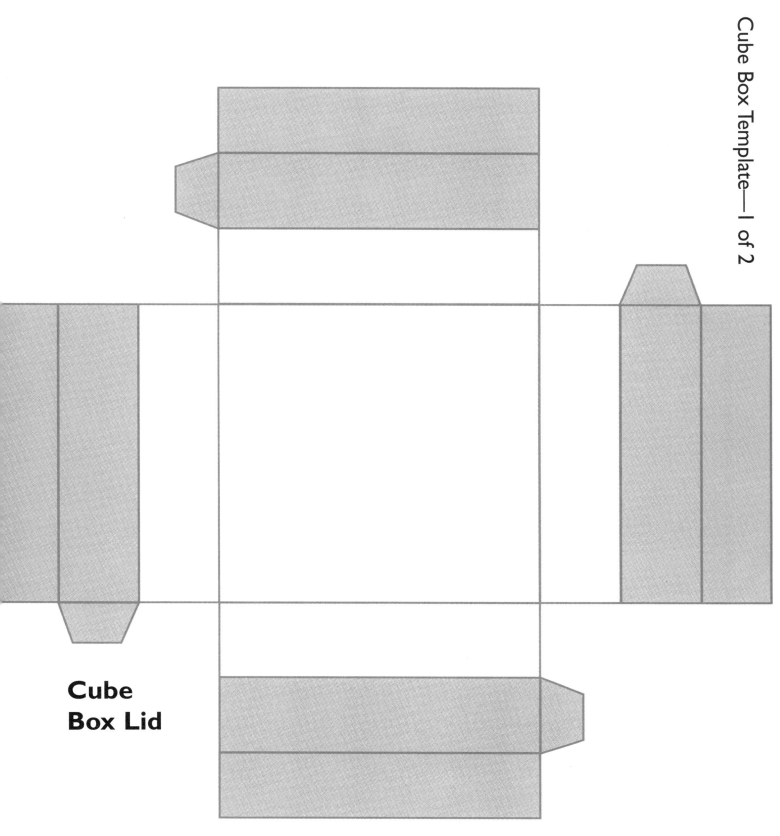

**Cube
Box Lid**

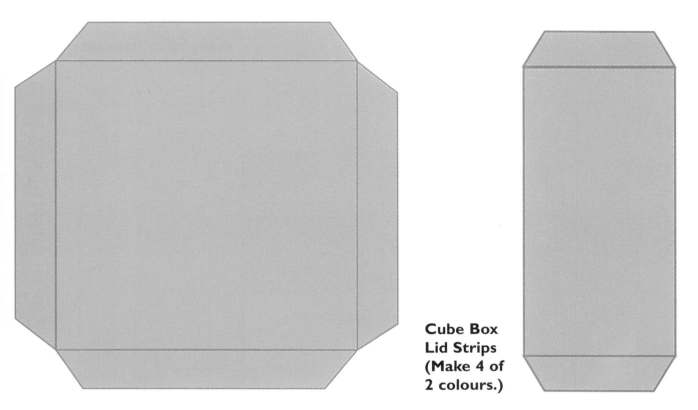

**Cube Box
Lid Strips
(Make 4 of
2 colours.)**

**Cube Box
Base Floor**

**Cube Box
Base Wall
(Make 2)**

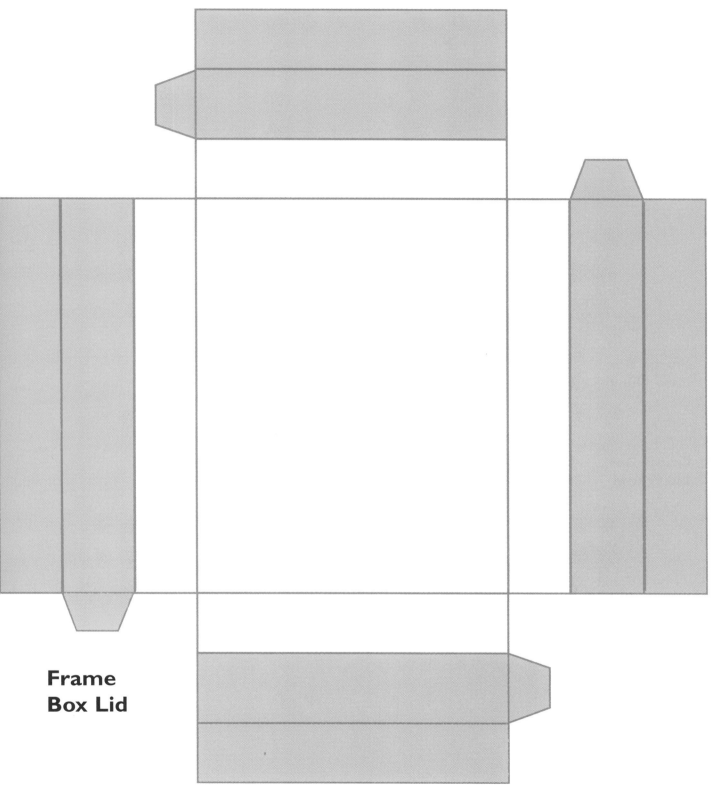

**Frame
Box Lid**

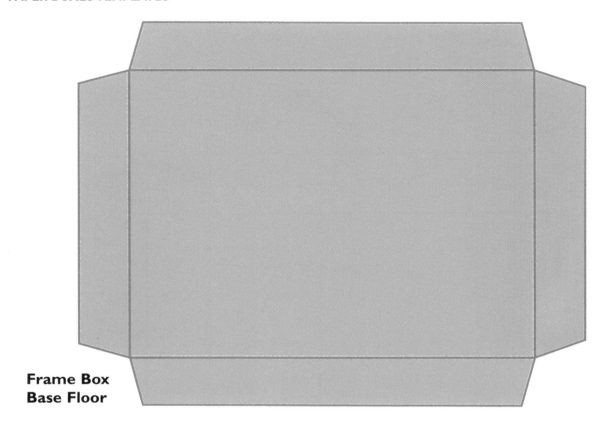

**Frame Box
Base Floor**

**Frame Box
Lid Frame**

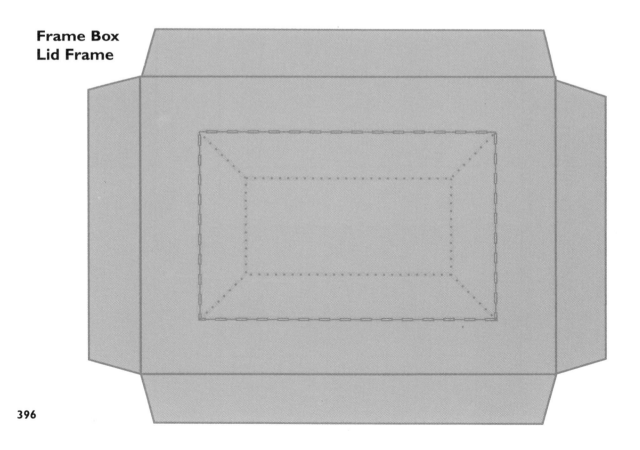

**Frame Box
Base Walls
(Make 2)**

Magician's Box Template—1 of 2

Magician's Box
Base Wall A
Magician's Box
Base Wall B
Magician's Box
Base Floor

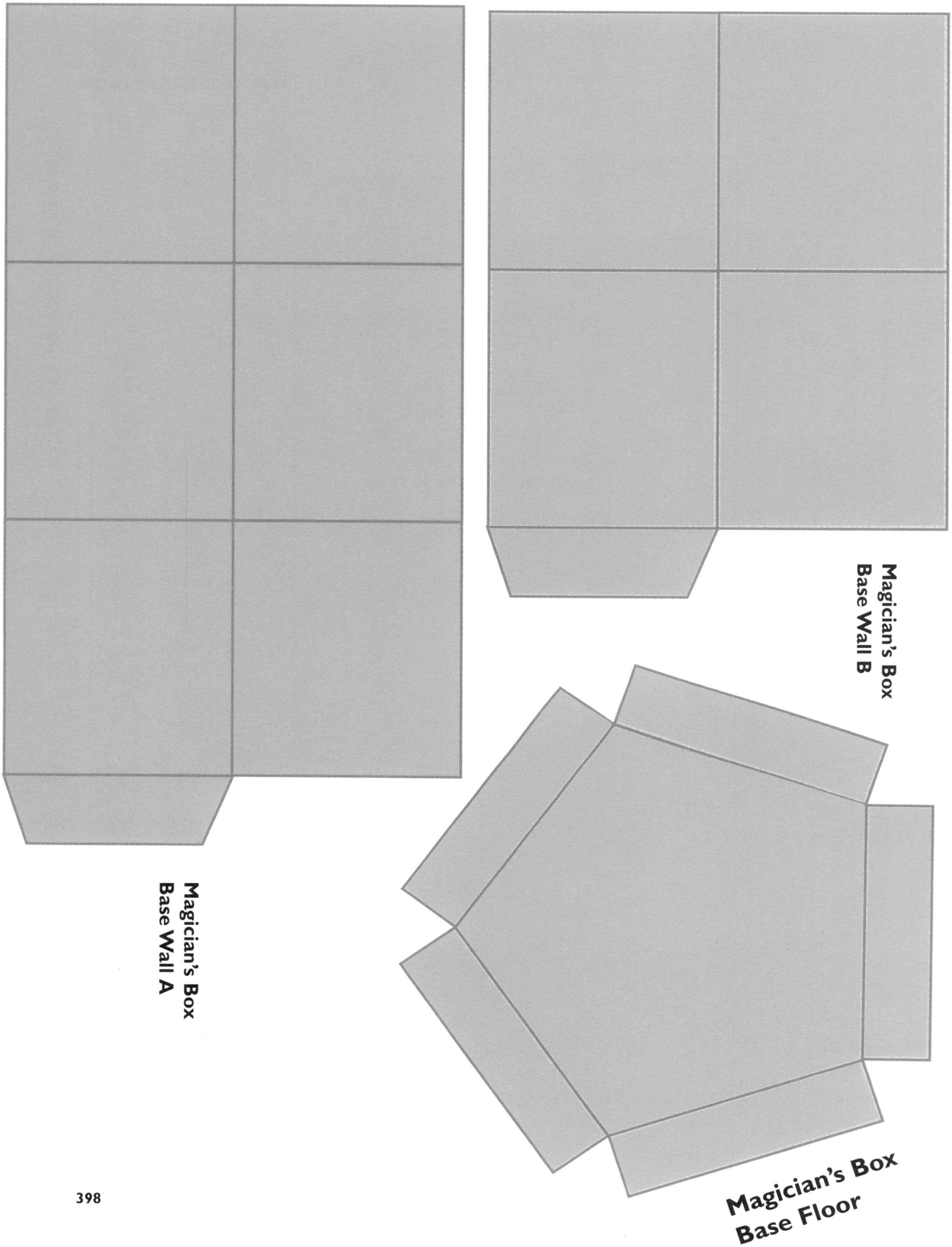

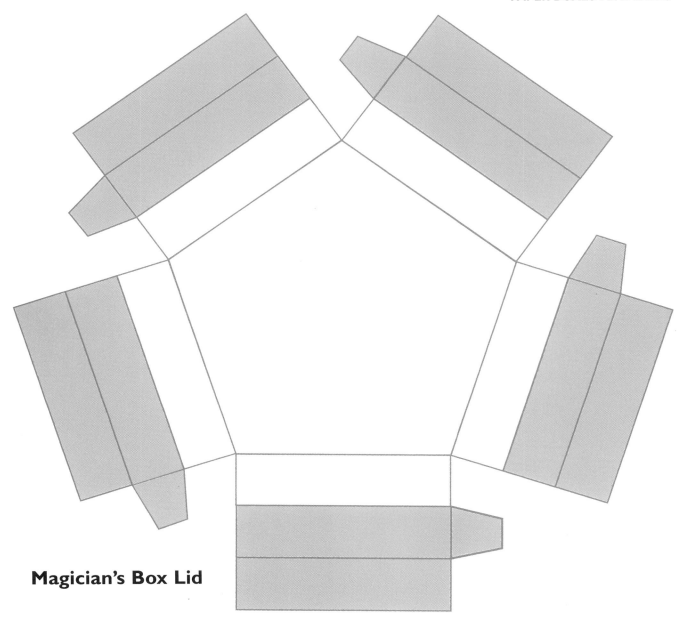

Magician's Box Lid

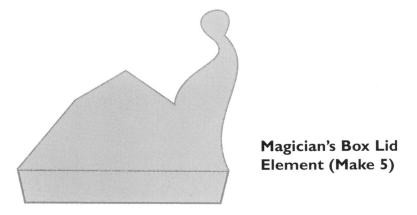

Magician's Box Lid Element (Make 5)

**Puzzle Box
Base Floor**

**Puzzle Box Base
Walls (Make 2)**

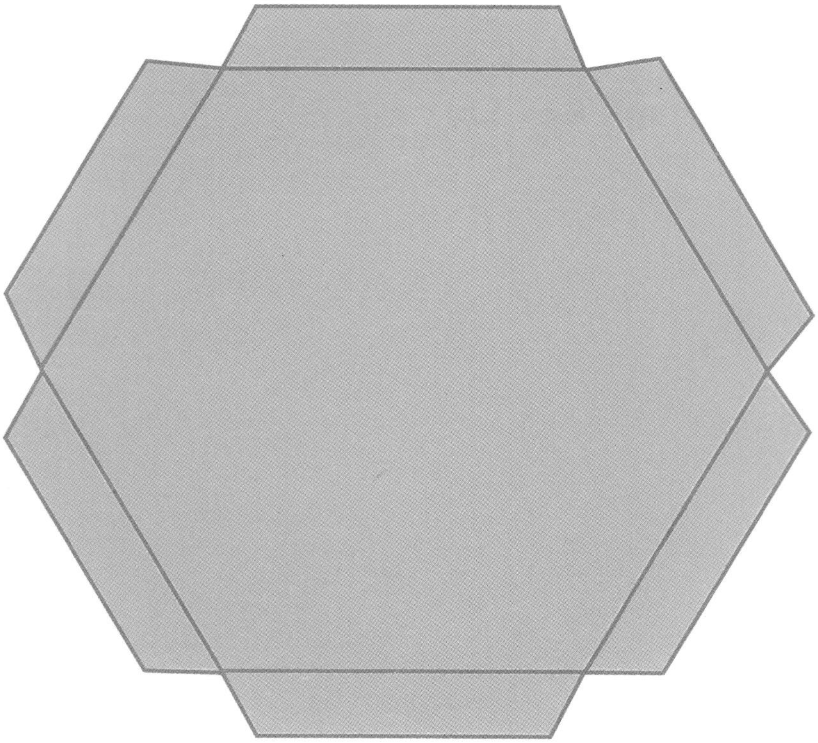

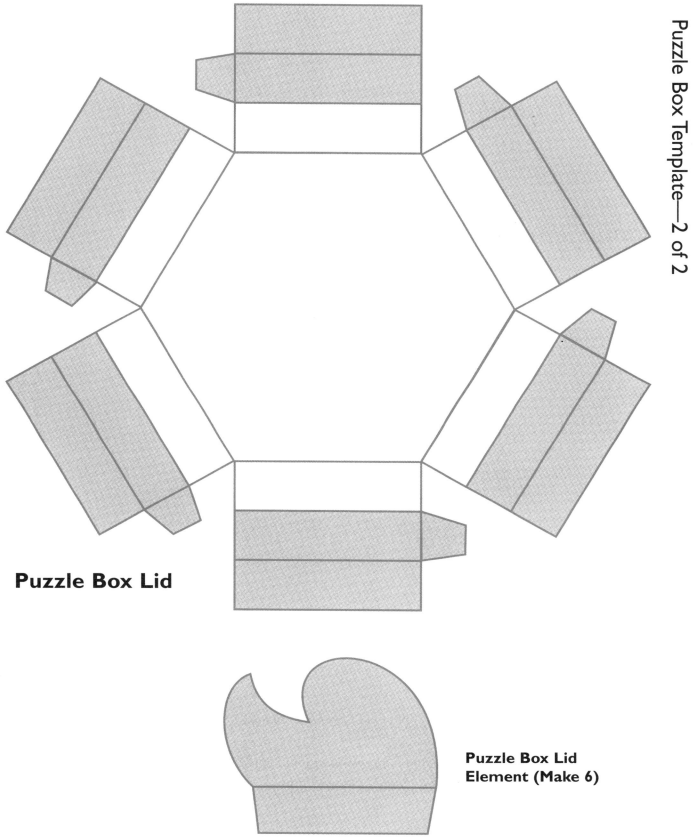

Puzzle Box Lid

**Puzzle Box Lid
Element (Make 6)**

Heart Box Template—1 of 2

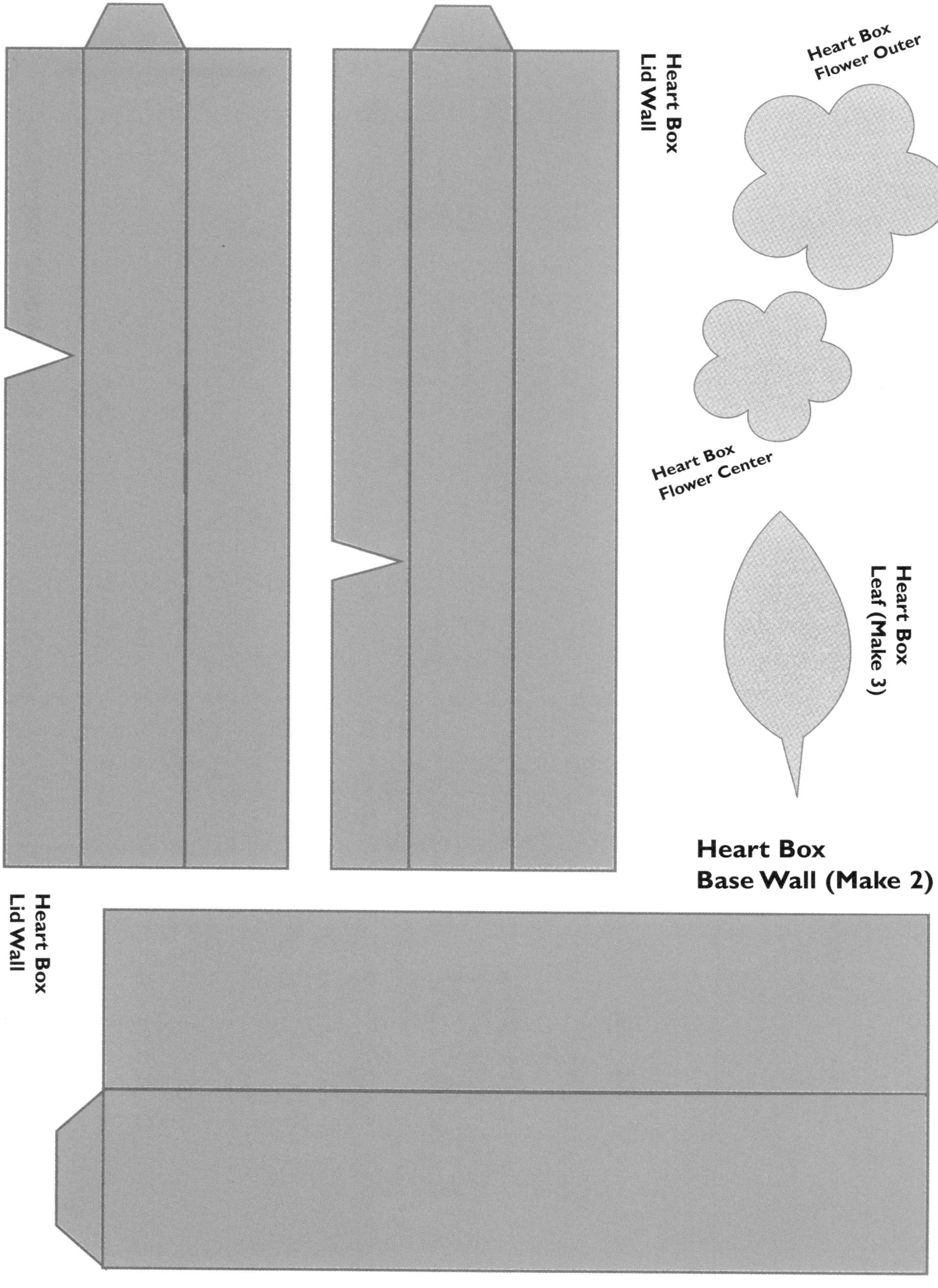
Heart Box
Lid Wall
Heart Box
Flower Outer
Heart Box
Flower Center
Heart Box
Leaf (Make 3)
Heart Box
Base Wall (Make 2)
Heart Box
Lid Wall

Heart Box Lid

**Heart Box
Base Floor**

Matchbox Cover

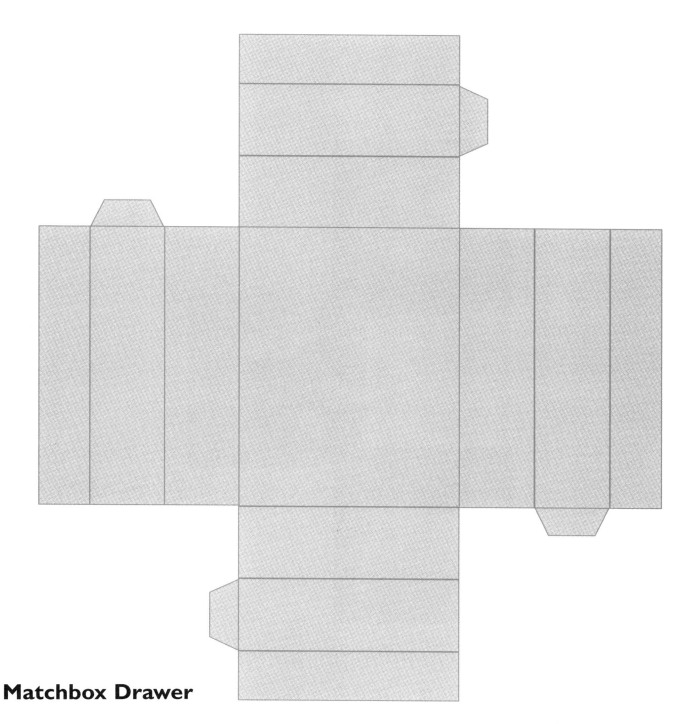

Matchbox Drawer

PAPER POP-UPS TEMPLATES

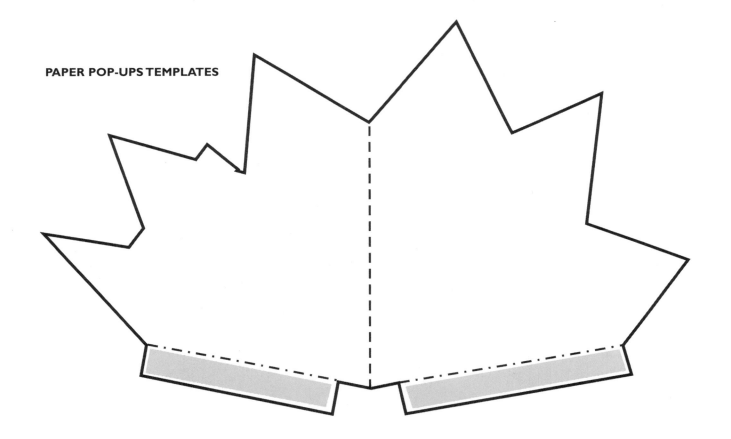

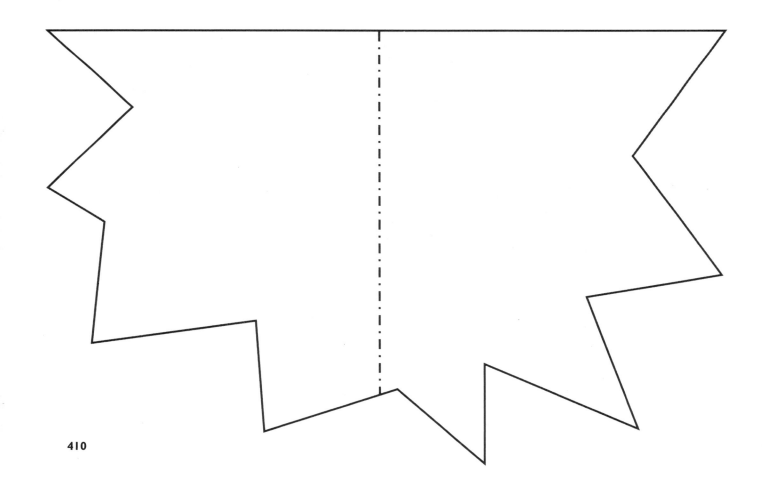

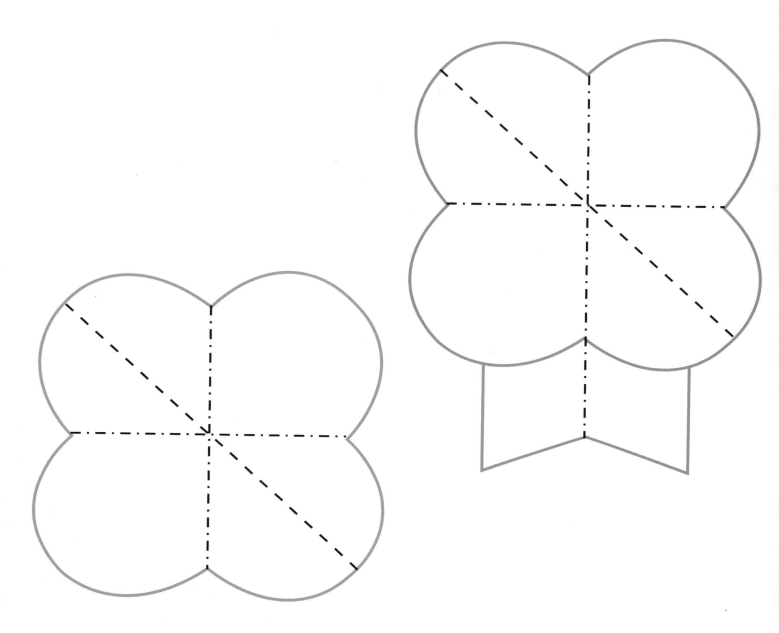

Swan & Cygnets Paper Elements

413

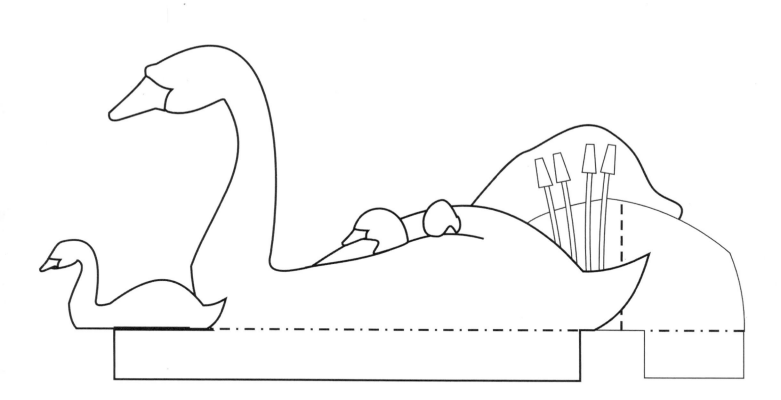

Monster Jaws Paper Elements

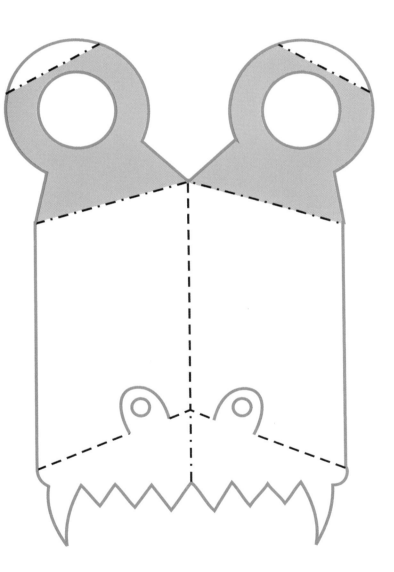

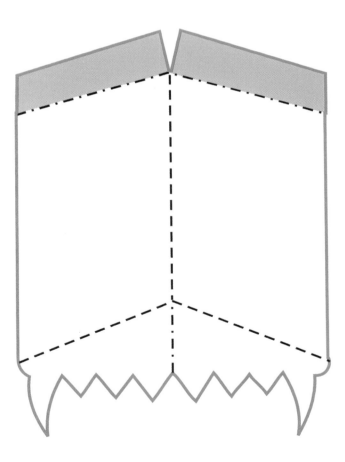

415

Guitar Paper Elements

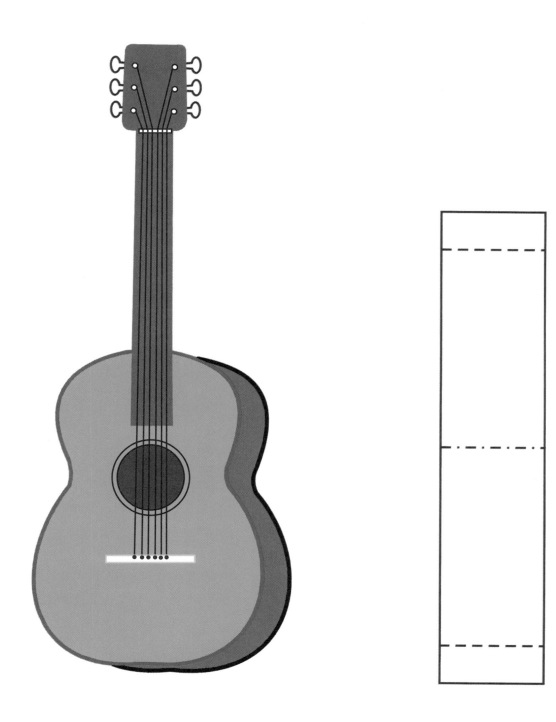

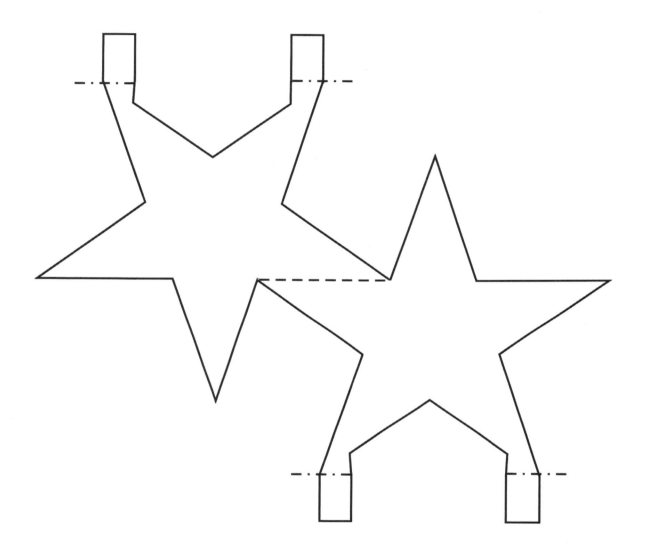

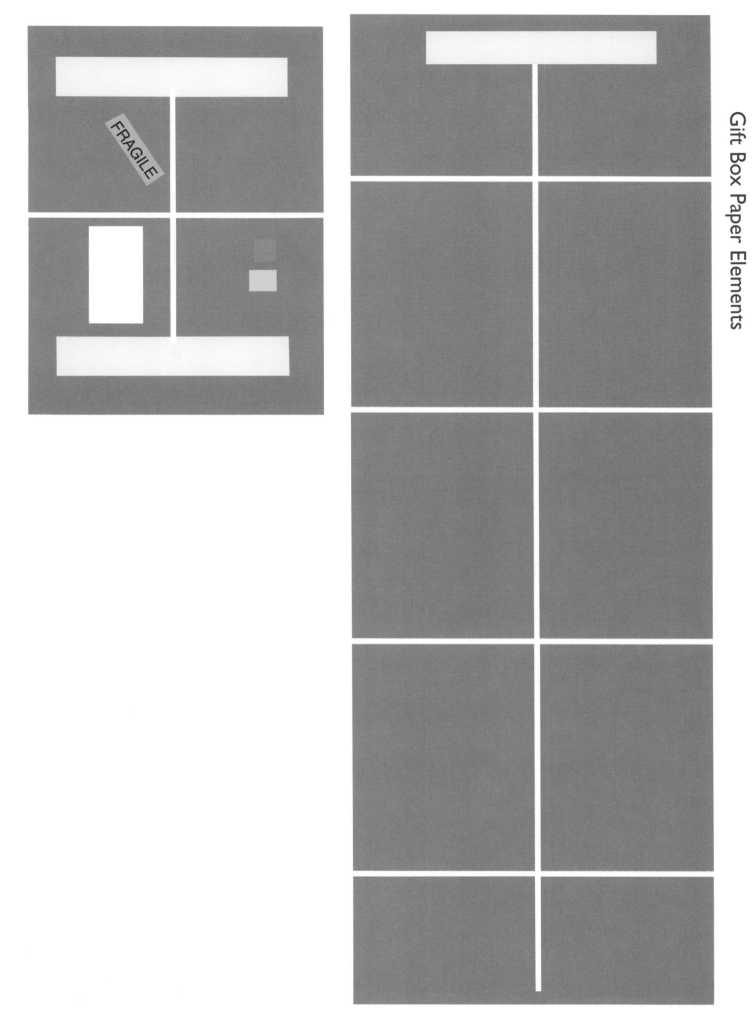

Gift Box Paper Elements

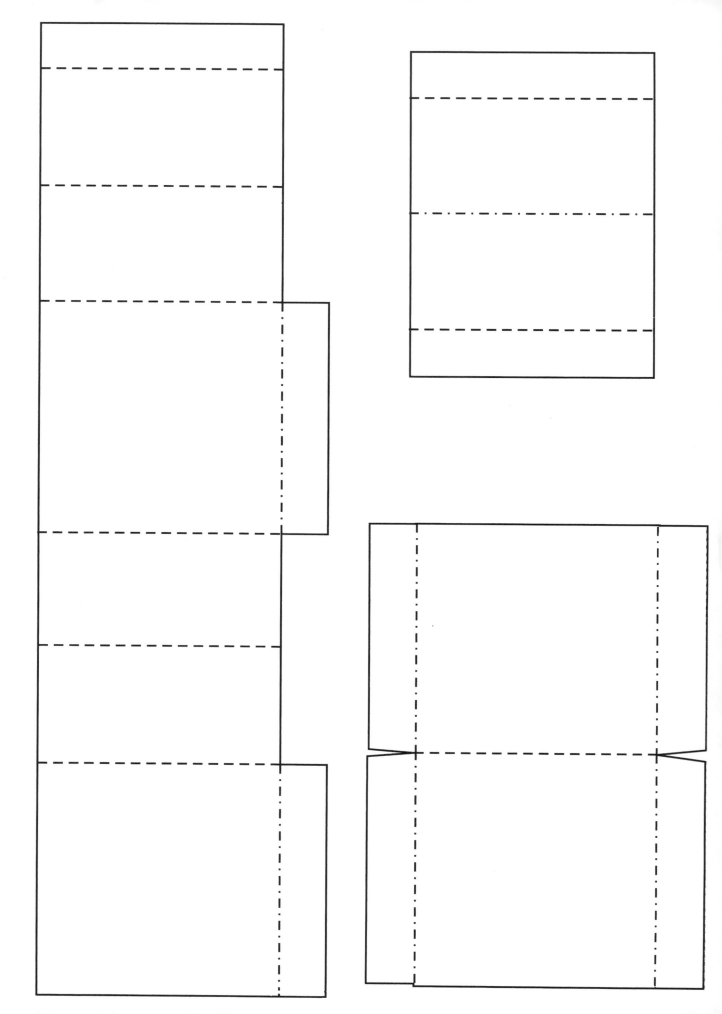

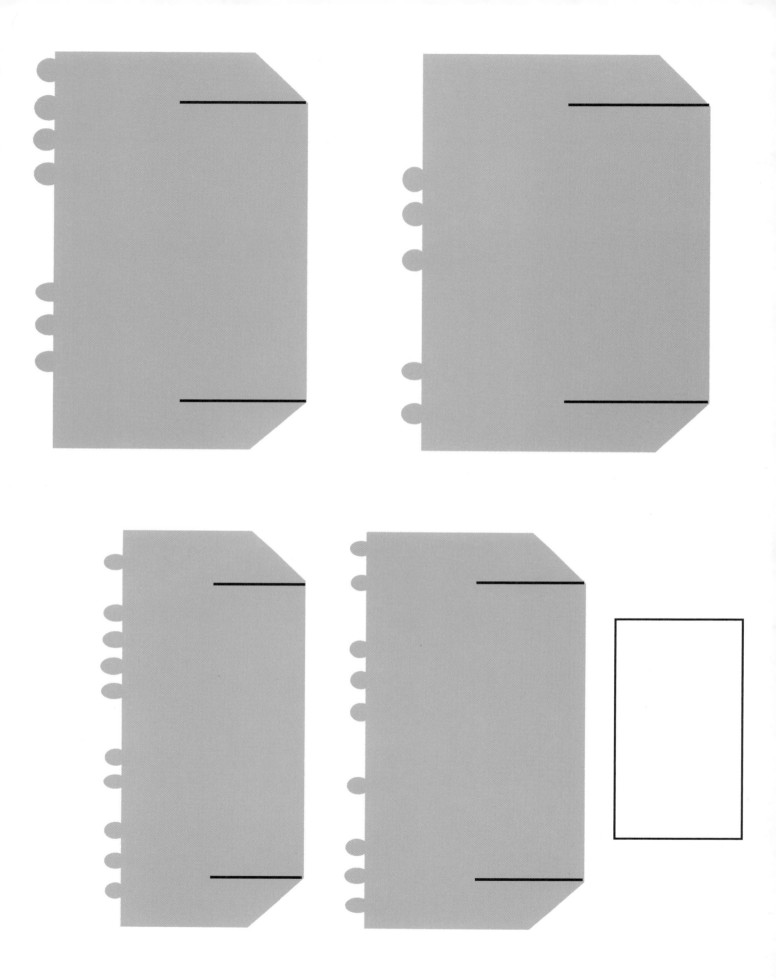

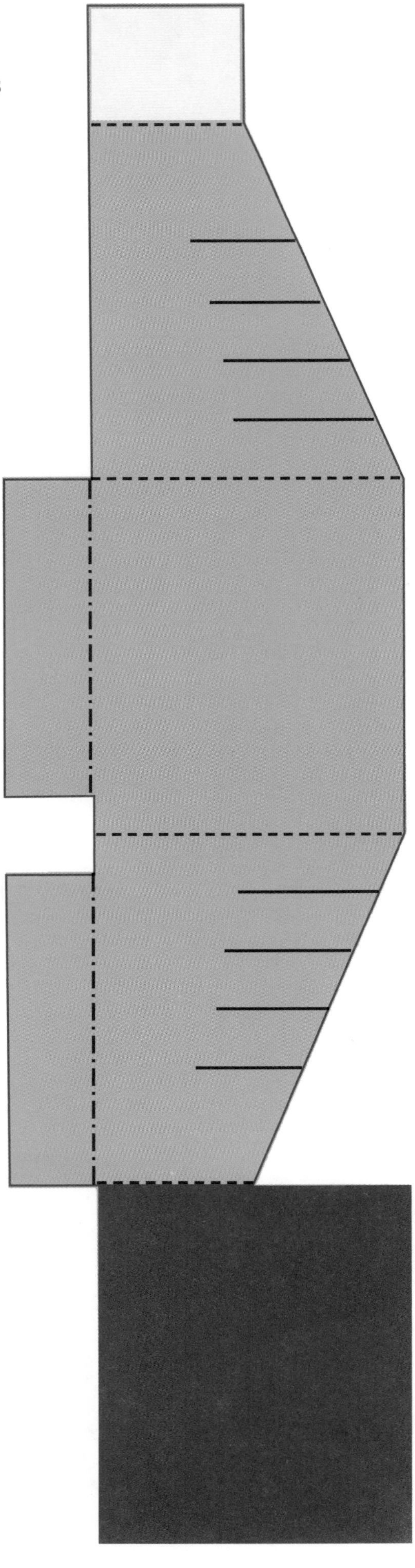

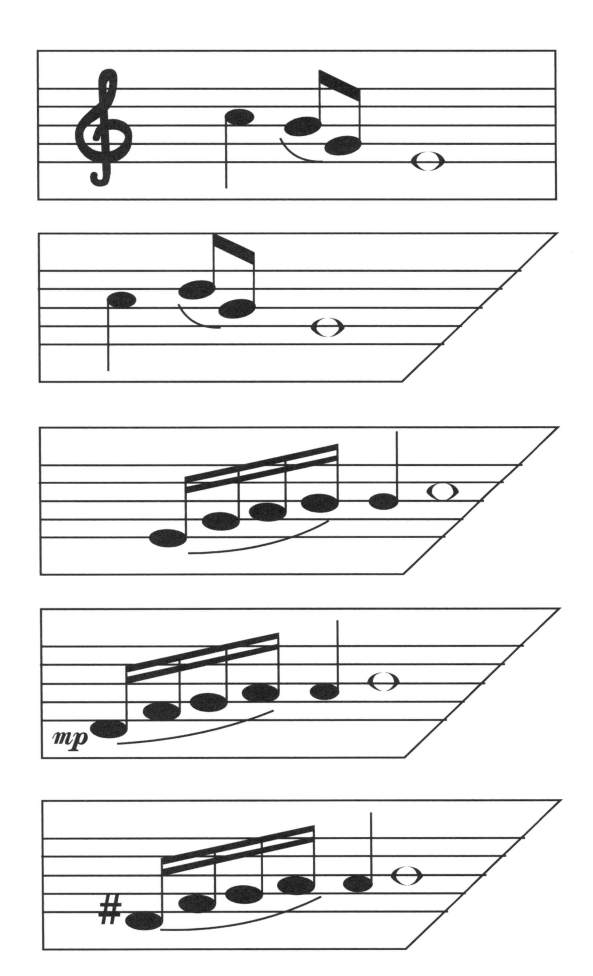

Musical Score Paper Elements

429

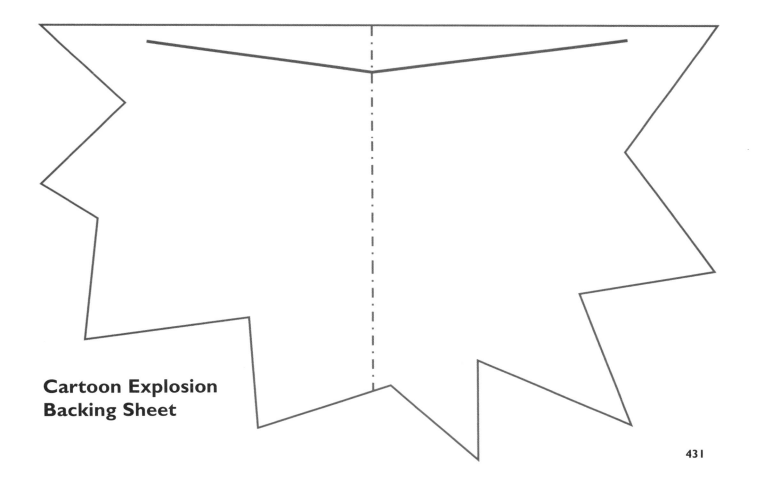

Cartoon Explosion Pop-up

**Cartoon Explosion
Backing Sheet**

431

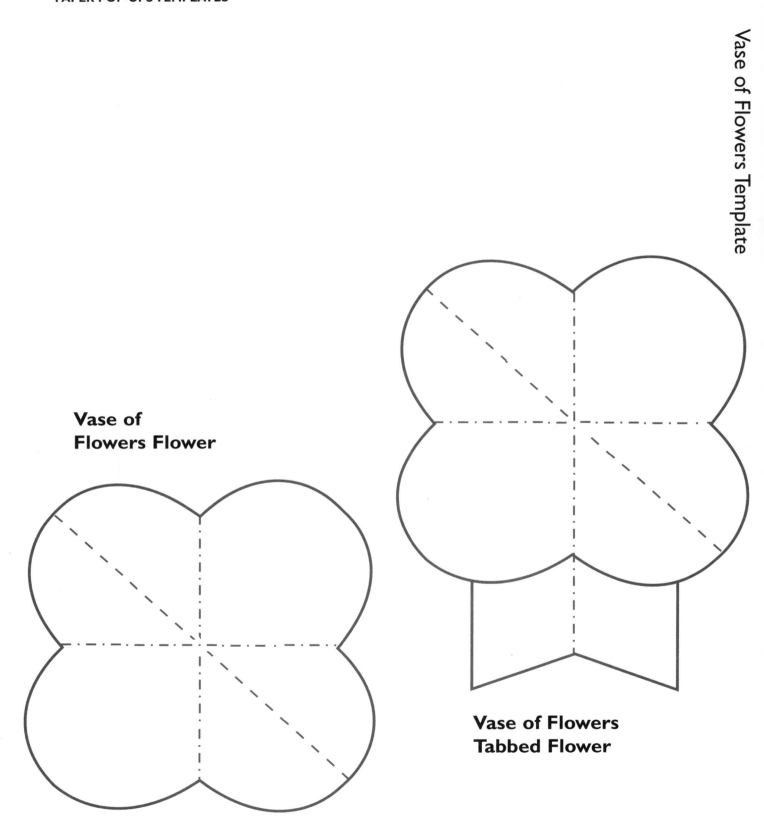

**Vase of
Flowers Flower**

**Vase of Flowers
Tabbed Flower**

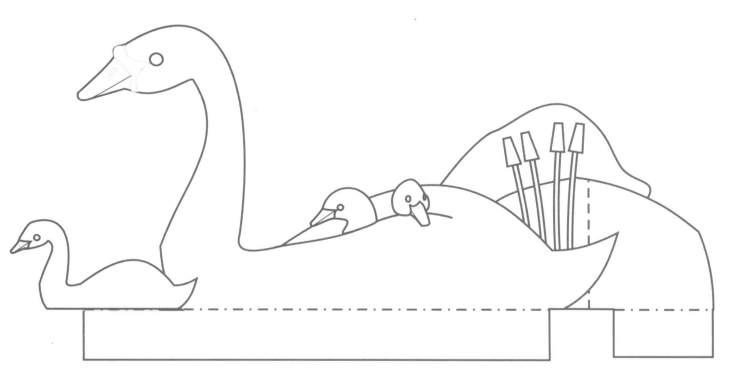

Swan & Cygnet

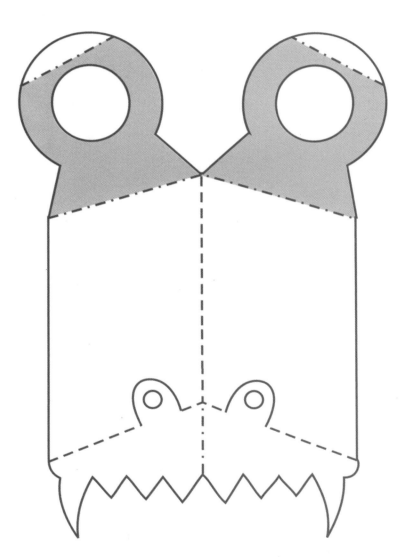

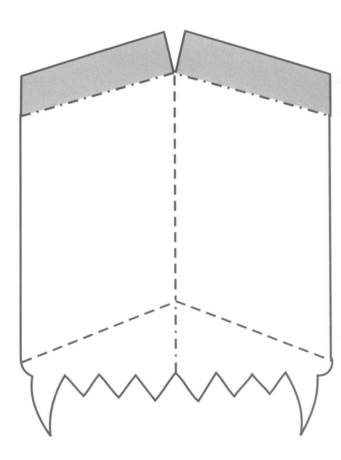

**Monster Jaws
Upper Jaw**

**Monster Jaws
Lower Jaw**

Guitar Template

Guitar

Guitar Supporting Tab

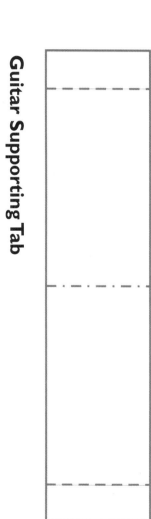

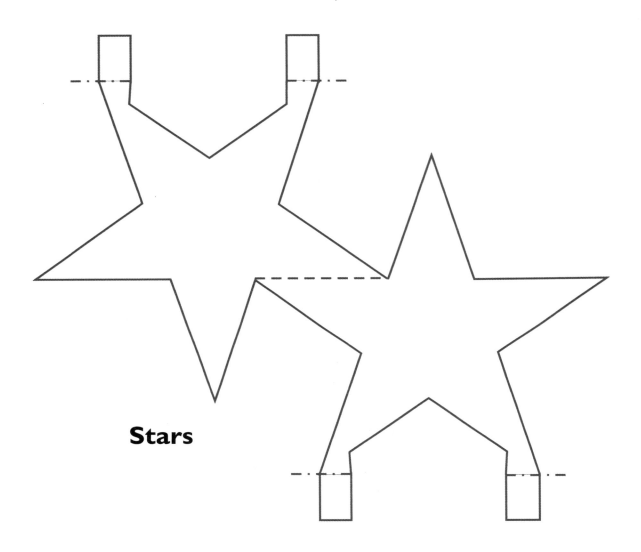

Stars

Gift Box Template

Gift Box Walls

Gift Box Lid

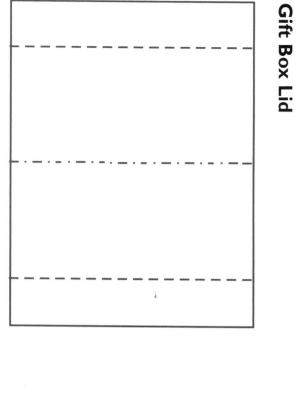

Gift Box Support

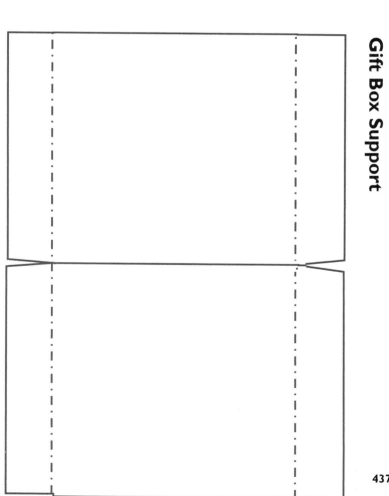

437

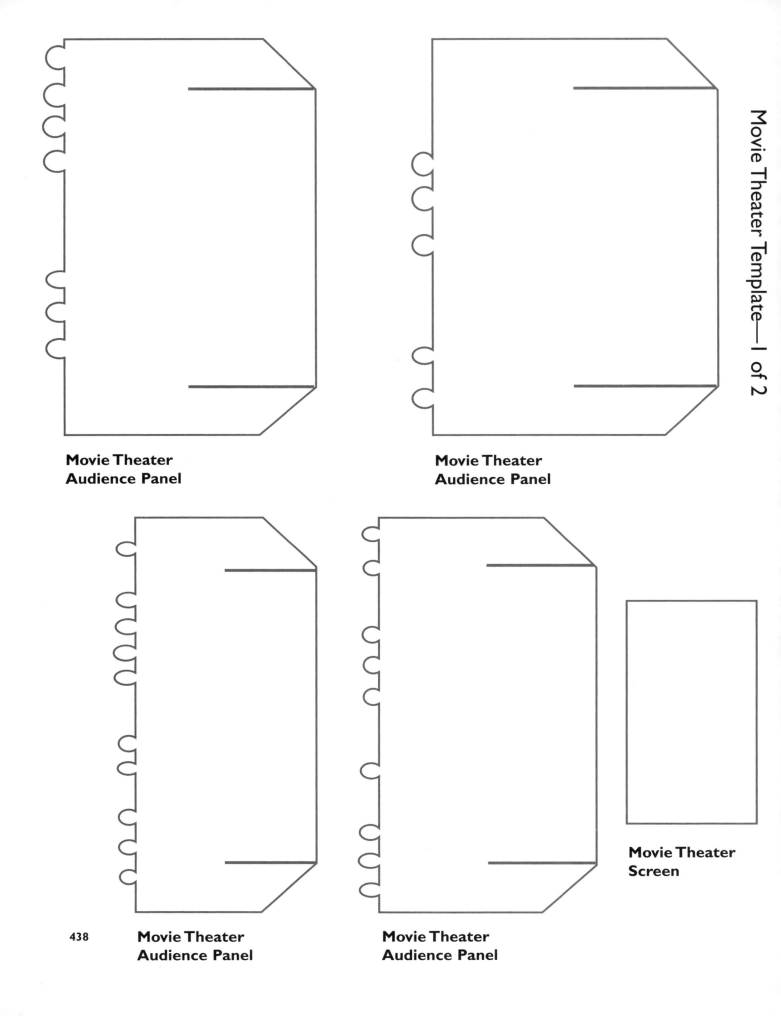

**Movie Theater
Audience Panel**

**Movie Theater
Audience Panel**

438 **Movie Theater
Audience Panel**

**Movie Theater
Audience Panel**

**Movie Theater
Screen**

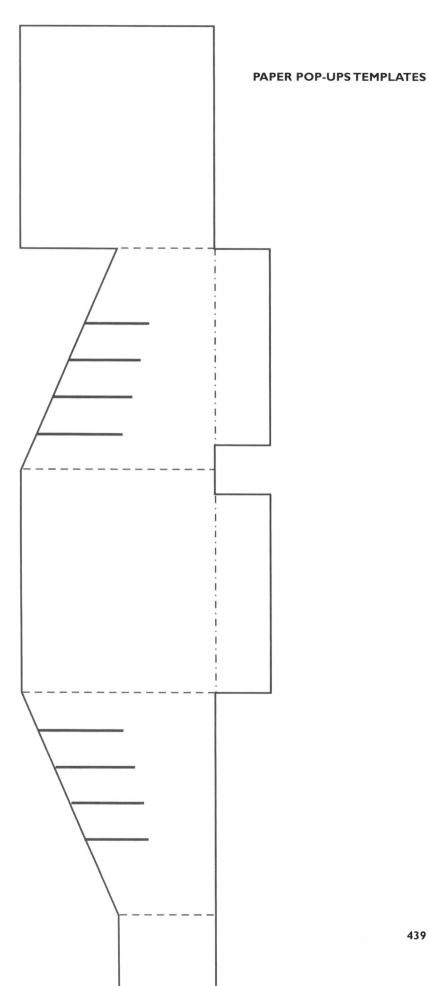

Movie Theater
Large Theater Piece

Note: To make an
accurate template, enlarge
on a photocopier at 125%

439

Coil Heart

Solid Heart

**Musical Score
Rectangular Shape**

**Musical Score
Beveled Shape**

Musical Score
Rectangular Shape

Musical Score
Beveled Shape

Celebration Template

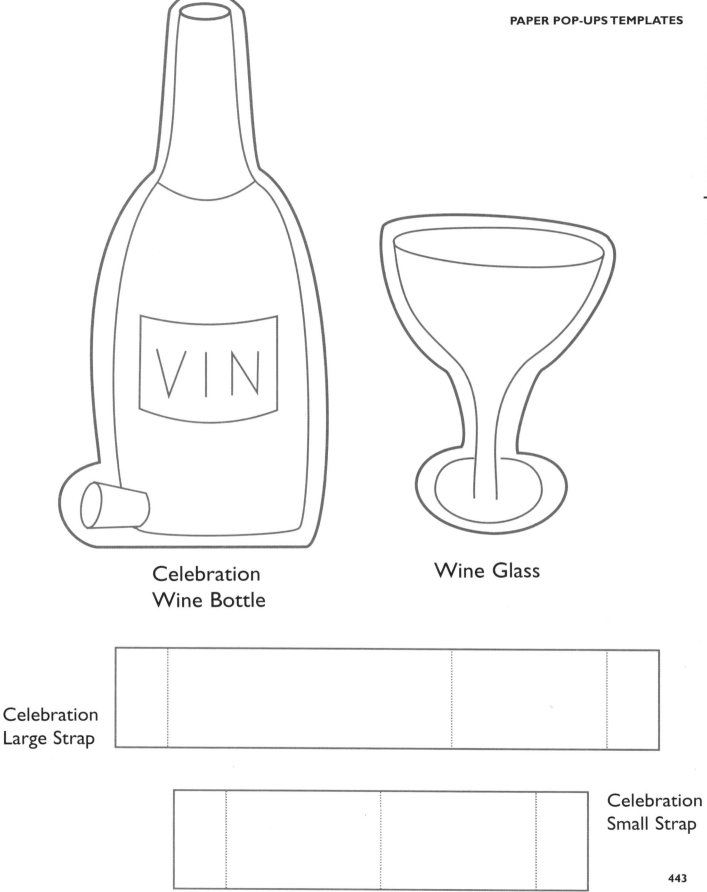

Celebration
Wine Bottle

Wine Glass

Celebration
Large Strap

Celebration
Small Strap

443

INDEX